KU-220-719

The Revolutionary Ideas of Karl Marx

Alex Callinicos

BOOKMARKS

London, Chicago and Melbourne

The Revolutionary Ideas of Karl Marx – Alex Callinicos
First published 1983
Second Edition published 1995
Reprinted with corrections November, 1996
Bookmarks, 265 Seven Sisters Road, London N4 2DE, England
Bookmarks, PO Box 16085, Chicago Il. 60616, USA
Bookmarks, GPO Box 1473N, Melbourne 3001, Australia
Copyright c Bookmarks Publications Ltd

ISBN 1 898876 13 4

Printed by BPC Wheatons, Exeter
Cover by Sherborne Design

Bookmarks is linked to an international grouping of socialist organisations:
- **Australia:** International Socialists, GPO Box 1473N, Melbourne3001
- **Belgium:** Socialisme International, Rue Lovinfosse 60, 4030 Grivengée
- **Britain:** Socialist Workers Party, PO Box 82, London E3
- **Canada:** International Socialists, PO Box 339, Station E, Toronto, Ontario M6H 4E3
- **Cyprus:** Ergatiki Demokratia, PO Box 7280, Nicosia
- **Denmark:** Internationale Socialister, Postboks 642, 2200 København N
- **France:** Socialisme International, BP 189, 75926 Paris Cedex 19
- **Greece:** Organosi Sosialisliki Epanastasi, c/o Workers Solidarity, PO Box 8161, Athens 100 10
- **Holland:** International Socialists, PO Box 9720, 3506 GR Utrecht
- **Ireland:** Socialist Workers Party, PO Box 1648, Dublin 8
- **Norway:** Internasjonale Socialisterr, Postboks 5370, Majorstua, 0304 Oslo 3
- **Poland:** Solidarność Socjalistyczna, PO Box 12, 01-900 Warszawa 118
- **South Africa:** International Socialists of South Africa, PO Box 18530, Hillbrow 2038, Johannesberg
- **Spain:** Socialismo International, Apartado 563, 08080, Barcelona
- **United States:** International Socialist Organisation, PO Box 16085, Chicago, Illinois 60616
- **Zimbabwe:** International Socialists, PO Box 6758, Harare

Contents

Alex Callinicos is a leading member of the Socialist Workers Party. He teaches politics at York University and is the author of, among other things, *Marxism and Philosophy* (1983), *Making History* (1987), *Against Postmodernism* (1989), *The Revenge of History* (1991) and *Theories and Narratives* (1995).

Foreword

My aim in this book has been to fill a gap in the literature on .
Marx by providing an accessible modern introduction to his life
and thought by someone who shares his basic beliefs on history,
society and revolution. I am grateful to a number of people for
their help and encouragement: to Peter Clark and Tony Cliff who
had the idea in the first place; to Tony Cliff for his searching criticisms of the book in manuscript; and to Peter Goodwin and Peter
Marsden, who performed the same task as well as the more difficult one of trying to make the book readable. Although the general political standpoint taken in this book is that of the Socialist
Workers Party, the errors it undoubtedly contains are all my own.
I would like to dedicate *The Revolutionary Ideas of Karl Marx* to
Joanna Seddon, to whom I owe, among other things, such knowledge as I have of the Utopian Socialists.

Key to references

Only references to the writings of Marx and Engels have been
included. The following abbreviations have been used:

AD	Engels, *Anti-Dühring* (Moscow, 1969)
C	Marx, *Capital*: i (Harmondsworth, 1976), ii (Moscow, 1956), iii (Moscow, 1971)
CW	Marx and Engels, *Collected Works*, 50 vols published or in preparation (London, 1975-)
CWF	Marx, *The Civil War in France* (Peking, 1966)
G	Marx, *Grundrisse* (Harmondsworth, 1973)
SC	Marx and Engels, *Selected Correspondence* (Moscow, 1965)
SW	Marx and Engels, *Selected Works*, 3 vols (Moscow, 1973)
TSV	Marx, *Theories of Surplus Value*, 3 vols (Moscow, 1963-72)
V	*Value: Studies by Marx* (London, 1976)

Introduction (1995)

T *he Revolutionary Ideas of Karl Marx* first appeared in
1983, 100 years after Marx's death. The political climate
was very different then. Ronald Reagan had recently
become president of the United States. Margaret Thatcher was
still in her first term as British prime minister. The offensive of
the free market right over which they presided was only beginning to make itself felt in the working class movement.

In Britain the Labour Party was being torn apart by the divisions created by its disastrous period in office between 1974 and
1979. The breakaway of the Social Democratic Party was pulling
the party to the right and the left wing movement headed by Tony
Benn was disintegrating. The Great Miners' Strike of 1984-5 was
still in the future. Its defeat would make the triumph of the right
inside the Labour Party inevitable.

Internationally the world was still in the grip of what was sometimes called the Second Cold War, the period of renewed tension
between the superpower blocs that started in the late 1970s. NATO
plans to install a new generation of cruise nuclear missiles in Western Europe—finally implemented in the autumn of 1983—
provoked the revival of the peace movement on an enormous scale.
After the crushing in December 1981 of the great Polish workers'
movement, Solidarnosc, the Stalinist regimes in the East seemed as
ossified and entrenched in power as ever. In Russia itself Mikhail

Gorbachev was still only a rising star in the Politburo.

The world is a very different place today. Fundamentally this is a consequence of what has been called the 'double revolution' of 1989/91—the 1989 revolutions which swept aside the Stalinist regimes in Eastern Europe, and the fall of the Communist Party of the Soviet Union which saw the disintegration of the USSR itself in 1991. This enormous transformation ended the partition of Europe between the superpower blocs and, with it, the Cold War between those blocs.

But as important as these geopolitical changes have been the ideological consequences of 1989/91. The collapse of the Communist regimes was widely taken definitively to refute Marx's ideas. The free market right seized on the fall of Stalinism and proclaimed it the triumph of capitalism. Indeed Francis Fukuyama, at the time an official in the State Department under President George Bush, announced 'the end of history'. Liberal capitalism had, Fukuyama claimed, decisively defeated Marxism and with it any serious challenge to its dominance. All that humankind had to look forward to was century upon century of capitalism.

It was natural enough for the right to exploit 1989/91 in this way. More surprisingly, many on the left went at least part of the way with Fukuyama. This reflected the fact that they had (like the right) equated the USSR and the other Stalinist regimes with socialism. The fall of what had been up to then 'existing socialism' was therefore interpreted as a defeat for the left worldwide.

The resulting mood of pessimism in which this left many socialists was summed up by the historian Eric Hobsbawm. In his recent book *Age of Extremes* (1994) Hobsbawm grimly views a world dominated by a dynamic and increasingly international capitalism and various forms of political reaction—religious fundamentalism and the like. As for Marxism, 'clearly, if Marx would live on as a major thinker, which could hardly be doubted, none of the versions of Marxism formulated since the 1890s as doctrines of political action and aspiration for socialist movements were likely to do so in their original forms.'

Marxism as a political and intellectual tradition was thus thrown onto the defensive. Academic Marxism, already weakened by its isolation in the universities through the 1980s, entered a further stage in its decline. The 1980s had seen the rise of postmodernism which proclaimed the death of all large truths and in particular of the 'grand narratives', above all Marxism, that sought to weave together all human history into a single process of development.

With the academic left in disarray, postmodernists proclaimed themselves the real radicals, even though they denounced any attempt to change the world through political action.

Politically, the events of 1989/91 strengthened the hand of those on the left who argue that there is no real alternative to market capitalism. The British Labour Party moved strongly in this direction. For them, socialism amounts to what the former Polish dissident Adam Michnik called 'the market with a human face'. Such is Labour's message since Tony Blair became its leader in July 1994. Blair's successful attack on Clause Four of the party's constitution, with its commitment to achieving common ownership of the means of production, served to underline that 'New Labour' intends no significant change in the structure of capitalism in Britain.

The odd thing about this embrace of the market is that it comes at a time when capitalism is doing pretty badly. After a wave of speculative euphoria during the Reagan-Thatcher era in the 1980s, the world economy entered a major recession at the beginning of the 1990s. This was the third great global slump since the early 1970s. By the mid-1990s those economies to go first into recession—the United States and Britain in particular—were experiencing uneven and unstable recoveries, but Japan, the most successful major economy in the postwar era, was stuck in the depths of a slump which, if anything, was getting worse.

It is now clear, moreover, that the free market right, with their call for a return to unrestrained, unregulated capitalism, offer no solution to this crisis. Britain, which took the right's policies furthest amongst major economies, is stuck in a century long process of relative decline. The chief effect of the new right in power has been a massive transfer of wealth and income from poor to rich and the more general growth of social and economic inequality. The resulting social polarisation sparked off explosions like the 1990 poll tax riots, which brought down Thatcher, and the 1992 Los Angeles rebellion. It is hard to see the new generation of right wing politicians—epitomised by Newt Gingrich in the US and Michael Portillo and John Redwood in Britain—producing anything except more of the same.

All of this suggests that the central strand in Marx's thought—his critique of capitalism as a system profoundly rooted in exploitation and chronically prone to crisis—remains valid today. This raises the question of whether Marxist economic theory can survive when the entire tradition of which it is part has been refuted by great historical events. But has it been refuted?

The answer to this last question is to be found, I believe, in the pages of this book. The reader will discover a Marx who is the very opposite of the icon of a despised and now defunct despotism. This is the real Marx, for whom socialism is the self emancipation of the working class—not something to be imposed on the mass of people, but something that they can only achieve by and for themselves, through their own struggles and organisations.

One must then distinguish the real Marxist tradition—what is sometimes called classical Marxism—from its various distortions. The informing political theme of this tradition is the idea of (as the American socialist Hal Draper put it) 'socialism from below', a socialism that is inherently democratic because it is made by the mass of workers themselves. Classical Marxism was inaugurated, as I describe in chapter 1, by Marx and his great friend and collaborator Friedrich Engels and was continued by later generations of revolutionary socialists, above all by Vladimir Lenin, Leon Trotsky and Rosa Luxemburg. Counterposed to it are rival, distorting 'Marxisms', which made it variously a doctrine of piecemeal reform (Western social democracy), the state religion of the Stalinist societies (official 'Marxism-Leninism'), or a form of scholarly inquiry disengaged from political practice (academic 'Western Marxism').

In particular the distance between the ideas outlined in this book and the reality of 'existing socialism' in the Soviet Union and elsewhere should be obvious. This is one of the main issues I address, in conclusion, in chapter 8. Drawing on Tony Cliff's analysis of Stalinism, I argue that the USSR and its ilk can be understood, in Marxist terms, not as any kind of socialism but as instances of bureaucratic state capitalism, a variant of the same exploitive social system that exists in the West. I conclude, in words written seven years before the revolutions in Eastern Europe:

'Really existing socialism' in the Eastern bloc is thus the negation of socialism as Marx conceived it. It rests, not on the self emancipation of the working class, but its exploitation. Anyone who remains true to Marx's thought must work wholeheartedly for the downfall of these regimes.

From this perspective the fall of Stalinism was an occasion not for mourning but for celebration. It marked, as I argue in *The Revenge of History* (1991), not the final refutation of Marxism, but a moment to resume unfinished business. Freed from the monstrous encumbrance of Stalinism, the real Marxist tradition could begin to emerge from the political margins to which it had been driven in the 1920s and challenge a capitalism more barbarous and irrational than it was even in Marx's day.

The Revolutionary Ideas of Karl Marx may thus serve as a useful way into a body of thought that is still as relevant as when first formulated. I have left the text of this new edition almost wholly unchanged. No doubt (as is always true) I would write the book differently had I to do so today, but as it stands it has a coherence which tinkering about with the text could damage. There are some passages, particularly in chapter 8, where the reader should take into account the different political situation—sketched out at the beginning of this Introduction—in which it was written. To help in this task I have revised the suggestions for further reading at the end of the book to cover Marxist writing published since the early 1980s.

Understanding Marx, I should emphasise, is not simply an intellectual exercise. His ideas are indispensable to making sense of a world that seems to be getting more irrational and chaotic by the day. But what is the point of gaining a deeper insight into the driving forces of the contemporary world unless it is a means of changing that world?

Capitalist crisis is not just an impersonal economic process. It means mass unemployment in the rich countries and famine and epidemics in many parts of the Third World. The terrible suffering this represents can produce political reactions that tip humankind further down the slope towards outright barbarism. Already the 1990s have seen in Western Europe the large scale revival of fascism, in the Balkans a senseless civil war and in many African countries the disintegration of the entire society as it is torn apart by warring bands.

'Socialism or barbarism' declared the great Polish revolutionary Rosa Luxemburg during the First World War. Barbarism we can see growing everywhere. The future of socialism depends on the ideas outlined in this book becoming, as Marx himself put it, a material force that moves millions of workers against a capitalist system overdue for replacement.

Introduction (1983)

arl Marx died 100 years ago, on 14 March 1883. So much has happened since then—two world wars, Auschwitz, the atomic bomb, the internal combustion engine, television, the microchip. What point is there now in writing a book about the life and thought of this man?

There are three answers to this question. First, Marx was one of a handful of thinkers who have fundamentally changed the way we see the world. In this he ranks with Plato, Aristotle, Copernicus, Galileo, Newton, Darwin, Freud and Einstein. The materialist conception of history—'the simple fact,' as Marx's lifelong collaborator Friedrich Engels put it at his graveside, 'hitherto concealed by an overgrowth of ideology, that mankind must first of all eat, drink, have shelter and clothing, before it can pursue politics, science, art, religion, etc' (**SW** iii 162)—is so powerful that even Marx's critics and opponents cannot ignore it.

However, and this is the second answer to our question, Marx was 'before all else a revolutionist', as Engels said (**SW** iii 163). Theory was, for Marx, a means to understand the world around him, but only as a step to transforming that world. His life work—the materialist conception of history, and the enormous economic studies culminating in *Capital*—was dedicated to one single goal: the self emancipation of the working class.

It is easy to forget the heroism involved in the task Marx set himself. He was a man of enormous and obvious brilliance. One contemporary described him in his mid-twenties: 'Imagine Rousseau, Voltaire, Holbach, Lessing, Heine and Hegel fused into one person...and you have Dr Marx.' Had he conformed politically and led a conventional academic career, he would have risen to the top of the intellectual establishment of the day. He could have died rich and famous.

Instead, Marx devoted his life to the cause of socialist revolution. He and his family were, as a result, hounded and spied on by the police forces of half of Europe. They lived in miserable poverty, with the bailiff always at the door, and survived thanks only to Engels' self sacrifice. When Marx died, his passing was ignored in his adopted country, England. The *Times* learned of his death only from the French press. Compare this career with that of one of the pampered pundits of our own day, Bernard Levin for example, constantly assured of their brilliance by the admiring media.

Marx commands our attention because an understanding of his thought is essential for anyone who considers him or herself a socialist, who wishes, like Marx, to do away with the exploitation, suffering and violence that is built into the capitalist system whose laws of motion he sought to uncover. For the questions which Marx raised are with us still. There are 30 million people without work in the Western industrial world alone. A number of major socialist experiments have taken place in the more developed countries—Chile 1970-3, Portugal 1974-5, France today. All have failed. None took the step Marx considered to be essential, of forcibly breaking the organised power of the capitalist class and setting up in its place a new and radically democratic form of workers' power. No serious socialist can avoid Marx's thought, because in it are found all the questions pressing on us now—crises and unemployment, revolution and reform.

Unfortunately, understanding Marx is not always as simple as it should be. This is not mainly because, as legend has it, Marx's writings are obscure, ponderous and Germanic—he was, on the whole, a clear writer, and his works are hard going usually only when the subject matter they deal with is itself complex. The main difficulty, and the third reason for writing this book, is that Marx's ideas have suffered the most enormous distortion.

The harm has been done partly, of course, by Marx's enemies, by the defenders of the existing order, the 'hired prizefighters' of capitalism, as he called them. So many lies have been written about Marx. He has been called many things—fanatic, anti-Semite and forerunner of Hitler (although he was a Jew and an internationalist), even a 'fundamentally religious' thinker (Marx was a life long atheist!). His enormous correspondence has been quarried by bourgeois 'scholars' in the hope, sometimes fulfilled, of catching him out in the odd vulgarity or racist remark.

These calumnies are, however, comparatively easy to refute. More difficult to deal with are the distortions that Marx's thought has suffered at the hands of his followers. 'All I know is that I am no Marxist,' he said towards the end of his life—'God save me from my friends!'

There have been two main sources of this 'friendly' misinterpretation of Marx's ideas. The first, and much the more important, arises from the fact that 'Marxism-Leninism' has become the official ideology of a number of important and powerful states, most notably the Soviet Union and the People's Republic of China. Marx's socialism, as I shall try to show, was socialism 'from below'. It foresaw the working class liberating themselves through their own activity, and remaking society in their own image. 'Really existing socialism' in the Eastern bloc, however, is based on the denial of the self activity of the workers and the denial of popular democracy. The rise and fall of Solidarnosc in Poland showed that beyond any doubt. One issue that I shall deal with in the final chapter is whether Marx's ideas can make sense of the states which rule in his name.

The other source of distortion is the fact that Marx has been discovered by the academics. It isn't just that his works have become the subject of hundreds of commentaries and doctoral theses. A new species of Marxism has arisen, based not in the labour movement but in the universities and polytechnics, and whose aim is not to overthrow capitalism but to study Marxism itself.

'Western Marxism' is the polite name for this species, because its members are found mainly in Western Europe and North America. 'Academic Marxism' would be a more accurate name. Its practitioners remind one of Narcissus, who in the Greek legend fell in love with his own reflection. Not all the output of these academic Marxists can be dismissed out of hand.

Sometimes it is necessary to devote time to clarifying and developing the concepts that we use, but for Western Marxists this activity has become an end in itself. The result is a body of writing incomprehensible to all but a tiny minority of highly qualified intellectuals.

The aim of this book, then, is to rescue Marx from the distortions he has suffered; to present, in as clear and simple a manner as possible, his basic ideas. It should already be obvious that this isn't an easy task. In the first place, socialists of all varieties read Marx in order to find justification for their political views—social democrats, orthodox communists, Maoists, different sorts of Trotskyists, and so on. It should be made clear from the start that this book is written from a revolutionary socialist standpoint. In other words, I share with Marx the belief that capitalism is an exploitive social system whose contradictions must lead either to socialism or to barbarism, and that the only hope for humanity lies in the working class destroying the capitalist state machine and replacing it with their own rule. This doesn't mean that this book has no criticisms to make of Marx. The man whose favourite motto was 'Doubt everything' would have despised the Soviet cult of him as an infallible sage. But the book is, first and foremost, an exposition and defence of Marx's ideas.

Secondly, any account of Marx's ideas is bound to be controversial. His writings are surrounded by such a mass of conflicting interpretations that to explain what they say is to walk through a minefield. Moreover, Marx, being human, was sometimes ambiguous and inconsistent, and changed his mind on matters both large and small. In picking one's way through these difficulties, one has to tread a narrow path. It is easy to slip from 'What Marx really meant to say...' to 'What Marx should have said, but didn't...' I hope I have avoided the latter. The only place where I might reasonably be accused of doing this is in chapter 5, on Marx's theory of history. Here I believe that Marx's views did change, and develop, between *The German Ideology* and *Capital*, and have based my account on the latter and more mature work.

Thirdly, there is the question of how far Engels' writings can be taken as a reliable guide to Marx's thought. Having been treated as the touchstone of orthodoxy by the Second International and in the Eastern bloc, Engels is now regarded by many

Marxists in the West as Marx's evil genius, who distorted the latter's thought. Both these views of Engels must be rejected. Engels himself would never have claimed to be as great or original a thinker as Marx. 'Marx was a genius,' he wrote, 'we others were at best talented' (**SW** iii 361). Nevertheless, Engels made his own independent contribution to Marxism, both as a writer on scientific, philosophical, political and military subjects, and as a populariser of Marx's ideas. He deserves to be studied in his own right. I shall cite his writings in so far as they complement, clarify or develop Marx's own views.

This book is a contribution to the struggle against capitalism, and for socialism. To the extent that it succeeds in changing a few people's beliefs, and persuading them that Marx was right, it must also alter their practice. For one cannot accept Marx's scientific theory and reject his revolutionary politics: the two go together. That is the fundamental point about Marxism—it is, in Antonio Gramsci's words, the philosophy of practice.

If this book convinces only one person of the necessity of working to bring about the self emancipation of the working class, then I shall be content.

economically and socially backward country, a patchwork of petty princedoms each claiming absolute power over its subjects, dominated by the reactionary Holy Alliance of Austria, Prussia and Russia. Yet intellectually the country flourished. The early decades of the 19th century were the golden age of German philosophy. It was almost as if this overdevelopment of abstract thought was a compensation for Germany's political impotence and economic backwardness. 'In politics the Germans *thought* what other nations did', as Marx later put it (**CW** iii 181).

The contradictions of German society were reflected in Hegel's thought. At first an enthusiast for the French Revolution, and for Napoleon, Hegel later became a pessimist and reactionary, believing that the absolutist Prussian state was the embodiment of reason. In the 1830s and 1840s he was, to all intents and purposes, the official Prussian philosopher, and his followers received appointments in the state controlled universities .

This situation did not last. A number of younger philosophers began to interpret Hegel in an increasingly radical way. Hegel identified reason with God, calling it the Absolute. History was, for him, simply the story of the Absolute's gradual journey towards consciousness of itself, a process whose climax was the Protestant Reformation. For the Young, or Left Hegelians, as they came to be called, the Absolute was simply humanity. God vanished from the picture. They agreed with Hegel that the state should be the embodiment of reason, but they disagreed that the Prussian monarchy fulfilled this role. They were atheists, rationalists and liberals. At first they hoped that the Prussian crown prince would introduce the democratic reforms they wanted. After he had succeeded to the throne as King Friedrich Wilhelm IV in 1840, and had shown himself as reactionary as his predecessors, the Young Hegelians' opposition to the *status quo* in Germany became more and more radical.

Into this intellectual and political scene Marx was drawn after his introduction to philosophy. The Hegelian left congregated in the Berlin Doctors' Club. Marx soon became a prominent member of the club and a close friend of Bruno Bauer, one of the foremost Young Hegelians. They were a drunken, loose living bunch. Heinrich Marx complained that 'as if we were men of wealth, my Herr Son disposed in one year of almost 700 thalers contrary to all agreement, contrary to all usage, whereas the

21

richest spend less than 500.'

Marx's links with his family were virtually broken off after his father's death in May 1838. He does not seem to have got on very well with his mother, although she provided him with quite large sums of money over the years. A satirical poem by the young Engels and Bruno's brother Edgar Bauer describes Marx at this time as 'a swarthy chap of Trier, a marked monstrosity/He neither hops nor skips, but moves in leaps and bounds/Raving aloud…/He shakes his wicked fist, raves with a frantic air/As if ten thousand devils had him by the hair.'

Marx seems to have hoped to pursue a career as a professional philosopher. He devoted much time to studying the early Greek thinkers, and in April 1841 received his doctorate for a thesis entitled 'Difference between the Democritean and Epicurean Philosophy of Nature'. Although obscurely written, and strongly Hegelian, the thesis shows Marx's growing impatience with the highly idealistic philosophy of his friend Bruno Bauer, who sought to reduce everything to human consciousness. The growing confrontation between the Prussian state and the Young Hegelians put paid to Marx's hopes of an academic career. Friedrich Wilhelm IV suppressed the main Left Hegelian journal, Arnold Ruge's *Hallische Jahrbücher,* and appointed Hegel's old enemy, Schelling, professor of philosophy at Berlin, with instructions to root out the 'dragon seed of Hegelianism'. Finally, in March 1842, Bauer was sacked from his teaching post at Bonn University.

Marx, who had returned to Trier in 1841, now threw himself into political journalism. *The Rheinische Zeitung* had been set up by Rhineland industrialists to press for their economic interests. To its bourgeois shareholders' bemusement, however, it soon fell under the control of the Young Hegelians, led by Moses Hess, one of the first German communists. Marx began writing for the paper in April 1842, and in October moved to Cologne to become its editor-in-chief. He was at this stage a radical liberal democrat, who hoped to see in Germany a republic and universal suffrage such as France had achieved after the revolution of 1789. When another paper accused the *Rheinische Zeitung* of communism he replied that 'the *Rheinische Zeitung*…does not admit that communist ideas in their present form possess even theoretical reality, and therefore can still less desire their practical realisation' (**CW** i 220).

Nevertheless, the *Rheinische Zeitung* was a turning point. I was then, Marx later reminisced, that 'I experienced for the first time the embarrassment of having to take part in discussions on so called material interests.' Marx, like the other Young Hegelians, followed their master in believing that the state was, or should be, above classes: as the representative of the universal interests shared by every citizen, the function of the state was to reconcile the differences of interest and conflicts between classes.

Studying the debates in the local Rhenish Estates (or parliament) on proposals for tightening up the law against thefts of wood, Marx realised that both the industrial capitalists who financed his newspaper and the feudal landowners who supported Prussian absolutism shared a common interest in the preservation of private property. An investigation of the wretched conditions of the peasants in the Moselle wine country brought home to him the effects of private property. As Engels put it 50 years later, 'I heard Marx say again and again that it was precisely through concerning himself with the wood-theft law and with the situation of the Moselle peasants that he was shunted from pure politics over to economic conditions, and thus came to socialism.'

It was not only 'pure politics' that Marx abandoned while at the *Rheinische Zeitung*. The experience of persecution drove Bauer and the Berlin Doctors' Club to greater and greater extremes of verbal radicalism. Isolated in Berlin, the stronghold of the Prussian bureaucracy and far from the more economically developed and liberal Rhineland, they continued to see their task as the purely intellectual one of refuting error. The chief target was religion, which the 'Free', as they now called themselves, endlessly denounced. Meanwhile, every compromise which the harassed Marx made to keep Prussian censorship from closing down the *Rheinische Zeitung* they denounced as treason. He learned a lifelong lesson—that theory which loses contact with reality becomes impotent.

It was with Bruno Bauer and his other old cronies in Berlin in mind that Marx wrote a little later that:

…we do not confront the world in a doctrinaire way with a new principle: Here is the truth, kneel down before it! We develop new principles for the world out of the world's own principles. We do

23

not say to the world: Cease your struggles, they are foolish; we will give you the true slogan of struggle. We merely show the world what it is really fighting for, and consciousness is something that it has to acquire, even if it does not want to (**CW** iii 144).

Here we have the origins of Marx's later attitude towards the working class. The task of the theorist is not to lay down the law to workers, but rather to make sense of what they are fighting for, to show how they can achieve it.

It remained only for Marx to discover the working class. That he had not done so yet is shown by a manuscript he wrote in mid-1843 while on honeymoon with Jenny at Kreuznach (he had resigned from *Rheinische Zeitung* shortly before the censors finally suppressed it in March 1843). Called *Contribution to the Critique of Hegel's Philosophy of Right*, it was not to be published until 1927.

Here Marx set out to refute Hegel's idea that the state was above classes. He was clearly very much under the influence of the most radical of the Young Hegelians, Ludwig Feuerbach, when he wrote it. Feuerbach, whose *Essence of Christianity* created a sensation when it appeared in 1841, went much further than Bruno Bauer. Feuerbach argued that Hegel's philosophy should be rejected in toto: philosophy's starting point had to be, not God or the Idea, but human beings and the material conditions in which they live. Obviously, this attracted those such as Marx, Engels and Hess, who were beginning to believe that only a social revolution could bring radical political change in Germany. But Marx had not yet seized on the working class as the agent of this revolution. He still looked towards 'true democracy'—universal suffrage—as the means of bringing the state under the control, not of the propertied minority, but of the mass of the population.

A year after writing the *Critique*, Marx was an open advocate of working class revolution, a communist. The decisive factor behind this shift was his move to Paris. The Prussian censorship had made work in Germany impossible. Marx and Arnold Ruge decided to produce a Young Hegelian journal abroad, the *Deutsch-Französische Jahrbucher*. In October 1843 the Marxes arrived in Paris to join Ruge.

Paris was very different from Berlin or Cologne. The cultural capital of 19th century Western civilisation, it was also the metropolis of a country undergoing rapid industrialisation, under the rule of a corrupt clique of courtiers and bankers gathered around the 'bourgeois monarchy' of Louis-Philippe. In Paris a swarm of communist and socialist sects—some of them with mass followings—coexisted and quarrelled. There were also 40,000 expatriate Germans, most of them artisans, many of them under the influence of a revolutionary secret society, the League of the Just.

Marx's contacts with the French and German communist societies in Paris were his first experience of an organised working class movement. The impact was enormous. He wrote to Feuerbach in August 1844:

> You would have to attend one of the meetings of the French workers to appreciate the pure freshness, the nobility which burst forth from these toil-worn men... It is among these 'barbarians' of our civilised society that history is preparing the practical element for the emancipation of mankind (**CW** iii 355).

This new view of the working class was expressed in Marx's two contributions to the only issue of the *Deutsch-Französische Jahrbucher* to appear, in March 1844 (its editors quarrelling, banned by the Prussian government, ignored by the French, the journal sank without trace when its publisher withdrew his backing). In 'On the Jewish Question' Marx argued, against Bauer, that a purely political revolution, such as that of 1789 in France, would liberate man only as 'an individual withdrawn into himself, into the confines of his private interests and private caprices, and separated from the community' (**CW** iii 164). Only a social revolution which swept away private property and individualism could offer 'human emancipation'.

In the second essay, which had been intended as the Introduction to Marx's unpublished *Contribution to a Critique of Hegel's Philosophy of Right*, he argued that only such a revolution was possible in Germany. The German bourgeoisie—the middle class—was too weak to play the role taken by its French counterpart in 1789, leading the whole people against the monarchy. Only the proletariat—the industrial working class—could play this role:

25

THE REVOLUTIONARY IDEAS OF KARL MARX

...a class with *radical chains*, which cannot emancipate itself without emancipating itself from all other spheres of society and thereby emancipating all other spheres of society, which, in a word, is the *complete loss* of man and hence can win itself only through the *complete rewinning of man* (**CW** iii 186).

As this last passage makes clear, Marx's approach to politics was still steeped in philosophy. He thought in terms of an alliance between philosophy and the working class—one, indeed, in which philosophy would play the leading role. He called the workers the '*passive* element' of the revolution and wrote that 'the *head* of this emancipation is *philosophy*, its *heart* is the *proletariat*' (**CW** iii 183,187). Workers were to play a revolutionary role because they were the most wretched of classes, not—as he later came to believe—the most powerful.

This rather patronising and elitist attitude soon changed—for two reasons. First, while in Paris, Marx undertook his first serious study of the writings of Adam Smith, David Ricardo and the other political economists. As a result, he wrote, between April and August 1844, the *Economic and Philosophic Manuscripts*. First to be published in 1932, these writings contain an early version of Marx's materialist theory of history. Most important of all, the revolutionary role of the working class is explained in terms of their role in the production of goods, which compels them to struggle against capitalism. 'From the relationship of estranged labour to private property it follows that the emancipation of society from private property etc, from servitude, is expressed in the *political* form of the *emancipation of the workers*' (**CW** iii 280).

The second reason for Marx's change of attitude was that the German working class gave dramatic proof that they were more than just a 'passive element'. In June 1844 the Silesian weavers rebelled against their masters, and the army had to be called in to restore order. Ruge published an anonymous article in a German emigré paper in Paris in which he dismissed the revolt and attacked the weavers. He was probably speaking for most of the Young Hegelians. The article was attributed to Marx, who wrote a furious reply denouncing Ruge and championing the workers for their courage and the high level of their organisation and consciousness. He regarded the working class no longer as the passive but as the 'dynamic element' of the German revolution (**CW** iii 202). Marx the revolutionary communist had finally emerged.

Friendship and revolution

At the end of August 1844, Friedrich Engels spent ten days in Paris. During his stay Engels visited Marx, a meeting which resulted in a lifelong partnership.

Engels was then 23, nearly three years Marx's junior, but had already enjoyed a brilliant career as a radical journalist and Young Hegelian. Although Engels had contributed to the *Rheinische Zeitung*, Marx had distrusted him as one of the Berlin 'Free' whose toy revolutionism he had come to despise. However, in November 1842 Engels moved to Manchester to work in the family firm of Ermen & Engels, to be confronted with the industrial revolution, working class poverty and Chartism, the first mass working class movement in history, then still recovering from the defeat of the general strike of August 1842. This experience, recorded most memorably in *The Condition of the Working Class in England,* led Engels, like Marx, to recognise the revolutionary role of the working class. An essay published in the *Deutsch-Französiche Jahrbucher*, 'Outlines of a Critique of Political Economy', anticipated Marx's later writings.

Marx and Engels were, then, natural partners. Their first work together was an attack on Bauer and the 'Free', who were reacting to the repression they had suffered at the hands of the Prussian state by adopting an increasingly elitist and anti-democratic attitude. Bauer, who was to become an anti-Semite and supporter of the Tsarist autocracy in Russia, wrote that 'it is in the masses and there alone that one should look for the true enemy of the Mind'. The reply by Marx and Engels, *The Holy Family*, was intended originally to be a short pamphlet. However, and not for the last time, Marx's zeal got the better of him. His contribution swelled it into a 200 page book ranging from philosophy to literary criticism, and defending the principle of working class self emancipation. Engels protested mildly at the inclusion of his name on the title page, since 'I contributed practically nothing to it', and at its length. 'Otherwise the book is splendidly written and enough to make you split your sides.'

Marx was by this time a prominent figure among the exiled revolutionaries who populated Paris in the 1840s. He was on

27

friendly terms with the fathers of anarchism, Pierre-Joseph Proudhon and Mikhail Bakunin, with whom he would discuss Hegel. The Marxes were also close to the poet Heinrich Heine, whom they persuaded for a while to overcome his fear of the masses and write socialist verses. It was of Marx and Engels that Heine later wrote: 'The more or less occult leaders of the German communists are great logicians, the most powerful of which have come from the school of Hegel; and they are, without doubt, Germany's most capable thinkers and most energetic characters.'

Marx's prominence may have helped to persuade the French government, under Prussian pressure, to expel him from France. In February 1845 he moved from Paris to Brussels, where he was soon joined by Engels, who gave up his job in the family firm to become a full time revolutionary. Here their partnership began in earnest. They visited England together in the summer of 1845, and then settled down to produce one final reply to Bauer and company.

The 'Free' had by now become extreme individualists, an attitude summed up by Max Stirner in *The Ego and his Own*, which argued that nothing except the individual self existed. *The German Ideology*, written by Marx and Engels between September 1845 and August 1846, was intended as a demolition of Stirner. Running to over 600 pages, mainly by Marx, it is that and a lot more. The first part, on Feuerbach, contains the first systematic account of historical materialism. They were unable to find a publisher for the book. As Marx later put it, 'We abandoned the manuscript to the gnawing criticism of the mice all the more willingly as we had achieved our main purpose—self clarification.'

The German Ideology provided the theoretical foundation for Marx's and Engels' politics. It argued that the possibility of social revolution depended on the material conditions which capitalism itself was creating. The most important of these conditions was the working class. 'Communism', Engels wrote around this time, 'is the doctrine of the conditions for the emancipation of the proletariat' (**CW** vi 341).

Having thus formulated their theory of revolution, Marx and Engels threw themselves into political activity. They concentrated their attentions on the League of the Just, an international secret society consisting mainly of German artisans living outside their own country. The dominant influence on the League was Wilhelm Weitling, a tailor whose views on socialism were extremely confused, but who believed that the mass of workers could not be won to communism, and that it was up to the revolutionary minority to seize power on behalf of the masses. This elitist attitude he shared with Auguste Blanqui, the great French revolutionary, and the League was banned in France after it had taken part in Blanqui's abortive insurrection in 1839. The headquarters of the League shifted to London, where it was split between Weitling's followers, and those who believed that gradual and peaceful education could achieve socialism.

In February 1846 Marx and Engels set up the Communist Correspondence Committee, with the aim of winning control of the League of the Just. At a stormy meeting of the committee, Marx told Weitling that 'to call to the workers without any strictly scientific ideas or constructive doctrine…was equivalent to vain dishonest play at preaching which assumed on the one side an inspired prophet and on the other only gaping asses.' He responded to Weitling's attempt to defend himself by attacking theory and theoreticians with the words: 'Ignorance never yet helped anyone!'

Paul Annenkov, a Russian acquaintance of Marx's who was present at this meeting, has left behind a vivid picture of him in his late twenties:

> Marx himself was the type of man who is made up of energy, will and unshakeable conviction. He was most remarkable in his appearance. He had a shock of deep black hair and hairy hands and his coat was buttoned wrong; but he looked like a man with the right and power to demand respect, no matter how he appeared before you and no matter what he did. His movements were clumsy but confident and self-reliant, his ways defied the usual conventions in human relations, but they were dignified and somewhat disdainful; his sharp metallic voice was wonderfully adapted to the radical judgements that he passed on persons and things.

Another contemporary writes of Marx at this time:

> Marx was a born leader of the people. His speech was brief,

convincing and compelling in its logic. He never said a superfluous word; every sentence contained an idea and every idea was an essential link in the chain of his argument. Marx had nothing of the dreamer about him.

This formidable intellect was set to work to refute what Marx and Engels regarded as the erroneous versions of socialism current in the German workers' movement. One target was the 'true socialists', intellectuals who had discovered the 'social problem' after the weavers' revolt, and who believed that society could be transformed through the moral conversion of the mass of the people. Another target was Proudhon. Marx wrote to him in May 1846 inviting him to become the Paris correspondent of the Brussels Committee. Proudhon replied with a patronising letter in which he told 'my dear philosopher' that he was opposed to revolution, preferring instead 'to burn property by a slow fire'. In 1847 Marx published *The Poverty of Philosophy*, in which he demolished Proudhon's *The System of Economic Contradictions*—which had as its subtitle *The Philosophy of Poverty*.

After lengthy manoeuvres Marx and Engels succeeded in winning control of the League of the Just. A congress in June 1847 transformed the League from a conspiratorial secret society into an open revolutionary organisation, the Communist League. Its slogan was no longer 'All men are brothers' (Marx said there were plenty of men whose brother he did not want to be) but 'Working men of all countries, unite!' The second congress of the Communist League, meeting in December 1847, instructed Marx and Engels to draw up a manifesto stating its principles. The result was the *Manifesto of the Communist Party*, written by Marx in February 1848 and published that same month in London. It opens with the words: 'A spectre is haunting Europe—the spectre of communism' (**CW** vi 481). It was the first popular exposition of Marxism, and is by far the most famous of all socialist writings.

By the time the *Manifesto* appeared, Europe was being swept by revolution. In February Louis-Philippe of France was overthrown and the Second Republic proclaimed; in March uprisings broke out in Vienna and Berlin. The reactionary Europe of the Holy Alliance had suddenly crumbled. The frightened Belgian government expelled Marx at the beginning of March. After a brief stay in Paris, he returned to Germany, to become editor-in-chief of the *Neue Rheinische Zeitung*, based, like its predecessor, in Cologne. According to Engels, 'The editorial constitution was simply the dictatorship of Marx.' Werner Blumenburg writes of the *Neue Rheinische Zeitung* that 'with its 101 numbers it is not only the best newspaper of that revolutionary year; it has remained the best German socialist newspaper.'

The revolutions of 1848 represented the moment at which the struggle between capital and labour took on greater importance than that between the bourgeoisie and the old feudal landowning classes. This was confirmed by the events of June 1848 in Paris, when a workers' uprising was brutally crushed by the republican government. Here, Marx wrote at the time, '*fraternité*, the brotherhood of antagonistic classes, one of which exploits the other, this *fraternité* [brotherhood] which in February was proclaimed and inscribed in large letters on the facades of Paris, on every prison and every barracks, this *fraternité* found its true, unadulterated and prosaic expression in *civil war*, civil war in its most terrible aspect, the war of labour against capital' (**CW** vii 144,147).

Marx and Engels continued to believe, however, that in backward Germany the bourgeoisie could be pressed into playing a revolutionary role like its English and French forebears. The Communist League, with its few hundred members, found itself swamped in the mass movement which followed the March revolution in Berlin. Rather than, as Engels put it many years later, 'preach communism in a little provincial sheet and…found a tiny sect instead of a great party of action', they decided 'to take on the role of the forward-pressing, extreme left wing of the bourgeoisie' (**SW** iii 166). The League was effectively dissolved and the *Neue Rheinische Zeitung* provided the focus of Marx's and Engels' political activity. Its 'political programme', Engels explained, 'consisted of two main points: a single, indivisible, democratic German republic and war with Russia' (**SW** iii 166).

The Russia of Tsar Nicholas I was the most powerful counter-revolutionary state in Europe and her armies were to play a crucial role in restoring order in 1848-9. Marx and Engels hoped that a republican Germany could, like the French Jacobins in the 1790s, liberate Europe by waging a revolutionary war against the reactionary powers. These hopes were to be dashed. The German bourgeoisie, terrified of the rising workers' movement, sought an accommodation with the Prussian monarchy. The *Neue Rheinische Zeitung* had to record the triumph of the counter-revolution in country after country—Austria, Bohemia, Hungary, France and Germany itself.

Marx found himself waging an increasingly uphill struggle to keep the paper going. In February 1849 he and other editors of the *Neue Rheinische Zeitung* were put on trial twice, but were acquitted by sympathetic juries. Finally, in May the Prussian authorities suppressed the paper and expelled the editors. The last issue, of 19 May 1849, was printed entirely in red. The editorial by Marx concluded: 'In bidding you farewell the editors of the *Neue Rheinische Zeitung* thank you for the sympathy you have shown them. Their last word everywhere and always will be: *emancipation of the working class*!' (**CW** ix 467)

Exile and the 'wretchedness of existence'

After his expulsion from Germany, Marx made his way first to Paris, and then, in August 1849, to London. At first he expected this exile to be brief, believing that the revolution had suffered only a temporary defeat. He was soon joined by Engels, who had taken part in the unsuccessful defence of the last republican stronghold in Germany, the Palatinate, from Prussian invasion.

The two friends played an active role in reviving the Communist League, whose central committee was based in London, and launched a new journal, the *Neue Rheinische Zeitung: Politisch-Oekonomisch Revue*. In its pages Marx published *The Class Struggles in France*, an analysis of the revolution of 1848-9. In March 1850 he drafted an address by the central committee which declared that 'the revolution…is near at hand' (**CW** x 279), and the following month the League concluded an alliance with the followers of Blanqui, the Universal Society of Revolutionary Communists, whose objective was 'the downfall of all privileged classes, [and] the submission of these classes to the dictatorship of the proletariat by keeping the revolution in continual progress [*en permanence*] until the achievement of communism' (**CW** x 614).

This revolutionary optimism began gradually to evaporate in the course of 1850. In June Marx obtained a ticket to the

Reading Room of the British Museum. Once installed there, he launched himself into intensive economic studies, drawing especially (as many have done after him) on the *Economist*. The conclusion he drew, spelled out at length in the last issue of the *Revue*, was that there was no immediate prospect of revolution. The upheavals of 1848 had as their background the general economic crisis which had gripped Europe after 1845. By 1850, however, the world economy had entered a new phase of expansion, stimulated by such developments as the discovery of gold in California and the improvement in communications brought about by the widespread use of steamships:

> With this general prosperity, in which the productive forces of bourgeois society develop as luxuriantly as is at all possible within bourgeois relationships, there can be no talk of a real revolution. Such a revolution is possible only in the periods when *both these factors*, the *modern* productive *forces* and the *bourgeois forms of production,* came *in collision* with each other... *A new revolution is possible only in consequence of a new crisis. It is, however, just as certain as this crisis* (**CW** x 510).

This pessimistic analysis angered and horrified the other leaders of the Communist League. After a bitter debate at a central committee meeting on 15 September 1850, Marx and Engels effectively withdrew from the League, which was in any case broken by mass arrests in Prussia the following May. When members of the League were put on trial, Marx sprang to their defence, writing a pamphlet which (typically) became a small book, *Revelations Concerning the Communist Trial in Cologne.*

To all intents and purposes, however, Marx ceased to take part in political activity, from time to time sniping at some of the vast numbers of refugees who congregated in London after the defeat of the 1848 revolutions. 'I am very pleased with the public and genuine isolation in which we too, you and I, find ourselves,' he wrote to Engels in February 1851:

> It entirely suits our position and principles. We have now finished with the system of mutual concessions, with half truths admitted for reasons of propriety and with our duty of sharing in the public ridicule in the party with all these asses.

33

Withdrawal from activity freed Marx to concentrate on his economic studies. He resumed work on the great book on 'Economics' which he had originally decided to write in 1845, but had given up for political work. Much of 1851 was spent in the British Museum, filling 14 notebooks with excerpts from the works of political economy that he read. 'When you visit him', one acquaintance wrote, 'you are received with economic categories instead of compliments.' In April 1851 Marx told Engels, 'I am so far advanced that in five weeks I will be through with the whole economic shit. And that done, I will work over my Economics at home and throw myself into another science in the museum. I am beginning to tire of it.'

When he died 32 years later, the 'Economics' was still unfinished: Marx left behind him the manuscripts of two of the three volumes of *Capital* for Engels to edit. One reason for this tardiness was that Marx was a perfectionist, constantly rewriting and expanding his drafts, and reading more books and articles till his researches seemed endless. Another reason was the need to analyse and comment on current developments. In 1852 Marx published one of his most brilliant works, *The Eighteenth Brumaire of Louis Bonaparte*, which sought to explain why the Second French Republic had given way to the Second Empire of Napoleon III.

Dominating these years, however, were the sheer pressures of poverty. The Marxes were constantly short of money. Between 1850 and 1856 they lived at first at 64 then 28 Dean Street in Soho, where three of their six children died. Life was a constant struggle with creditors—landlord, butcher, baker, greengrocer, milkman. 1852 seems in many ways to have been the worst year. When her daughter Franziska died that Easter, Jenny Marx could find the money to pay for her coffin only by borrowing from a French emigré. In December Marx told a correspondent that he could not leave the house because he had pawned his coat and shoes. But the worst blow came in April 1855, when the Marxes' eight year old son, Edgar, died of consumption (tuberculosis). Marx wrote to Ferdinand Lassalle a few months later:

Bacon says that really important men have so many relations with nature and the world that they recover easily from every loss. I do not belong to these important men. The death of my child has deeply shaken my heart and mind and I still feel the loss as freshly as on the first day. My poor wife is also completely broken down.

It was during these terrible years that Helene Demuth, a von Westphalen family servant who had been the Marxes' maid since 1845, gave birth to an illegitimate son, Frederick, whose father was almost certainly Marx. The scandal was hushed up. Engels agreed to pretend to be the child's father, only revealing the secret to Eleanor Marx on his deathbed in 1895. The affair revealed that Marx himself was not wholly hostile to the conventions of bourgeois respectability. Indeed, he and Jenny constantly sought to maintain a middle class household, complete with Helene as loyal retainer. They brought up their three surviving daughters, Jenny, Laura and Eleanor, to the extent it was possible, as good bourgeois girls. None of this should come as any surprise, for there is no way in which individuals can escape the pressures of the society in which they live, however much they oppose that society.

In 1856 Jenny Marx received two small bequests which enabled them to move out of their cramped Soho lodgings to 9 Grafton Terrace, as she put it, 'a small house at the foot of romantic Hampstead Heath, not far from lovely Primrose Hill.' But their troubles were far from over. In January 1857 Marx wrote: 'I have absolutely no idea what I shall do next, and now I am in an even more desperate situation than I was five years ago. I thought I had swallowed the ultimate filth. *Mais non.*'

A year or so later he told Engels that 'there is no greater stupidity than for people of general aspirations to marry and so surrender themselves to the small miseries of private and domestic life.' In 1862 things were so bad that Marx tried to get a job as a railway clerk: his handwriting was so illegible that he was turned down. A few months afterwards he wrote:

Every day my wife tells me she wishes she and the children were dead and buried. And really I cannot argue with her. For the humiliations, torments and terrors that have to be gone through in this situation are really indescribable... I pity the poor children all the more because this has happened during the 'Exhibition' season, when all their friends are enjoying themselves, while they are only terrified in case someone should visit us and see the filth.

That the Marxes survived at all during these years was due to Engels' self sacrificing and constant support. In November 1850 he had returned to Manchester to take up his old job at Ermen & Engels. That he did so very much against his own inclinations is made clear by a letter to Marx of January 1845: 'This penny-grabbing is too horrible…it is too horrible to continue to be, not only a bourgeois, but a manufacturer, a bourgeois in active opposition to the proletariat.'

Engels' biographer, Gustav Mayer, writes:

> A man who wrote so fluently as Engels had no need to worry about his future. If he did, nevertheless, return to 'filthy business', it was for the sake of Marx; for Engels felt that Marx's great talents were of vital importance to the future of the cause. Marx could not fend for himself and his family: he must not become a victim of emigré life. To avoid that, Engels was glad to go back to the office desk.

Without Engels' regular subsidies, the Marxes would have sunk without trace. Marx acknowledged this debt after he had sent the first volume of *Capital* to the printers:

> Without you I could not have completed the book, and I assure you that it has always been a load upon my conscience to think that you, chiefly for my sake, were wasting your brilliant powers in business routine, and perforce had to share all my *petites mis-ères* [small wretchednesses] into the bargain.

Engels' importance to Marx was far more than as a source of money. Engels always insisted that he was the junior partner in their relationship. But he brought to their partnership a number of gifts. He had a quick and lively mind, and had developed into a revolutionary communist much more quickly than Marx. ('You know that I am slow to grasp things,' the latter wrote 20 years afterwards, 'and that I always follow in your footsteps.') Writing was not the laborious process for Engels that it was for Marx: he wrote rapidly and fluently. He had a marvellous gift for languages, and wide interests in the natural sciences. It has also been argued that his *historical* judgements were nearly always superior to those of Marx, and that he had a deeper knowledge of

European history. Finally, he was, far more than Marx, a man of action (his nickname among the Marxes was 'The General' because of his interest in military affairs) and was much more of a practical organiser. In all these ways, his talents complemented those of Marx.

Even Engels' companionship and financial assistance could not prevent the struggles and privations of the 1850s and 1860s from leaving their mark. There is little doubt that Jenny Marx suffered the most. She was frequently physically ill, and her experiences took a mental toll as well, as this letter to Marx shows: 'Meanwhile I sit here and go to pieces. Karl, it is now at its worst pitch...I sit here and almost weep my eyes out and can find no help. My head is disintegrating.' As early as 1851 Marx told Engels:

> At home everything is constantly in a state of siege, streams of tears exasperate me for whole nights at a time and make me completely desperate... I pity my wife. The chief burden falls on her, and *au fond* she is right... All the same you must remember that by nature I am *très peu endurant* [impatient] and *quelque peu dur* [rather hard], so that from time to time I lose patience...

As this last letter suggests, Marx's response to their domestic circumstances was to retreat into himself, adopting a cold and tough exterior. He described himself as having 'a hard nature', and told Engels that 'in such circumstances, I can generally save myself only by cynicism.' Nevertheless, he fell victim to a variety of physical complaints: insomnia, attacks of the liver and gall, and carbuncles or boils ('I hope the bourgeoisie will remember my carbuncles all the rest of their lives', he once wrote to Engels). Anxiety caused by his domestic distress and his liver troubles often impeded Marx's work. He wrote to Engels in July 1858, when he was working on the *Grundrisse*, the first draft of *Capital*: 'The situation is now absolutely unbearable...I am completely disabled as far as work goes, partly because I lose most of my time running around trying to make money and partly (perhaps a result of my feeble physical condition) my power of intellectual concentration is undermined by domestic problems. My wife's nerves are quite ruined by the filth'. As Werner Blumenburg remarks:

It has often been asked why Marx was unable to complete his masterpiece *Capital*, to which he devoted three decades of his life, and it has been thought that the reason lay in theoretical difficulties. But the circumstances of the author's life make it rather seem miraculous that he was able to complete so much.

Marx's sufferings undoubtedly made him more suspicious of other people, and harsh and bitter in what he said about them. The brutal and sometimes anti-Semitic remarks in his correspondence with Engels concerning the German socialist leader Ferdinand Lassalle reflect not only their political differences, but also Marx's resentment of a man who moved in the smartest social circles, was wealthy, and basked in popular acclaim. Their relationship never recovered from Lassalle's visit to the Marxes in 1862, when he infuriated Marx by spending a pound a day just on his cigars, while (Marx told Engels) Jenny 'had to take to the pawnbroker everything that was not actually nailed down' to entertain their guest in the style to which he was accustomed.

Early the next year Marx's hard and cynical front nearly cost him his friendship with Engels. When Engels wrote to him with news of the death of his companion, Mary Burns, Marx replied with a letter which, after some rather perfunctory condolences, treated Engels to a lengthy account of his latest financial difficulties. Only after a Marx family row and the most profuse apologies was the understandably hurt Engels reconciled.

Marx's writings of the 1850s also reflect his circumstances. In these years Engels could not afford to provide the Marxes with more than a pound or two at a time, so Marx had to supplement his income by writing for the *New York Daily Tribune* (many of the articles were in fact written by Engels, whose English was at first better). Marx's judgement was not always wholly sure. When Britain and France went to war with Russia in the Crimea (1854-6), Marx, who was fanatically anti-Russian because of the Tsar's role in cementing the reactionary Holy Alliance, formed a rather dubious alliance with an eccentric Tory MP, David Urquhart, in whose paper, the London *Free Press*, many of Marx's articles appeared. Marx also allowed himself to be dragged into emigré squabbles, most notably when a French government agent produced a pamphlet libelling him. The result was a 300 page book, *Herr Vogt* (1860), notable chiefly for Marx's talent to abuse.

One should not exaggerate the gloom of these years. There were regular Sunday outings to Hampstead Heath, when family and friends read the Sunday papers, rode donkeys, and recited Dante and Shakespeare. Marx was not an ascetic socialist. He liked a drink, preferring wine but being happy to settle for beer. On one memorable occasion, Marx, Edgar Bauer, an old friend and sparring partner from his Young Hegelian days, and Wilhelm Liebknecht went on a pub crawl in London from Oxford Street to Hampstead Road, stopping at every pub on the way. All went well till they reached the end of Tottenham Court Road, where they nearly got into a fight with a party of celebrating Oddfellows and started to throw paving stones at street lamps. Naturally, the police appeared, and chased them. They got away, thanks partly to a surprising burst of speed on Marx's part.

A Prussian police spy who visited Dean Street in 1852 painted this picture of the Marx household:

> As father and husband, Marx, in spite of his wild and restless character, is the gentlest and mildest of men...When you enter Marx's room smoke and tobacco fumes make your eyes water so much that for a moment you seem to be groping about in a cavern, but gradually, as you grow accustomed to the fog, you can make out certain objects which distinguish themselves from the surrounding haze. Everything is dirty, and covered with dust, so that to sit down becomes a thoroughly dangerous business. Here is a chair with only three legs, on another chair the children are playing at cooking—this chair happens to have four legs. This is the one which is offered to the visitor, but the children's cooking has not been wiped away; and if you sit down you risk a pair of trousers. But none of these things embarrass Marx or his wife. You are received in the most friendly way and cordially offered pipes and tobacco and whatever else there may happen to be; and eventually a spirited and agreeable conversation arises to make amends for all the domestic deficiencies, and this makes the discomfort tolerable. Finally you grow accustomed to the company, and find it interesting and original.

Capital and the First International

In 1857 the world economy entered the crisis which Marx had predicted would follow the prosperity of the early 1850s, to Engels' enormous delight. While all was gloom at the Manchester stock exchange, he told Marx, 'People are worrying themselves to death about my sudden and strange good humour.' The two friends hoped that the economic depression would revive the revolutionary movement. 'In 1848 we said, "Now our time is coming," and in a certain sense it came,' Engels wrote. 'But this time it is coming in full measure: a life and death struggle. My military studies will at once become more practical.'

Alas, The General's hopes were to be dashed. There was no revolution of 1858. But the crisis did have the effect of encouraging Marx to resume his economic studies. He told Engels in December 1857: 'I am working madly through the nights on a synthesis of my economic studies so that, before the deluge, I shall at least have the main outlines clear.' Fortified by lemonade and 'an immense amount of tobacco', Marx succeeded in producing, between August 1857 and March 1858, the work now known as the *Grundrisse*, the first rough draft of *Capital*.

Although Lassalle found a German publisher for the manuscript, Marx decided that it was too much of a mess ('in everything that I wrote I could detect an illness of the liver,' he told Lassalle). All that appeared of this manuscript in Marx's lifetime was a completely rewritten version of the first part, on money, which was published in June 1859 as *A Contribution to the Critique of Political Economy*. The preface to this contained an important statement by Marx on his intellectual development and on the basic principles of historical materialism.

During the following eight years, during which the Marxes suffered some of their worst domestic crises and Marx himself resumed serious political work for the first time since 1850, *Capital* itself took shape. Marx had originally intended the *Contribution* to be merely the introduction to the 'Economics' which would encompass six volumes: (1) Capital, (2) Landed Property, (3) Wage Labour, (4) The State, (5) International Trade, (6) The World Market. Between August 1861 and July 1863 Marx set to work on continuing the *Contribution*. The result was 23 notebooks covering 1,472 pages, the work known as the

1861/63 manuscript, which has still to be entirely translated into English. Marx's investigations during these years led him to change his mind about the 'Economics'. He had already discovered the concept of surplus value, the key to his economic theory, in the *Grundrisse*, but it was only in the 1861/63 manuscript that he formulated his theory of profit. Marx abandoned the six volume scheme, and decided instead to call the whole work *Capital*, which would be divided into four volumes—on production, circulation, the system as a whole, and theories of surplus value, incorporating much of the material he had intended to deal with in later volumes of the 'Economics'.

In 1863-4 the Marxes' finances improved thanks to two bequests, from Marx's mother and from his old comrade Wilhelm Wolff. The first volume of *Capital* is dedicated to the latter. On the strength of this money, the household moved from Grafton Terrace to a much larger house nearby, at 1 Maitland Park Road. The money soon ran out, and Engels had yet again to dig into his pockets to support them. To add to the renewed money worries, Marx suffered terribly from carbuncles from 1863 onwards. He dosed himself on arsenic, creosote and opium and sometimes cut the boils out himself. Despite all these distractions, Marx wrote the manuscripts of Volumes 1, 2 and 3 of *Capital* in 1864 and 1865. (He never managed Volume 4, but the relevant sections of the 1861/63 manuscript were published after his death as *Theories of Surplus Value*.)

In 1865 Marx signed a contract with the Hamburg publishers Meissner & Behre. Urged on by Engels, he spent much of 1866 preparing *Capital* Volume 1 for the printers, polishing it up into a finished form. When the relieved Engels heard that the first batch of manuscripts had gone off to Meissner, he drank 'a special glass' in celebration. On 16 August 1867 Marx announced that he had finished the proofs of *Capital* Volume 1:

> It was thanks to you alone that this became possible. Without your self sacrifice for me I could never possibly have done the enormous work for the three volumes. I embrace you, full of thanks. Enclosed two sheets of corrected proofs.
> The £15 received with best thanks.
> Greetings, my dear, beloved friend!

41

The book appeared a few weeks later. A thousand copies were printed of the first edition.

Other political involvements in the mid-1860s began to draw Marx away from his economic studies. Although the revolution Marx and Engels had expected after the crisis of 1857-8 did not materialise, the early 1860s saw a revival of the European workers' movement. Trade unionism made rapid strides in Britain and France, while Lassalle was able to launch the first mass workers' political organisation in Germany, the General Union of German Workers (ADAV). Political events stimulated the labour movement to think in terms of international solidarity. The American Civil War, even though it caused a depression in the English cotton industry, led the Lancashire textile workers to support the cause of the North. The Polish insurrection of 1863 against Russian rule won the backing of socialists and democrats throughout Europe.

In this climate the International Working Men's Association (IWMA), to give the First International its proper name, was launched. A delegation of French workers, followers of Proudhon, attended a mass meeting of solidarity with Poland called by the English trade unions in London in July 1863. These contacts led to a mass meeting at St Martin's Hall in London on 28 September 1864 at which the IWMA was launched. Marx was one of the 34 members of its general council elected at that meeting. Soon he was its effective leader, writing most of its manifestos and addresses, and attending to a large portion of the administrative work and correspondence.

The International was, however, a very different kettle of fish from the Communist League. Werner Blumenburg writes:

> The Communist League had been a secret propagandist society in which Marx enjoyed dictatorial powers. But the International was a union of independent (and jealously independent) organisations of working men in various different countries. Marx had no dictatorial powers; he was only one among a number of members of the general council. It was always a matter of convincing the other members. For the International contained many other different currents of thought; there were supporters of Fourier, Cabet, Proudhon, Blanqui, Bakunin, Mazzini and Marx himself. There were all shades of opinion ranging from peaceful Utopian Socialists, to the

anarchists for whom the revolution was a matter of fighting on the barricades. There were the English trade union leaders, whose unions—the organisational mainstay of the International—were rooted in a section of society where the old professional pride of the guilds still lived on. There were the Germans, easily organised and disciplined, and also the inflammable revolutionaries of the Latin countries.

These political differences were eventually to doom the International, but its first five years were remarkably successful. The effectiveness of the International in preventing the use of foreign blacklegs to break the London tailors' strike of 1866 won it increased British trade union supporters and it played a leading role in the Reform League, established with union support to win universal suffrage. The successive congresses of the International (London 1865, Geneva 1866, Lausanne 1867, Brussels 1868, and Basle 1869) took positions on a variety of issues such as working hours and child labour. A number of effective anti-blackleg operations were mounted on the continent.

Marx also waged an ideological struggle for influence within the International, especially against the followers of Proudhon. It was to the general council in June 1865 that Marx read the lectures which were to become the pamphlet *Wages, Price and Profit*, showing that, contrary to the arguments of John Weston, a follower of Robert Owen, trade unions could win higher wages for workers. In Germany, although the Lassallean ADAV remained aloof from the International, the formation at Eisenach in 1869 of the Social Democratic Workers Party, under the leadership of Wilhelm Liebknecht and August Bebel, gave Marx's ideas the backing of an organisation in his native country for the first time since the split in the Communist League nearly 20 years earlier.

Two developments decisively altered the situation of the International. First, war broke out between France and Prussia in July 1870. Prussia's rapid and crushing victory led to the abdication of Napoleon III of France and the proclamation of the Third Republic. The reactionary nature of the French provisional government under Thiers then led the workers of Paris to take up arms in March 1871 and proclaim their own government, the Commune. Thiers retreated to Versailles, and despatched an army

43

which, despite the Parisians' heroic defence, suppressed the Commune, drowning the uprising in blood.

The International had little influence over the Commune, and Marx himself was doubtful whether the rising had any hope of success. But he sprang to its defence. On 30 May 1871, three days after the fall of the Commune, the general council adopted an address entitled *The Civil War in France*, drawn up by Marx. It is one of the finest of Marx's writings, at once a moving vindication of the Communards, a bitter denunciation of their murderers, and an important statement of Marx's theory of the state, which was later to inspire Lenin's *The State and Revolution*.

The fall of the Commune led to an international hue and cry against all socialists. The International naturally became one of the main targets of this campaign. Marx was lifted by the press from obscurity to notoriety as the 'Red Doctor', puppet master of the Commune and, according to some of the more lurid accounts, an agent of Bismarck. *The Civil War in France* was a popular success, selling 8,000 copies. One result was that the English trade unions, which at this stage represented chiefly a comparatively privileged craft elite, withdrew their support from the International. Odger and Lucraft, the British members of the general council, resigned after *The Civil War in France* was published.

The second, and more serious, blow to the International was the result of Mikhail Bakunin's activities. Bakunin, a Russian aristocrat, had worked his way from orthodox to Left Hegelianism in the late 1830s and early 1840s, concluding in 1842 that 'the urge to destroy is a creative urge'. He stuck to this basically anarchist position for the rest of his life. After 1848 Bakunin fell into the hands of the Tsar, and was imprisoned in the dreadful Peter-Paul Fortress, where he wrote a secret 'Confession' addressed to Nicholas I as his 'spiritual father'. In 1861 he turned up in London, having escaped from Siberia.

Marx had been on friendly terms with Bakunin in the 1840s and sent him a copy of *Capital* Volume 1 as an 'old Hegelian'. They were, however, very much opposites. Bakunin's fellow Russian exile, Aleksandr Herzen, wrote that 'to a passion for propaganda, for agitation, for demagogy, if you like, to incessant activity in founding and organising plots and conspiracies and establishing relations and in ascribing immense significance to them, Bakunin added a readiness to be the first to carry out his ideas, a readiness to risk his life, and recklessness in accepting all the consequences.' His reaction to the fall of Napoleon III was to rush to Lyons, where he declared the state abolished outside the town hall, and was carried off by the police. He also fell under the influence of the sinister Nechaev, whose murderous activities were immortalised by Dostoevsky in his novel *The Devils*.

In 1868 Bakunin joined the International. At the same time he set up the Alliance for Social Democracy, which soon assumed the role within the International of 'a state within a state', in Engels' words. The anarchists were especially strong in the Swiss, Italian and Spanish sections of the International. The differences between Marx and Bakunin became especially pronounced after the defeat of the Commune. In a sense, it was a repetition of the split in the Communist League after 1848. Marx argued that revolutionary prospects were receding, while the Bakuninists urged immediate uprisings everywhere. Realising that his position was becoming untenable with the effective withdrawal of the British unions, previously the mainstay of the general council, Marx decided to dissolve the International. This took place at the Congress of the International held at the Hague in September 1872, ironically the only one Marx ever attended. His supporters succeeded in beating off an attack on the general council, expelled Bakunin from the International, and moved its headquarters to New York, thus depriving it of any influence. The International was formally dissolved in 1876.

Last years

After the collapse of the First International, Marx ceased to play much of an active part in politics. Financially, life for the Marxes was much better than it ever had been. Ermen bought Engels out in 1869, which meant that The General now had a sizeable capital sum whose income could support himself and the Marxes in comfort. The next year he moved to London and bought a large house in Regents Park Road, less than ten minutes walk away from the Marxes. For the next quarter of a century, long after his friend's death, this house was to be the centre of the international working class movement.

Withdrawal from the International should have freed Marx to

complete Volumes 2 and 3 of *Capital*. Certainly he was not idle. He closely supervised the French translation of *Capital* Volume 1, revised the original German manuscript for a second edition which appeared in 1873, and undertook detailed studies of the agrarian question in Russia for his analysis of rent in Volume 3. (The first translation of *Capital* Volume 1 appeared in Russia in 1872; the censors let it through because they thought 'few would read it and still fewer understand it', but it was an enormous success among the radical intelligentsia.)

According to Engels, after 1870 Marx studied 'agronomics, rural relations in America and, especially, Russia, the money market and banking, and finally natural sciences such as geology and physiology. Independent mathematical studies also figure prominently in the numerous extract notebooks of this period' (C ii 3-4). But Marx did little work on the manuscripts of *Capital* Volumes 2 and 3. The years of 'bourgeois misery' had taken their toll. Marx suffered from constant headaches and insomnia, and went on regular health cures, visiting Karlsbad annually in 1874-6. As David McLellan puts it, 'He was now mentally and physically exhausted: in a word, his public career was over.'

Exhausted Marx may have been, but he did not lose that toughness of mind that had made him feared and respected among European radicals since the 1840s. H M Hyndman, an ex-Tory who became one of the main promoters (and vulgarisers) of Marx's ideas in England, recalled 'saying to him once that as I grew older I thought I became more tolerant. "Do you," he said, "*do* you?" It was quite certain that he didn't.' Marx's most important intervention in these years came when the two German workers' parties fused in 1875 to form the German Social Democratic Party (SPD). Marx and Engels believed that the programme adopted by the new party's founding congress at Gotha made too many concessions to Lassalle. In the *Critique of the Gotha Programme* Marx called his followers to order, in the process writing his most important discussion of the transition from capitalism to communism. (The SPD leaders, Bebel and Liebknecht, prevented the publication of the *Critique* till 1891.)

Marx and Engels were often in conflict with the German socialists. Engels had to write *Anti-Dühring* in 1877 to defend their ideas against an academic socialist, Eugen Dühring, who was gaining some influence in the SPD. In 1879 they wrote a circular letter denouncing certain SPD leaders influenced by Dühring (including the future father of 'revisionism', Eduard Bernstein), whose version of socialism was little different from liberal democracy. It was in these years that Marx declared: 'All I know is that I am no Marxist.'

The final years of tranquillity suited Marx. An acquaintance portrayed him at this time as:

> ...highly cultivated gentleman of the Anglo-German pattern. Intimate relations with Heine had endowed him with a cheerful disposition and a capacity for witty satire. Thanks to the fact that the conditions of his personal life were now as favourable as possible, he was a happy man.

In a questionnaire he filled out for his daughters in 1865, Marx described his favourite activity as 'bookworming'. The sheer range of Marx's reading is extraordinary. S S Prawer, professor of German at Oxford University, has shown in a recent study the extent to which Marx was acquainted with, and drew on an enormous variety of European literature:

> He felt at home in the literature of classical antiquity, German literature from the Middle Ages to the age of Goethe, the worlds of Dante, Boiardo, Tasso, Cervantes, and Shakespeare, the French and English prose fiction of the 18th and 19th centuries; and he showed himself interested in any contemporary poetry which might help—as that of Heine had certainly done—to undermine respect for traditional authority and arouse hopes of a socially juster future. On the whole, however, his gaze was directed more to the past than to the present, more towards Aeschylus, Dante and Shakespeare than towards the writings of his own contemporaries.

Greek and Roman literature was one of Marx's special loves. At a time of great mental and physical discomfort Marx took to reading 'Appian's account of the Roman civil wars in the original Greek... Spartacus appears as the most capital fellow to be found in the whole of ancient history. A great general...a noble character, a true representative of the ancient proletariat. Pompey [the Roman general who crushed the slave revolt led by

Spartacus] is nothing but a turd.'

In a famous passage from the *Grundrisse*, Marx wondered why, even though 'the Greek arts and epic are bound up with certain forms of social development...they still afford us artistic pleasure and...count as a norm and an unattainable model'(G 111). Marx also greatly admired Balzac for his realistic portrayal of class relations in post-revolutionary France. One of his many unrealised projects was a study of Balzac.

Marx's two elder daughters got married, Laura to Paul Lafargue in 1868, and Jenny to Charles Longuet in 1872. Marx was not an especially easy father in law. Lafargue in particular had to submit to careful cross-examination before Marx would consent to the match. But it was his youngest daughter, Eleanor, or Tussy, as she was known by the family, the most like her father ('Tussy is me,' he once said), who had to face the toughest opposition when she fell in love with a young French journalist called Lissagray, the first historian of the Commune. (London was full of French exiles after 1871.) The row embittered relations between father and daughter for some years.

Eleanor had pretensions to be an actress, and a Shakespeare reading club used to meet at Maitland Road. One of its members described Marx thus:

> As an audience he was delightful, never criticising, always entering into the spirit of any fun that was going on, laughing when anything struck him as particularly comic, until the tears ran down his cheeks—the oldest in years, but in spirit as young as any of us.

1881 marked a turning point. The Longuets moved to Paris: Marx bitterly missed their three children. By this time, Jenny Marx had been diagnosed as suffering from incurable cancer of the liver. Marx himself was ill with bronchitis. Eleanor recalled:

> It was a terrible time. Our dear mother lay in the big front room, Moor [Marx's family nickname] in the small room behind. And the two of them, who were so used to one another, so close to one another, could not even be together in the same room... Never shall I forget the morning when he felt strong enough to go to Mother's room. Then they were young again—she a young girl and he a loving youth, both on the threshold of life, not an old

man devastated from illness and an old dying woman parting from each other forever.

On 2 December 1881, Jenny Marx died.

Engels told Eleanor, 'Moor is dead, too.' Marx spent some time in Algiers, visited the Longuets in Paris, taking refuge in 'the noise of children, this "microscopic world" that is much more interesting than the "macroscopic",' and went to Vevey in Switzerland with Laura. He returned to England and caught a cold in the Isle of Wight, only to learn of his daughter Jenny's death at the age of 38. On 14 March 1883 Engels visited Maitland Road to find 'the house in tears. It seemed that the end was near.' When he and Helene Demuth went upstairs to see Marx, they found that he had died quietly in his sleep. Engels wrote to Friedrich Sorge with the news: 'Mankind is shorter by a head, and that the greatest head of our time.'

Socialism before Marx

Marx was the genius who continued and consummated the three main ideological currents of the 19th century, as represented by the three most advanced countries of mankind: classical German philosophy, classical English political economy, and French socialism combined with French revolutionary doctrines in general.

T hus wrote Lenin in 1914. Marx was not the first socialist—far from it. Since ancient Greece and Rome people have aspired to a society in which poverty, exploitation and oppression were abolished. But only in the first half of the 19th century, and especially in France, did socialism develop into a coherent set of ideas enjoying mass support. To understand Marx's thought, we must know something of his predecessors, and of the intellectual, social and political context in which they emerged.

The years between 1789 and 1848 have been called the epoch of the 'dual revolution'. Politically there was the French Revolution of 1789; economically, there was the industrial revolution. The industrial revolution meant the emergence of the 'factory single workplaces which increasingly depended for their operation on artificial sources of energy such as steam. This radically new form of economic organisation originated in the British textile industry and spread with gathering speed to other sectors of the economy and other countries. Industrialisation accelerated in Europe in the 1830s, with the building of the railways, and then again in the great boom that followed the defeat of the revolutions of 1848.

The result was a new world of great industrial centres, towns and cities such as Manchester and Lyons, in which were gathered a new class, the industrial working class or proletariat, as Marx called it to distinguish industrial workers from peasants. The miserable conditions in which these workers lived and laboured became a matter of increasing concern among the educated classes in the 1840s, a concern that reflected fear as well as philanthropy. After the first of the great working class revolts of the 19th century, by the Lyons weavers in 1831, a French journalist warned:

> Every manufacturer lives in his factory like the colonial planters in the midst of their slaves, one against a hundred... The barbarians who menace society are neither in the Caucasus nor in the steppes of Tartary; they are in the suburbs of our industrial cities.

The industrial working class were a danger to the power of a new ruling class. For the 'dual revolution' had also established the political dominance of the owners of industrial and trading wealth, the bourgeoisie. Before 1789, absolute monarchy was the rule in Europe, except in Britain, the Dutch United Provinces, and the Swiss cantons. The peasants who made up the overwhelming majority of the population were subject to the economic and political tutelage of their lords, backed by the repressive power of the state

The revolution which began in France in 1789 struck the doom of this system. Before it was over, the French king had been executed, a republic proclaimed, liberty, equality and fraternity declared the right of every Frenchman (although not of any Frenchwoman), and revolutionary armies had carried this republican message from one end of Europe to the other. Neither the degeneration of the revolution into the Empire of Napoleon I,

51

degeneration of the revolution into the Empire of Napoleon I, nor the attempts of the Holy Alliance of Austria, Russia and Prussia to turn back the clock after his final defeat in 1815 could wipe out the effects of the Great French Revolution of 1789. Much of the politics of the 19th century was concerned with restoring the republic in France, and copying its achievements elsewhere in Europe.

The revolution began with the demand of the Third Estate—all those who belonged to neither of the two great feudal Estates, the nobility and the clergy—to have the dominant say in the nation's affairs. But the chief beneficiary was one particular section. Although the common people of Paris, the shopkeepers, artisans and labourers, gave the revolution its impetus, and although the peasantry provided the republic and the empire with its armies, the French bourgeoisie emerged strongest from the turmoil of 1789-1815. The revolution swept aside the remnants of feudalism which had clogged up society, and which had interfered with the efficient pursuit of profit. And it created a powerful and centralised bureaucratic state, capable of providing capital—the new trading and industrial wealth—with the services it required, and of crushing any threat from below.

So the effect of the 'dual revolution' was paradoxical. On the one hand, the principle that every member of society, however lowly his position, was entitled to equal rights of citizenship was established, even if not fully realised. (One person one vote is an achievement of the 20th, not the 19th century.) On the other hand, the differences in wealth and economic power remained vast. The industrial revolution merely changed the form of social and economic inequality—to lord and peasant was added capitalist and worker. The essence remained the same.

So the outward form of political equality was accompanied by real economic and social inequality. The aim of the French revolutionaries, to liberate the entire people, the whole of humanity, had not been achieved. For what good is the *right* to dine at the Ritz, if you haven't got enough money to pay for a meal there? Or perhaps any meal? Out of this contradiction between the political and economic aspects of the 'dual revolution'—between the promise of liberty, equality and fraternity, and the real inequalities and exploitation of industrial capitalism—the modern socialist movement developed.

The Enlightenment

The decades that led up to the dual revolution saw a bitter struggle of ideas between the defenders of the feudal order and the supporters of the emerging capitalist society. At the centre of this struggle was the movement known as the Enlightenment.

The system of ideas, or ideology, that dominated feudal Europe had been wrought by the philosophers of the Catholic Church, who had modified the ideas of Aristotle, one of the greatest Greek thinkers, until they fitted in with Christianity. The result was a way of looking at the world which could explain much in considerable detail, without in any way placing in question the power of the feudal lords and the monarchy.

According to Aristotle, everything in the world had a *purpose*. That purpose gave the thing its place in the world. So, for example, he argued that bodies were naturally at rest. Motion, change, was abnormal, something which happened when bodies were disturbed, shaken out of their natural places. And when disturbed, bodies would move back to their natural places, where they would be, once again, at rest.

The purposes of individual beings, and the places they naturally occupy, all dovetailed together, according to Aristotle, to form the pattern of the universe.

This way of looking at the world served two purposes.

First, it provided a sophisticated version of the Christian myth, of the belief that the universe and everything in it had been created by God. For the idea that everything has a *purpose* implies that it fits into a design, a design made by an all powerful, all knowing deity with some particular end in view. Secondly, it corresponded to the structure of feudal society, in which everyone had their place, whether nobleman, guildman or serf, a place into which you were born and in which your children would follow. At the apex of the feudal system stood the king, just as God was at the centre of the universe. According to this system of ideas, the stable and harmonious feudal order, in which everyone had their place, mirrored the stability and harmony of God's universe.

But two developments began to challenge this system of ideas: the growth of science and the growth of a new class. The new traders and manufacturers, the new bourgeoisie, derived their power, not from the armed men they could command or the land that they owned, but from their control of money, 'capital', and

53

their ability to make profit. So they chafed against the restraints of feudalism, just as the new scientists chafed against the feudal worldview as it increasingly clashed with what they were able to observe.

The great scientific revolution of the 17th century with which the names of Galileo, Kepler, Descartes, Boyle, Huygens and Newton are associated cannot be reduced to this ideological struggle. However, its effects on feudal ideology were devastating. Already in the late 15th century Copernicus had argued that the earth revolves around the sun, rather than being, as Aristotle would have it, the stable centre of the universe. Galileo went much further, introducing the law of inertia, according to which every object is naturally in motion, and not at rest. Suddenly, the minority of Europeans who could read found themselves thrust into a strange new world, in which everything was in motion, and the earth was merely one small and insignificant planet in an infinite universe. 'The silence of these infinite spaces fills me with dread,' wrote Blaise Pascal, one of the most sophisticated defenders of 17th century Catholicism.

The strongholds of feudal ideology, in the shape of the Inquisition, tried to crush the new science with repression. Giordano Bruno was burned at the stake in 1600 for agreeing with Copernicus, while Galileo was silenced after being threatened with the same fate. Nevertheless, a century later their followers had triumphed. Sir Isaac Newton's *Mathematical Principles of Natural Philosophy* provided the physical sciences with their basis until the early 20th century. Acceptance of Newton's physics reflected the ideological and political supremacy which the bourgeoisie won in England as a result of the revolutions of 1640 and 1688 as much as it did its scientific merits.

We have seen that Aristotelian physics explained things from the standpoint of their purpose: bodies each had their rightful place in God's scheme, would move only when disturbed from this natural place, and would stop once they had regained it. The physics of Galileo and Newton, on the other hand, explained the movement of bodies *mechanically*. In other words, what objects did depended on the action of outside forces. The classic case of this is Galileo's law of free fall, according to which a falling object of whatever weight will accelerate at a rate of 32 feet per second per second. It does so as a result of gravitation, that is, of the attraction exercised by a much larger object, namely the earth.

The new science was *materialistic*. Its theories involved no purpose, no design, no God. We could understand the world just by taking into account the action of different bodies upon each other. It was a natural inference to say that physical bodies were all that there was. Souls, angels, devils and God himself—everything that lacked a body, that had a purely 'spiritual' existence—did not exist at all. Galileo, Newton and the other great scientists of the 17th century did not, on the whole, make this inference, but others soon did. When Napoleon I asked one French physicist what role God played in his theories, he received the reply: 'Sire, I do not have any need of this hypothesis.'

Obviously, just by expelling God and purpose from physics, the new science dealt a shattering blow to the ruling ideology. But there was a logical next step, which was to extend its method from the study of nature to the study of society. And indeed, during the English Revolution of 1640-60, Thomas Hobbes, the greatest of bourgeois political philosophers, took this step. His materialism earned Hobbes the epithet of the 'Demon of Malmesbury' from the Jesuits, and none of his successors went as far as he had, but in Hobbes' masterpiece, *Leviathan* (1651), the scientific study of society was begun.

The starting point was to find some basic principle similar to that of the principle of inertia (according to which all bodies are naturally in motion) in the study of nature. The candidate which they came up with for this role was the human passions. For Hobbes and the Enlightenment, the starting point of any study of society was the study of human nature. And human nature was in turn conceived as being unchanging. People's passions, the desires and inclinations which move them to act, are the same in every society and at every period of history. All that changes is the degree to which social and political institutions make it easier or more difficult for people to pursue these desires and inclinations.

From the standpoint of earlier political theory, the ideas of the Enlightenment represented enormous progress. In the 17th century Sir Robert Filmer had argued that the power of kings arose from the fact that they were the rightful heirs of Adam and Eve! Obviously, an approach to society which started from a serious attempt to understand human nature was infinitely superior to this sort of nonsense. Moreover, the idea that society should be judged by the degree to which it fitted people's desires and inclinations was highly subversive of the feudal order, which assigned everyone to a preordained position.

But the Enlightenment suffered from three serious defects. The most basic was that it treated human nature as unchanging. More than that, the philosophers of the Enlightenment read into what they called 'human nature' the self interested behaviour characteristic of people living in a capitalist society. This is true even of Adam Ferguson, one of the leading members of the Scottish historical school, a group of thinkers who were well aware of the differences between societies.

Ferguson wrote in his great *Essay on the History of Civil Society* (1767) that the 'instinctive desires' tending 'to the preservation of the individual':

> ...give rise to his apprehensions on the subject of property, and make him acquainted with that object of care which he calls his interest... He finds in a provision of wealth...an object of his greatest solicitude, and the principal idol of his mind... Under this influence...[men] would enter, if not restrained by the laws of civil society, on a scene of violence or meanness, which would exhibit our species, by turns, under aspects more terrible and odious, or more vile and contemptible, than that of any animal which inherits the earth.

Secondly, the Enlightenment theory of human nature was, in the main, a study of the human *mind*. People's passions and their thoughts were treated as being of greater importance than their economic and social position. This meant that the Enlightenment philosophers' view of human history was *idealistic*, it was centred on ideas rather than the material world of the new science: in other words, change was seen as a result of old ideas being discarded and new ones adopted. This view was summed up by Condorcet in a book titled *Sketch for a Historical Picture of the Progress of the Human Mind*. The title says it all: for Condorcet history was precisely the 'progress of the human mind', society improving as knowledge expanded. Condorcet believed that this progress could continue indefinitely into the future.

This view of history underlay the Enlightenment philosophers' political strategy. Political change—the reform or abolition of absolutism—would come about as a result of a battle of ideas. It would arise from enlightenment, that is, from the triumph of reason over superstition, science over faith. In line with their stress on the role of ideas, the Enlightenment philosophers saw organised religion as the main obstacle to progress. 'Despotism is the work of superstition,' wrote Holbach. Consequently, the mere power of reason would be enough to dissolve religion, and thereby to undermine absolutism. *'As soon as man dares to think,'* said Holbach, *'the priest's empire is destroyed.'*

This belief in the omnipotence of reason was a natural consequence of the philosophers' position as a tiny, highly educated minority living off the labour of (so they believed) an illiterate and superstitious majority. Their social position helps to explain the Enlightenment's third defect, its elitism. 'What does it matter,' wrote Voltaire to Helvetius, 'that our tailor and cobbler are governed by [the priests]? The point is that those with whom you live are forced to lower their eyes before the philosopher. It is in the interest of the king, that is, of the state, that the philosophers run society.'

The Enlightenment philosophers were far from being revolutionaries. Most were happy to act as advisers to the 'enlightened despots' of the 18th century such as Frederick the Great of Prussia. At most they wanted a constitutional monarchy like the British. Had they lived till the 1790s they would have been horrified by the effect of their work in undermining feudal ideology. One of them, Condorcet, did indeed survive to see the French Revolution, and died on the guillotine.

Despite these defects, the ideas of the Enlightenment played an essential role in providing the intellectual framework for the early socialists.

Utopian Socialism

Modern socialism emerged, chiefly in France, in the aftermath of the revolution of 1789. Its two main wings, the Utopian Socialism of the Comte de Saint-Simon, Charles Fourier and Robert Owen, and the revolutionary communism of Gracchus Babeuf and Auguste Blanqui, are distinguished chiefly by their attitude to the French Revolution. The first rejected it, the second sought

57

to complete it.

Saint-Simon and Fourier had both lived through the revolution, and suffered much as a result of it. Saint-Simon was imprisoned during the Terror, and Fourier was ruined by the siege of Lyons in 1793. So they rejected revolutionary action because of its violence and destructiveness. Moreover, precisely because the revolution had, if anything, widened the divisions between rich and poor, they concluded that political action was hopeless as a means of improving the condition of humanity. Only peaceful propaganda offered any hope of achieving genuine and constructive change.

The gap between the revolution's pretensions to liberty, equality and fraternity, and the capitalist realities of post-revolutionary French society provided the Utopians with their starting point. They made what is still the most powerful critique of capitalism, of its economic anarchy and suppression of human needs, and they aimed towards a new society in which these needs would be realised.

The Utopians' debt to the Enlightenment is most obvious in Fourier. Fourier too started from a conception of human nature. But where Enlightenment philosophers had held self interest to be the most basic of human instincts, Fourier vastly widened the scope. According to his account of the twelve basic passions, human beings desire love and friendship as well as material satisfaction; they wish to enjoy a variety of different pursuits, as well as to compete successfully with each other. The implication of this argument was that capitalism, far from being as the Enlightenment thinkers had believed the most natural form of human society, was the most *unnatural* because it denied some of the most important human needs and desires. So where the Enlightenment had criticised despotism and superstition, Fourier mounted an assault on the whole of 'Civilisation', by which he meant class society.

To the 'social hell' of contemporary society, the Utopians counterposed a vision of the future. Saint-Simon spoke for them all when he said that 'the golden age of the human race lies not behind but ahead of us.' Again, it was Fourier who developed the most powerful (if also sometimes the dottiest) account of what socialism would be like. The basic unit of Harmony, as he called the new society, would the the Phalanstery, a primarily agricultural community of exactly 1,620 people who would live, work and eat together. According to Fourier's theory of attractive labour, people would change their occupations every few hours, and compete in groups and series of fellow workers, in order to satisfy their desire for, respectively, variety and emulation. Every human passion would be realised.

It is easy to make fun of the more fantastic aspects of Utopian Socialism. (Fourier believed that in Harmony the seas would turn to lemonade.) What was important about the Utopians, however, was their stress on the liberating aspects of socialism. All the different ways in which people's desires and abilities had been suppressed by class society, the cultural and sexual as well as the economic and political, would be done away with in their new society. Fourier was the most virulent critic of the bourgeois family, and an advocate of women's liberation: it was he who coined the term 'feminism'.

The problem was, of course, how to get from Civilisation to Harmony. Here again, the influence of the Enlightenment was decisive. Saint-Simon and his followers, the most historically minded of the Utopians, followed Condorcet in believing that social change was a consequence of 'the progress of the human mind'. Saint-Simon was aware of the role of class struggle in history. Thus he divided contemporary French society into the *industriels* and the *oisifs*—those who worked, and the rich parasites who lived off their labour. But he believed that change came about as a result of new scientific discoveries. The followers of Saint-Simon distinguished between 'organic' epochs, in which everyone shared the same beliefs, and 'critical' epochs, in which they did not, and so society fell apart. Ideas are thus the motor of historical change.

The Utopian Socialists believed that reason would triumph as a result of a process of enlightenment. Education, the gradual spread of socialist ideas, would transform the world. And they appealed especially to capitalists. Both Fourier and Saint-Simon were opposed to the abolition of classes. Fourier, for example, hoped to get enlightened businessmen to finance a Phalanstery, which he believed would bring a good return on their investment as well as do away with the evils of Civilisation. Once a few Phalansteries had been set up, Fourier expected they would propagate by example until Harmony had conquered the globe. He even advertised for investors, announcing in the press that he could be found in a certain cafe at the same time every week if any capitalist wished to find out about his projects. (No one came.)

In the 1830s and 1840s, as the French working class movement began to develop, the idea that there would be a place for capital in the new society came under increasing fire. The followers of Saint-Simon had argued that distribution under socialism would be governed by the principle, 'From each according to his capacities, to each according to his works', implying that those with greater than average talent and skill would receive more than others. Louis Blanc coined the egalitarian slogan, 'From each according to his capacities, to each according to his needs.'

In the highly regimented utopia depicted by Etienne Cabet in his *Voyage en Icarie* (1840), there was no place for capital. Thus was born French communism, which under Cabet's leadership won mass working class support. Cabet, despite his belief in equality, was no revolutionary. 'If I held a revolution in my hand,' he declared, 'I would keep my hand closed, even if this should mean my death in exile.' The same was true of Cabet's opponent, Pierre-Joseph Proudhon, who rejected the communists' conception of a centralised future society in which everything was owned and managed in common. Proudhon's utopia was a paradise of the small peasant and artisan, in which the banks and big capital had been abolished, but private property preserved. Like Cabet, however, Proudhon believed that socialism could be introduced as a result of peaceful propaganda.

There were others who preferred action to words. Blanqui said: 'Communism [meaning the ideas of Cabet] and Proudhonism stand by a river bank arguing whether the field on the other side is maize or wheat; let's cross and see.'

The revolutionary communist tradition of which Blanqui, before Marx, was the greatest representative, stemmed from the extreme left wing of the radical republicans in the French Revolution. At the high point of that revolution, in 1793-4, the Jacobins had imposed a centralised dictatorship which saved France from enemies both abroad and at home, crushed internal opposition by the use of the guillotine, and imposed restrictions such as price controls on the free play of the market, before it was overthrown by the moderates. In 1797 Babeuf and his fellow members of the Conspiracy of Equals were executed for planning to restore the revolutionary dictatorship. They had intended this time to go much further than the Jacobins, hoping to realise the ideals of liberty, equality and fraternity by abolishing private property and imposing absolute equality.

Blanqui followed the Utopians in virulently criticising capitalism, and in looking forward to a future society, which he called communism. He followed Babeuf, however, in believing that communism could be achieved only through the armed overthrow of the existing state, and the establishment of a revolutionary dictatorship. It was Blanqui who coined the expression 'dictatorship of the proletariat'. By this he meant, however, a dictatorship *over* the proletariat. For Blanqui believed that the influence of the ruling ideology, and especially of religion, would prevent the mass of the population from actively supporting the revolution. Power would have to be taken *on behalf of* the working class, not by it. The 'first duty' of the dictatorship would be to wipe out all religions as 'assassins of the human race': only once this task had been achieved would the workers be ready for communism.

Blanqui's strategy clearly followed from his conception of how socialism would come about. A secret society of professional revolutionaries was necessary in order to organise the armed insurrection. Capitalism would be overthrown, in other words, by the action of an enlightened minority. The reason, Blanqui's German co-thinker, Wilhelm Weitling, made clear:

> To want to wait, until everyone is sufficiently enlightened, as people usually propose, means to give the matter up completely; for an entire people will never be equally enlightened, at least as long as inequality and the struggle of private interests in society continue to exist.

With great consistency and courage, Blanqui acted on his beliefs. In the 1830s he was involved in two conspiracies, which led to the insurrection of May 1839, easily crushed by the forces of the state. Blanqui's life followed a cycle of brief periods of revolutionary activity followed by prolonged imprisonment or exile. He was jailed by every regime that ruled France between 1815 and 1880.

Despite their other differences, the Utopian Socialists and the

61

Blanquists shared a common inheritance from the Enlightenment. They all believed historical change to be the result of a battle of ideas. The establishment of socialism would depend upon the enlightenment of the mass of the population. This led naturally to elitism. For since most workers and peasants were manifestly not enlightened, social change could be initiated only through the action of the few people who had grasped the truth. Whether the action took the form of setting up Phalansteries or organising armed uprisings was less important than the fact that the workers were expected to be passive witnesses of their own liberation.

Marx wrote of the Utopians:

> In the formation of their plans they are conscious of caring chiefly for the interests of the working class, as being the most suffering class. Only from the point of view of being the most suffering class does the proletariat exist for them. The undeveloped state of the class struggle, as well as their own surroundings, causes socialists of this kind to consider themselves far superior to all class antagonisms. They want to improve the condition of every member of society, even that of the most favoured. Hence, they habitually appeal to society at large, without distinction of class, nay, by preference to the ruling class. For how can people, once they understand their system, fail to see in it the best possible plan of the best possible state of society? (**CW** vi 515)

Blanqui was no believer in class collaboration. When asked his profession, he replied, 'Proletarian'. He had mass working class support. But, as with the Utopians, his strategy reflected 'the undeveloped state of the class struggle'. The highly repressive nature of most 19th century regimes, and the underdevelopment of French industry, which was still mainly in small workshops, meant that open organisation based on the collective economic power of the working class was difficult, if not impossible, and underground activity essential. But the effect was an attitude to workers remarkably similar to that of the Utopian Socialists. For revolutionary communists and pacific Utopians alike, the working class was the object and not the subject of change.

Ricardo, Hegel and Feuerbach

The Utopian Socialists developed a brilliant critique of capitalist 'Civilisation', and produced some marvellous anticipations of a future communist 'Harmony'. Their weakness lay in a lack of any real understanding of how to get from one to the other, from capitalism to communism.

The French socialists were still prisoners of the Enlightenment. Their materialism did not extend to society: history was still seen as the 'progress of the human mind'. Moreover, neither Blanqui nor the Utopians had any scientific analysis of capitalism itself. To go further two things were needed—first, a new scientific method, superior to that of the Enlightenment, and, secondly, a better understanding of capitalism. The elements of these were provided by the two other sources of Marxism—German classical philosophy and British political economy. We shall start with the second of these, and its greatest representative, David Ricardo.

The anatomy of civil society

The thinkers of the Enlightenment drew a distinction between the state and civil society. The state, they argued, represented the

63

common interests of all citizens. Civil society, on the other hand, was the realm outside the state where individuals pursued their private economic interests. Everyone agreed that, without the state, society would collapse into chaos. People were assumed to be naturally aggressive, greedy, selfish and violent. If left to themselves, without the restraints imposed by the state, the result would be a 'war of all against all', of which Hobbes painted such a terrifying picture in his *Leviathan*.

The economic orthodoxy of the time argued that prosperity depended on state intervention. Sir James Steuart, for example, tried to show that capitalists would earn a profit on their investments only if the government stepped in to fix prices at a level higher than the costs of production. This theory fitted closely with the way states operated in the 17th and 18th centuries, imposing strict controls on the economic activities of their subjects.

The school of thinkers known as the classical political economists shared with the rest the assumption that people were naturally competitive and self interested. But they argued that the pursuit by individuals of their own self interest would guide the economy onto the best course without state intervention.

Adam Smith, the greatest of the Scottish historians, wrote *The Wealth of Nations* in 1776, in which he argued that state intervention in the economy could only be harmful. If individuals were left to pursue their own private interests, this would bring about an economic equilibrium in which all the resources of society were fully used.

Adam Smith was a university professor in Glasgow, one of the main centres of the industrial revolution, and he enjoyed close connections with the industrial and commercial bourgeoisie of the city. He wrote *The Wealth of Nations* very much as the spokesman of an innovative and self confident capitalism impatient with what it saw as unnecessary state interference. (Smith was not opposed, however, to such government measures as the Navigation Acts, which gave British capitalists a monopoly of colonial trade. These he regarded as in the interests of the class he represented.)

The concept of 'the market' was central to Adam Smith's ideas. For the wealth of which he writes appears as an immense collection of products—or commodities—which are bought and sold. It was logical, therefore, to seek to establish the factors which govern the prices at which these products are bought and sold, to try to establish the value of these products. These factors Smith identified as supply and demand. If there are more of a particular product around than there are people wanting them, he said, then the price will fall to attract more buyers. On the other hand, if there are more buyers around than there are products, then the price will rise until some of the buyers drop out.

Smith's theory of value was based on the idea that every commodity has a 'natural' price. This is the price for which it will sell when supply and demand balance. The three main classes of society, capitalists, workers, and landowners, will then each earn their income (respectively profits, wages, and rent) out of this price at its 'natural' rate.

There are three very important implications of Smith's concept of natural price. First, there is the idea that the capitalist economy spontaneously tends towards equilibrium, that the forces of supply and demand will tend to balance out so that commodities are sold at their 'natural' price. One of Smith's followers, Jean-Baptiste Say, even tried to prove that supply and demand will *always* match each other, and so economic crises, which arise when goods go unsold, are impossible.

Secondly, Smith's theory of value uncovers a *capitalist* economy. Previous economists did not distinguish between capitalists, artisans and labourers. Smith's originality lay in his treating capitalists as a separate class earning their own distinct form of income, profit, which was entirely different from the rent of land and the wages of labour.

Thirdly, for Smith capitalism is *natural*. For an 18th century writer this meant 'good'. Many Enlightenment thinkers had tried to criticise existing society on the grounds that it was artificial, and did not correspond to human nature. The most important of these was Jean-Jacques Rousseau, who contrasted the early stages of society, in which people lived in small and idyllic rural communities (as he saw them), with the 'unnatural' contrast between rich and poor which followed the division of labour and the emergence of money and trade.

For the political economists, however, the natural society belonged not to the beginnings of history, but was emerging from the industrial revolution—capitalism. Smith traced the division of labour back to 'a certain propensity in human nature', namely 'the propensity to truck, barter and exchange one thing for another'. The market, money and trade sprang from human nature, he said, rather than contradicting it, as Rousseau had argued.

Thomas Robert Malthus took this tendency much further. His notorious *Essay on the Principle of Population* (1798) was written in reply to Condorcet and other Enlightenment thinkers, whose optimistic belief that humanity could indefinitely improve their condition had helped inspire the French Revolution. (Malthus was an Anglican clergyman whose economic writings are devoted to defending the interests of the English landed aristocracy.)

According to Malthus's principle of population (which is based on exceedingly scant facts), it is a law of nature that population increases geometrically while food production grows only arithmetically, so that society will, in the course of things, outstrip its resources. Malthus argues that if the living standards of the mass of the population are any higher than the level of subsistence, they will start to have more children, until the imbalance between population and food production forces down living standards below subsistence, and causes famine and disease which, by removing surplus mouths, restore equilibrium.

So according to Malthus, any attempt to improve the living standards of the mass of the population was doomed to failure by 'law of nature'. Any attempt to create a society based upon liberty, equality and fraternity:

> ...would, from the inevitable laws of nature, and not from any fault in human institutions, degenerate in a very short period into a society constructed upon a plan not essentially different from that which prevails in every known state at present—a society divided into a class of proprietors and a class of labourers, and with self love for the mainspring of the great machine.

Capitalism is thus natural. Any attempt to do away with it is based on pure delusion. It is little wonder that Malthus's theory of population was invoked by 19th century capitalists and their apologists in order to justify paying workers their bare subsistence and no more.

Committed though political economy was to justifying the existence of capitalism, it nevertheless undertook the first serious enquiry into what Marx called 'the economic anatomy of the classes' (**SC** 69). This was most true of David Ricardo. His *Principles of Political Economy* (1817) advanced beyond Adam Smith in two crucial ways. First, Ricardo argued that 'the value of a commodity, or the quantity of a commodity for which it will exchange, depends on the relative quantity of labour which is necessary for its production'. This is, to all intents and purposes, the labour theory of value which Marx was to make the basis of his own analysis of capitalism.

Smith had tended to regard the 'natural' price of a commodity as determined by the 'natural' rates of its components, wages, profit and rent. For Ricardo, on the other hand, the value, or natural price, is set by the labour required to produce the commodity. Capitalists, workers and landowners must then fight over the division of this value among themselves.

Secondly, and as an obvious result of this labour theory of value, the interests of labour, capital and landowners are antagonistic. Ricardo argued that 'there can be no rise in the value of labour without a fall in profits'. Wages and profits are thus inversely related, so that capital's gain is labour's loss, and vice versa. Moreover, rent is a deduction from the value of the commodity so that 'the interest of the landlord is always opposed to the interest of every other class in the community'.

The significance of this theory of value and profits is that it places the class struggle, and in particular the struggle over the distribution of the social product—who should have what share of the 'national cake'—at the centre of capitalist society.

This recasting of political economy must be seen as, in part, an attempt by Ricardo, a successful MP and banker, to find a framework in which to examine the practical problems facing British capitalism in the early 19th century. This was a time of bitter class struggle, which pitted weavers against their masters, whose introduction of new machinery into the textile industry provoked the Luddite machine-breaking movement. At the same time, both workers and factory owners were united in opposition to the Corn Laws, which protected British landowners from foreign competition and so kept food prices high. Ricardo's first major treatise, published in 1815, sought to prove that cheap food would mean lower wages, and therefore would increase profits. His political economy championed the interests of the industrial bourgeoisie against those of the politically dominant landed aristocracy, defended by his friend Malthus.

Nevertheless, as Marx later pointed out, 'Ricardo's conception is, on the whole, in the interests of the *industrial bourgeoisie*, only *because*, and *in so far as*, their interests coincide with that of production or the productive development of human labour. When the bourgeoisie comes into conflict with this, he is just as *ruthless* towards it as he is at other times towards the proletariat and the aristocracy' (**TSV** ii 118). For example, in the third edition of the *Principles*, published in 1821, Ricardo added a chapter on machinery which showed that technological improvements could lead to unemployment. His horrified disciple J R McCulloch protested: 'If your reasoning...be well founded, the laws against the Luddites are a disgrace to the statute book.' This example of what Marx described as Ricardo's 'scientific ruthlessness' (**G** 754) may explain why his followers gradually abandoned his theory of value and profits.

Nevertheless, Ricardo shared the basic assumptions of the other political economists. He held that class struggle took place over the *distribution* of the social product. The *division* of society into a class of capitalists, owning the means of production—the factories and machines—and a class of workers, owning only their labour power—their strength and skills—he saw as natural.

Similarly, although Ricardo, like Marx after him, believed that the rate of profit tended to fall, he looked *outside* society for the explanation. Following Malthus, he argued that since population would rise faster than food production, then the productivity of labour in agriculture would tend to fall over time (this is the 'law of diminishing returns'). As a result, the subsistence wages necessary to keep workers alive would rise, so profits would fall until society reached a 'stationary rate' at which production would cease to grow. As Marx put it, Ricardo 'flees from economics to take refuge in organic chemistry' (**G** 754).

The source of these weaknesses lay in a conception of history which the classical economists still shared with the Enlightenment. Not that they were unaware of historical change. On the contrary, the Scottish historians and the French economist Turgot distinguished four stages of human development: hunting, pasturage, agriculture and commerce, each of which represented progress from its predecessor. But they saw 'commerce', by which they meant capitalism, as the *last* stage in human history.

There weren't going to be any further changes because capitalism was 'natural', since, they said, it corresponded to human nature with its innate need to 'truck and barter'.

Marx summed this attitude up thus:

> Economists have a singular method of procedure. There are only two kinds of institutions for them, artificial and natural. The institutions of feudalism are artificial institutions; those of the bourgeoisie are natural institutions... When the economists say that present day relations—the relations of bourgeois production—are natural, they imply that these are the relations in which wealth is created in conformity with the laws of nature. These relations therefore are themselves natural laws independent of the influence of time. They are eternal laws which must always govern society. Thus there has been history, but there is no longer any (**CW** vi 174).

Hegel and the dialectic

Classical political economy had got itself into a peculiar situation. It had revealed the contradiction at the heart of the society that was emerging from the 'dual revolution'—the fundamental conflict of interest between capital and labour. But, having discovered this, the political economists then wanted to call the historical process to a halt.

There were obvious political and ideological reasons for this standpoint. But it also reflected the Enlightenment's chief intellectual weakness, the lack of any concepts which would permit them to explain why and how historical change takes place. They tended to treat history, as we have seen, as the unfolding of human reason.

This weakness arose from the limitations of the mechanical materialism which underlay the thought of the Enlightenment. The physics of Galileo and Newton explained the motion of bodies as the result of external forces, gravity for example. But such a theory is not very satisfactory when applied to living organisms. The changes which an acorn undergoes when it becomes an oak do not seem to be the result of the action of outside forces. Living things go through a process of *development*. They

69

come into existence, mature, decay and die. This process seems to arise from the inner nature of the organism, not from the pressures it experiences from outside.

The inability of mechanical materialism to explain development and change led in the late 18th century to the emergence, especially in Germany, of what was called *Naturphilosophie* or 'Philosophy of Nature'. This school challenged the idea that all there was to nature was bodies acting on each other. Their actual theories were usually mystical and reactionary or backward looking, invoking notions of purpose which suggested that the world had after all been designed by God. Later developments in the sciences—Darwin's theory of evolution, the discovery of the organic cell, Mendel's genetics—mean that we can now explain how living organisms work without falling back on God.

The emergence of *Naturphilosophie* was important, however, because it encouraged people to look on society as itself an organism gradually developing and changing. Mechanical materialism suggested a picture of society as a collection of separate individuals, each pursuing their own interests independently of everyone else. To see society as an organism, however, means two things. First, individuals cannot live outside society—man is a social animal, not an isolated individual. Secondly, history is as natural to society as growth and decay are to the living body—society can only be understood historically.

It was Georg Wilhelm Friedrich Hegel who made such a view of society the basis of one of the grandest of all philosophical systems—and at the heart of Hegel's system was the dialectic, the way of thinking that was to provide the basis for an understanding of the historical process.

The dialectic was based on two assumptions. First, that 'all things are *contradictory in themselves*'. Secondly, that 'contradiction is at the root of all movement and life, and it is only in so far as it contains a contradiction that anything moves and has impulse and activity.'

To see what Hegel meant by contradiction, let's go back to the acorn and the oak. The acorn, in becoming an oak, has itself ceased to be. The oak is different from the acorn. The oak is *not* that acorn. Hegel would say that the oak is *the negation of* the acorn.

Yet implicit within the acorn is the potential to become an oak.

The acorn contains within itself its own negation, and is thus *contradictory*. It is this contradiction, says Hegel, and *only* this contradiction, that allows it to grow. Indeed this sort of contradiction is present in everything: reality is the process through which, again and again, the negation within things comes to the surface and changes them. Reality *is* change.

Hegel then takes this a step further. When something negates itself it turns into its opposite, he says. A famous example of this process is what Hegel called the transformation of quantity into quality. By this he meant the way a succession of small changes, each of which leaves the basic character of a thing unaltered, can lead, beyond a certain point, to its complete transformation. For example, gradually reducing the temperature of water will make no significant difference to it, until it reaches 0°C, when it will freeze, changing from a liquid to a solid. Melt the ice, and gradually raise the temperature of the water. Again no significant change will occur until 100°C is reached, when the water will evaporate, turning from a liquid into a gas. Thus a series of changes in the quantity of temperature of water leads to a change in its quality. Quantity, says Hegel, becomes its opposite, quality.

But Hegel argues that beneath this apparent opposition is an underlying unity. 'Neither the one nor the other has the truth. The truth is in their *movement*.'

To get at what he is trying to say, let's return to the acorn and the oak. They are, clearly, different and distinct from each other. In that sense, they are opposites. Nevertheless, the oak developed out of the acorn. It was once that acorn. Acorn and oak mark the beginning and end of the same process.

Another example may reinforce the point. A 70 year old man is obviously very different from the week old baby he once was. Yet they are the *same* person. The old man was once that baby and they share a basic identity despite the many transformations that 70 years of living bring about.

So Hegel's broader argument is that if we merely concentrate on individual things, we see only the differences between them. Once we look at things from the standpoint of the dialectic, however, we see that they are all part of the same process. 'The truth is the whole.' Things acquire their real meaning only when we see them as moments in a process of change.

71

The dialectic, Hegel's new philosophical method, his new way of looking at things, thus has three stages. First, simple unity, when we see the object itself before any change takes place. Second, the negation, when we see the object give rise to its opposite. Third, the negation of the negation, when we see these opposites reconciled into a greater unity.

So far I have tried to illustrate Hegel's dialectic by choosing rather banal examples for the sake of simplicity. Hegel himself, however, regarded only thought and society as truly dialectical. Hegel's own purpose was to show how all the phenomena of nature and the stages of human history were merely aspects of what he called 'Absolute Spirit'. This 'Absolute Spirit' is really only another way of saying 'God'.

Hegel believed that everything existed in the infinite mind of God. The grand scheme of his philosophical system was to show how God, the 'simple unity' of the first stage of the dialectic, gave rise to his negation, Nature, in the second stage, while the third stage was the unification of God and Nature through the development of human consciousness and understanding—culminating in the philosophy of Hegel himself.

He drew a parallel picture of human consciousness. The human mind, he says, believes itself to be separate from nature, isolated and lost in a world that is not its own. This he called *alienation*. This is overcome by growing human consciousness, which recognises that both nature and itself are aspects of a wider unity—again Absolute Spirit, or God. Hegel was in fact still tied down with the Enlightenment's conception of history as 'the progress of the human mind', except that he had elevated this to the progress of God's mind, or Absolute Mind. 'History is mind clothing itself with the form of events,' he wrote. And on this he built an immense philosophical scheme which he outlined in several long books. Most of Hegel's own conclusions were ultimately backward looking and need not concern us here. It was his *method*, his new dialectical way of looking at the world, that was the step forward.

The fact that his dialectics emphasised the contradiction in everything meant that Hegel did see the contradictions in the society around him—but the solutions he proposed were reactionary and backward looking. In the *Philosophy of Right* (1821)

Hegel argued that the market economy, if left unregulated, would lead to poverty, stagnation and social unrest. The antagonisms of the bourgeois social order, he said, could only be overcome by a state that was independent of that order, and that had the bureaucratic, semi-feudal structures of the Prussian monarchy.

Ultimately, Hegel's belief that opposites were reconciled in the 'Absolute' led him to preach the status quo. He left it to others to draw the revolutionary conclusions that followed from his 'dialectics'.

Feuerbach sets Hegel on his feet

According to Hegel's ideas, contradiction was 'at the root of all movement and life', and the *only* reality was change and movement. Applied to society, these were highly subversive ideas. They implied, in the words of Engels:

> [that] all successive historical systems are only transitory stages in the endless course of development of human society from the lower to the higher. Each stage is necessary, and therefore justified for the time and conditions to which it owes its origin. But in the face of new, higher conditions which develop in its own womb, it loses its validity and justification. It must give way to a higher stage which will also in its turn decay and perish (**SW** iii 339).

This meant that capitalism could not be the end of history, but merely one stage, and that it contained within itself its own contradiction. It was with this in mind that the 19th century Russian revolutionary Aleksandr Herzen wrote: 'The philosophy of Hegel is the algebra of revolution.'

But Hegel had got the whole thing upside down. He had discovered the dialectical process at work in natural and historical events. He sought to isolate what all these had in common. He then made these shared features the basis of his logic. Finally, he claimed that these logical categories were themselves *responsible* for the life and movement of the real world. The dialectic, from being a way of understanding the world, a way of thinking, had been elevated into the controlling factor itself. Thought created reality, said Hegel, just as in the Bible God creates the world.

73

LIVERPOOL JOHN MOORES UNIVERSITY
LEARNING SERVICES

'Hegel fell into the illusion', wrote Marx, 'of conceiving the real as the product of thought,' but 'the real subject retains its autonomous existence outside the head' (**G** 101). The dialectic, he said, 'is standing on its head. It must be inverted, in order to discover the rational kernel within the mystical shell' (**C** i 103).

The dialectical categories, like all products of thought, merely reflect the real, material world. They could be a tool to understanding the material world, but first they had to be released from their 'mystical shell'. And it was Ludwig Feuerbach who set Hegel's ideas back on their feet.

Hegel had said that the first 'simple unity' was God, the 'Absolute Idea'. Then came the 'negation', the material world, which was opposed to and alienated from God, until the third stage of the dialectic, the growth of man's consciousness, which would reconcile God and the material world in Absolute Spirit. Feuerbach argued that Hegel had turned something that is merely the property of human beings, the faculty of thought, into the ruling principle of existence. Instead of seeing human beings as part of the material world, and thought merely as the way they reflect that material world, Hegel had turned both man and nature into mere reflections of the all powerful Absolute Idea.

This, said Feuerbach, is at the root of all religion. Religion takes what are human powers—the ability to think, to act on and change the world, and so on—and transfers them to an imaginary being, God. Thus they turn their own powers into something alien from themselves. So this product of human thought, God, is made all powerful and all knowing, while human beings themselves are devalued, regarded as sinful, weak and foolish creatures, the puppets of their own invention. They are alienated from their own powers.

Feuerbach's analysis of religion, and the materialist philosophy on which his analysis rested, had an enormous impact on the Left Hegelians of the 1840s. Engels writes of *The Essence of Christianity* (1841) that:

> ...it placed materialism on the throne again. Nature exists independently of all philosophy. It is the foundation upon which we human beings, ourselves products of nature, have grown up. Nothing exists outside nature and man, and the higher beings our religious fantasies have created are only the fantastic reflections of

our own essence... One must have experienced the liberating effect of this book to get an idea of it. Enthusiasm was general; we all became at once Feuerbachians (**SW** iii 344).

Feuerbach's achievement was that he reinstated the materialism of the Enlightenment. His most basic concept was that of human nature, which he called 'species being'. But Feuerbach did not simply return to the Enlightenment. Like Fourier and the other Utopian Socialists, he widened the concept of human nature so that it included more than mere self interest. 'The essence of man is contained only in community, in *the unity of man with man*', he wrote.

But, like the philosophers of the Enlightenment, Feuerbach still conceived human nature as something which did not change. What was necessary, he argued, was to make people aware of their true nature. This could be achieved only through a process of education whose aim would be to destroy the influence of religion on people's minds.

Marx aptly summed up Feuerbach's position when he wrote that 'in so far as Feuerbach is a materialist he does not deal with history, and in so far as he considers history he is not a materialist' (**CW** v 41).

Nevertheless, Feuerbach's critique of Hegel provided the starting point for Marx's own distinctive position. Materialism, the belief that thought reflects the world, and does not create it, lay at the basis of his conception of history. 'It is not the consciousness of men that determines their being, but, on the contrary, their social being which determines their consciousness' (**SW** i 503).

In *The Holy Family* Marx championed the materialism of the 17th century scientific revolution and the 18th century Enlightenment against the Young Hegelians. He lampooned the latter's belief that thought ruled the world in the preface to *The German Ideology*:

Once upon a time a valiant fellow had the idea that men were drowned in water only because they were possessed with the *idea of gravity*. If they were to get this notion out of their heads, say by avowing it to be a superstitious, a religious concept, they would be sublimely proof against any danger from water. His whole life long he fought against the illusion of gravity, of whole harmful

75

consequences all statistics brought him new and manifold evidence. This valiant fellow was the type of the new revolutionary philosophers in Germany (**CW** v 24).

For the Hegelian left, all that people had to do to become free, was to think themselves free, to rid themselves of the 'illusion of unfreedom'. Max Stirner, the main target of *The German Ideology*, dismissed the material apparatus of the state, with all its repressive power, as a 'spook', a phantom created by our own imagination. Marx's criticism of Feuerbach was that he did not go far enough. History as well as nature had to be understood materialistically.

capitalist, in which a non-worker controls, and profits from, the labour of others.

Capitalism, for Marx, is a world in which the worker is dominated by the products of his labour, which have taken on the shape of an alien being, capital. This vision, so powerfully developed in the *1844 Manuscripts*, is to be found in Marx's later writings, including *Capital*. But his analysis of alienated labour still bears the marks of his philosophical past.

In the first place, everything is built about the contrast between human nature as it is—debased, distorted, alienated—and as it should be. In the *Manuscripts*, capitalism is still primarily an *unnatural* society, the 'social hell' which Fourier and the other Utopians had denounced for its failure to fulfil human beings' genuine needs.

Such a primarily moral diagnosis of the weaknesses of capitalist society is an essential part of any socialist theory. But what would distinguish Marx's later writings from those of earlier socialists was his analysis of the way in which capitalism creates the material and social conditions of its overthrow. Marx is not yet in the *Manuscripts* really concerned with what he would call in *Capital* 'the economic law of motion of modern society' (**C** i 92), but primarily with showing how capitalism denies human nature.

Again, it is true that the class struggle is seriously considered by Marx for the first time here. The first of the *Manuscripts* begins with the words: '*Wages* are determined through the antagonistic struggle between capitalist and worker' (**CW** iii 235). Nevertheless, there is no real discussion of how the class struggle plays a crucial role in both the development and the overthrow of capitalism. Communism figures still in the *Manuscripts* as a philosophical category, as the goal from which the whole of history takes its meaning. Marx calls it 'the riddle of history solved' (**CW** iii 297). The influence of Hegel's circular dialectic, in which the outcome of history, the reconciliation of contradictions in Absolute Spirit, is determined from the outset, is still strong.

These philosophical traces have their political effects. One implication of the analysis of alienated labour is that the capitalists are themselves alienated, themselves condemned to live a less than human, debased existence. This sort of argument had been

83

used by the Utopian Socialists to justify appealing to capitalists as well as workers, arguing that they too stood to benefit from the overthrow of bourgeois society.

What Engels said in 1892 of his own early writings is true of Marx's *Economic and Philosophical Writings of 1844*:

> Modern international socialism...did not exist in 1844. My book represents one of the phases of its embryonic development; and as the human embryo, in its early stages, still reproduces the gill arches of our fish ancestors, so this book exhibits everywhere the traces of the descent of modern socialism from one of its ancestors, German philosophy. Thus great stress is laid on the dictum that communism is not a mere party doctrine of the working class, but a theory encompassing the emancipation of society at large, including the capitalist class, from its present narrow conditions. This is true enough in the abstract, but absolutely useless, and sometimes worse, in practice. So long as the wealthy classes not only do not feel the want of any emancipation, but strenuously oppose the self emancipation of the working class, so long the social revolution will have to be prepared and fought out by the working class alone (**SW** iii 444).

In later works, *The German Ideology, The Poverty of Philosophy, Capital* and its drafts, Marx fully developed his theory of history, and showed how capitalist exploitation forces workers to organise collectively for its overthrow. The analysis of alienated labour in the *1844 Manuscripts* is, as Engels says, an embryo of that later, mature theory.

The logic of *Capital*

'If Marx did not leave behind him a "*Logic*" (with a capital letter), he did leave behind the *logic* of *Capital*,' wrote Lenin. By this Lenin meant that although Marx never wrote 'two or three printer's sheets' extracting the 'rational kernel' of Hegel's dialectic, *Capital* shows his method at work. Its study, therefore, should enable us to understand the principles underlying Marx's version of the dialectic.

Marx's starting point was radically different from Hegel's:

My dialectical method is, in its foundations, not only different from the Hegelian, but exactly opposite to it. For Hegel, the process of thinking, which he even transforms into an independent subject, under the name of 'the Idea', is the creator of the real world, and the real world is only the external appearance of the idea. With me the reverse is true: the ideal is nothing but the material world reflected in the mind of man, and translated into forms of thought (**C** i 102).

Marx's approach was, in other words, materialist:

The premises from which we begin are not arbitrary ones, not dogmas, but real premises from which abstraction can only be made in the imagination. They are the real individuals, their activity and the material conditions of their life, both those which they find already existing and those produced by their activity. These premises can thus be verified in a purely empirical way (**CW** v 31).

It does not follow that we can come to understand 'the real individuals, their activity and the material conditions of their life' merely by observing and recording them. The reason is that appearances are sometimes deceptive. Things are not always as they seem. For example, to judge by our own observations, the earth stands still, and the sun goes round it. In fact, precisely the opposite is the case.

Marx himself gives this example in *Capital*, when he writes that 'the apparent motions of the heavenly bodies are intelligible only to someone who is acquainted with their real motions, which are not perceptible to the senses' (**C** i 433). He thus distinguishes between the real, but concealed, and the apparent, but misleading behaviour of objects. This distinction, between what he calls the *essence*, or inner structure, and the *phenomenon*, or outward appearance of things, runs right through *Capital*. Indeed, he declares that 'all science would be superfluous if the outward appearance and the essence of things coincided' (**C** iii 817).

Whatever general reasons there may be for appearance differing from reality, Marx had grounds for thinking this to be especially so of capitalism. For capitalism, as a class society, uses ideology systematically to distort our perception of how it works.

To penetrate beneath the appearances, Marx appeals to what he calls 'the power of abstraction' (**C** i 90). By this he means that we must form concepts which capture the most basic and general features of the reality we are trying to understand, and from which have been removed all secondary and irrelevant matters. For example, physics takes the *mass* of a body, setting aside such questions as its colour, its chemical composition, and whether it is composed of dead or living matter. On the basis of this concept of mass, scientists could formulate such theories as the principle of inertia, the law of gravitation and the law of free fall, which are applicable to all bodies.

Marx believed that Ricardo had performed a similar feat of abstraction when he formulated the labour theory of value: 'At last Ricardo steps in and calls to science: Halt! The basis, the starting point for the physiology of the bourgeois system—for the understanding of its internal organic coherence and life process—is the determination of *value by labour time*' (**TSV** ii 165-6).

The problem is that such abstractions usually contradict the appearances (indeed, if they didn't, then, as Marx says, there would be no need for science). The law of free fall, for example, according to which all bodies fall at an acceleration of 32 feet per second per second, is true only in a vacuum. In reality, because of air friction, a stone and a feather will not hit the ground at the same time. Again, as Ricardo and Marx both knew, commodities do not actually exchange in proportion to the labour time required to produce them.

What this means is that abstraction is only the *starting point* of any scientific analysis. It permits us to isolate the basic features. We must then explain how these features are related to what we can observe with our eyes. Marx was highly critical of Ricardo's method, objecting that he merely juxtaposed the abstract concept he had formulated (the labour theory of value) to the living reality which he wished to explain. The two were left quite unrelated to each other, merely sitting side by side. For Marx, on the other hand, abstraction was simply a means to an end, a detour through which better to understand the world.

Marx takes as an example the general rate of profit, which, as we shall see later, apparently contradicts the labour theory of value. Ricardo had simply accepted the existence of the general rate of profit, without (as Marx did) using the labour theory of value to explain it:

Instead of *postulating* this *general rate of profit*, Ricardo should
have examined how far its existence is in fact consistent with the
determination of value by labour time, and he would have found
that, instead of being consistent with it...it *contradicts* it, and that
its existence would therefore have to be explained through a
number of intermediary stages (**TSV** ii 174).

This process of explaining appearances by starting from abstractions, and working 'through a number of intermediary
stages', Marx called 'the method of rising from the abstract to the
concrete' (**G** 101). By 'concrete' Marx means the actually existing world, as we observe it. He writes:

[that] it seems to be correct to begin with the real and the concrete...thus to begin, in economics, with for example the population, which is...the foundation and the subject of the entire social
act of production. However, on closer examination this proves
false. The population is an abstraction if I leave out, for example,
the classes of which it is composed. These classes in turn are an
empty phrase if I am not familiar with the elements on which they
rest. For example wage labour, capital etc. These latter in turn
presuppose exchange, division of labour, prices etc. For example,
capital is nothing without wage labour, without value, money,
price etc. Thus, if I were to begin with population, this would be
a chaotic conception of the whole, and I would then, by means of
further determination, move analytically towards ever more
simple concepts, from the imagined concrete towards ever thinner
abstractions until I had arrived at the simplest determinations.
From there the journey would have to be retraced until I had finally arrived at the population again, but this time not as the
chaotic conception of a whole, but as a rich totality of many determinations and relations (**G** 100).

This, then, is Marx's method of analysis. First we must recognise that reality is complex, made up of many different elements.
As Marx puts it: 'The concrete is the concentration of many determinations, hence unity of the diverse' (**G** 101). To understand
this reality, we have then to use 'the power of abstraction' to
break it into these 'simplest determinations'. And having isolated
these, we can then use them to reconstruct concrete reality, 'this

time…as a rich totality of many determinations and relations.'

So we move first from concrete to abstract, breaking down the concrete into its 'simplest determinations', and then from abstract to concrete, using these to reconstruct the whole. We shall see this method at work when Marx analyses capitalist society in *Capital*.

Marx calls concrete reality, despite its complexity, a 'totality', '*unity* of the diverse'. The notion that society forms a whole is central to his method. The different aspects of society can only be understood as parts of the whole; they do not make any sense in isolation from one another. Resolving the whole into its 'simplest determinations' is only a preliminary to recomposing them into 'a rich totality of many determinations and relations'. Marx criticised the political economists because they tended to treat society as a collection of isolated individuals lacking any real relation to one another, so that 'the limbs of the social system are dislocated' (**CW** vi 166-7).

Once we see society as a totality, then the idea that it changes through time is easy to grasp. Another of Marx's criticisms of the political economists was that they treated the laws they established for capitalism as applicable to every form of society. 'Economists express the relations of bourgeois production…as fixed, immutable, eternal categories.' As a result, they 'explain how production takes place in the above-mentioned relations [of production], but what they do not explain is how these relations themselves are produced, that is, the historical movement which gave them birth' (**CW** vi 162).

Marx's approach, on the other hand, is always historical. Capitalist relations of production are those of a historically specific, and transitory, form of society. 'Economic categories are only the abstractions of the social relations of production,' says Marx (**CW** vi 165), so these too will change as society changes.

Marx is able to acquire this historical perspective thanks to Hegel. 'All things are *contradictory in themselves*,' said Hegel, including forms of society. But while Hegel dissolved the antagonisms of society ultimately into the Absolute, Marx believed that there is no end to contradiction. It is the contradiction that leads to change—as the contradictions in feudal society led to the change to capitalism. And capitalism contains its own contradictions which will lead to further change.

The dialectic thus becomes a theory of historical development, rather than, as in Hegel, the autobiography of God or Absolute Spirit. Each form of social organisation contains within it the contradictions that give it the potential for change. It is a 'unity of opposites', and historical development is the struggle of these opposites.

If we say that every class society is a unity of opposites, in which one class exploits another opposing class, then we are saying a number of important things. Firstly, that each class exists only in its antagonistic relationship to the other. Exploiter and exploited are mutually dependent on each other. Thus, capital is inseparable from wage labour, since it is the latter which creates the profits which are capital's life blood; while, says Marx, *'wage labour...is capital producing labour'* (**G** 462).

Marx's concept of class is thus very different from that used by sociologists, for whom classes are defined by the technical function they perform in the division of labour (white collar workers, manual workers, managers, professionals and so on). Classes for Marx only emerge through their antagonistic relationship to each other. In a sense, the class struggle comes before classes, since it is only when they clash and perceive their conflicting interests that social groups begin to behave as classes.

Another important implication of the notion of the unity of opposites is that the class struggle is inherent in societies divided into classes. Many sociologists and historians are prepared to admit the existence of, and to study 'social conflict'. However, this conflict is seen as something accidental, the product of abnormal and temporary tensions, which can be eliminated by skilful 'social engineering' without damaging the fabric of the existing order. Society, for most non-Marxist thinkers, is essentially harmonious.

Marx, on the contrary, conceived society as a unity of opposites, of which the class struggle was an essential part, and would continue until the basic contradiction, the exploitive social relationship at the heart of society, was eliminated.

This is entirely different from Hegel's position. The third stage of Hegel's dialectic involves a reconciliation of the opposites in which the mutually opposed and contradictory elements are dissolved into each other through the recognition that they are basically the same, both part of 'Absolute Spirit'. For Marx, on the other hand, contradictions can only be overcome through *struggle*, and through the victory of one opposite over the other. The antagonism between wage labour and capital is no mere illusion; it cannot be abolished through some mental change, some different way of seeing things, but only through revolutionary social change.

Marx's method involved, therefore, not merely conceiving society as a whole, in which all the different aspects were connected, but conceiving it as a unity of opposites. Indeed, he believed that only by seeing society as such a contradictory unity could it be understood as a totality. Marx made considerable fun of Proudhon's 'dialectical' method of dividing everything into a good and bad side, and then arguing that history could only progress by eliminating the bad side. 'What constitutes dialectical movement is the coexistence of two contradictory sides, their conflict and their fusion into a new category' (**CW** vi 168). 'It is the bad side that produces the movement which makes history by providing a struggle' (**CW** vi 174).

For Marx, without the 'bad side'—violence, exploitation and struggle—there would be no historical movement and development. Discussing the effects of British rule in India, Marx pitilessly described the greed and destructiveness of the colonisers, and the resulting disintegration of the 'industrious, patriarchal and inoffensive' communal village system. However, he argued that British colonialism had played a historically progressive role in sweeping away the 'idyllic village communities' which had been the 'solid foundation of oriental despotism', and replacing them with capitalist social relations which could provide the material basis for the complete abolition of classes:

> England, it is true, in causing a social revolution in Hindostan, was actuated only by the vilest interests, and was stupid in her manner of enforcing them. But that is not the question. The question is, can mankind fulfil its destiny without a fundamental revolution in the social state of Asia? If not, whatever may have been the crimes of England, she was the unconscious tool of history in bringing about that revolution (**CW** xii 132).

The violence and exploitation characteristic of capitalism are thus necessary conditions of the development of communism. They are unavoidable:

> When a great social revolution shall have mastered the results of the bourgeois epoch, the market of the world and the modern powers of production, and subjected them to the common control of the most advanced peoples, then only will human progress cease to resemble the hideous pagan idol, who will not drink the nectar but from the skulls of the slain (**CW** xii 222).

The philosophy of practice

Both Marx and Hegel, despite their other differences, saw history as an objective process, one that took place independently of the consciousness and will of the human beings caught up in it. Both would have agreed with Spinoza that the attitude of the true thinker was 'neither to laugh, nor to weep, nor to condemn, but to understand'.

Marx also took from Hegel a rejection of purely moral criticism. Such criticism, typical of both the Hegelian left and the Utopian Socialists, merely contrasts an existing state of affairs with an ideal one which is in some way preferable, a contradiction between how society 'is' and how it 'ought' to be. But this contradiction is one between mind and reality. It is not a contradiction in reality itself, so it is a contradiction which can never be overcome.

A *dialectical* understanding of reality, however, is able to detect within the existing state of affairs possibilities for change, to discover the tendencies within the present situation which will lead to its transformation. Political action must base itself on what is objectively possible, not on fantasies and good intentions spun from the thinker's brain.

This does not mean, however, that Marx believed that conscious human action was irrelevant to changing history. On the contrary, Marxism is best understood, in the words of the great Italian revolutionary Antonio Gramsci, as 'the philosophy of practice'. In the 'Theses on Feuerbach' Marx decisively rejected the view, shared by Hegel and his followers, the Enlightenment, and the Utopian Socialists, that thought can be isolated from

91

social practice, so that history is essentially a history of ideas, of changing conceptions of the world. According to Marx, thought can be understood only as part of social life, not as something which develops independently of that life:

> Men are the producers of their conceptions, ideas etc, that is, real active men, as they are conditioned by a definite development of their productive forces and of the intercourse corresponding to these, up to its furthest forms. Consciousness can never be anything else but conscious being, and the being of men is their actual life process (**CW** v 36).

Human thought is thus a response to the problems posed by 'the actual life process', that is, of the material and social conditions in which people live. It consists of 'the ideological reflexes and echoes of this life process' (**CW** v 36). It follows that the source of change is not the adoption by human beings of new ways of seeing the world. Rather, these new ways are a product of changes in material and social conditions:

> Men, developing their material production and their material intercourse, alter, along with this their actual world, also their thinking and the products of their thinking. It is not consciousness that determines life, but life that determines consciousness (**CW** v 37).

The eleventh 'Thesis on Feuerbach' declares: 'The philosophers have only *interpreted* the world in various ways; the point is to *change* it' (**CW** v 5). This is a direct attack on the Young Hegelians, who 'consider...all the products of consciousness, to which they attribute an independent existence, as the real chains of men...[their] demand to change consciousness amounts to a demand to interpret the existing world in a different way, ie to recognise it by means of a different interpretation' (**CW** v 30). In other words, the belief that a change of ideas will transform reality simply produces a new way of looking at reality, which itself remains unchanged. Idealism is thus a profoundly conservative viewpoint, because it allows us to think that the battle of ideas is a substitute for the struggle to change the material and social conditions of which thought is a reflection.

At the same time, Marx argued that it was an equally serious mistake to regard people as merely the victims of society. It is very easy for critics of capitalism to regard workers as being so shaped and deformed by their exploitation as to be incapable of independent thought and action. There are, for example, many socialists today who believe that the working class has been effectively corrupted by racist and sexist ideology, and by the economic concessions that have been wrested from the employers and the state in the advanced industrial countries.

Marx believed such a view (it was prevalent among the Utopian Socialists of his day) was profoundly elitist. The third of the 'Theses on Feuerbach' declares:

> The materialist doctrine that men are products of circumstances and upbringing, and that, therefore, changed men are products of other circumstances and changed upbringing, forgets that it is men who change circumstances and that the educator must himself be educated. Hence, this doctrine is bound to divide society into two parts, one of which is superior to society (**CW** v 7).

What Marx meant was this. Workers, according to the view he is attacking, are too debased and corrupt to do anything about capitalism. This situation will change only under socialism, which will create a new sort of human being, one that no longer suffers from the defects of people under capitalism. But this seems a counsel of despair. How will socialism ever be achieved if capitalism is able to prevent the masses from recognising that their interest lies in its abolition? Only if an enlightened minority of socialists who are somehow exempt from the conditioning of capitalism transform society *for* the masses.

This apparently highly materialist view thus collapses into idealism, since it supposes that there are people who have risen above the pressures of bourgeois society, and therefore above the class struggle. We are back then to the elitism of Utopian Socialism and Blanqui, both of which treat workers as the object rather than the subject of change.

Marx argues that this whole analysis is fundamentally mistaken, since it fails to grasp the role played by *struggle* in transforming both people and society. The third 'Thesis on Feuerbach' concludes: 'The coincidence of the changing of circumstances and of human activity or self change can be conceived and

93

rationally understood only as *revolutionary practice*' (**CW** v 4).

In other words, workers are not simply passively shaped by society. Capitalism, because it is a form of society based on exploitation, that is, on the contradiction between capital and labour, gives rise to the class struggle. The effect of this struggle is to transform the working class. The pressure of the battle with the employer forces workers to organise collectively, and to behave increasingly as a class conscious of its interest in transforming society. The experience of struggle makes workers aware that their interests differ from those of the capitalists. The victories they win, however small the issues involved may seem, give them the confidence necessary to engage in the political movement necessary to wrest power from the bourgeoisie.

The class struggle is also decisive in establishing socialism. Marx did not believe that capitalism would collapse under the pressure of its contradictions. The victory of the working class was in no sense inevitable. The outcome of his dialectic, unlike Hegel's, was not predetermined in advance. Everything depended ultimately on the consciousness, organisation and confidence of the working class.

We can sum this up by saying that at the heart of Marx's thought was the proposition that socialism is the self emancipation of the working class. It is only by their own efforts that workers can be rid of capitalism. They are their own liberators. No one else can achieve socialism for them, neither the well intentioned efforts of Utopian reformers, nor the conspiracies of Blanquist insurrectionists. The general rules of the International Working Men's Association, written by Marx, begin with the words: 'The emancipation of the working classes must be conquered by the working classes themselves' (**SW** ii 19).

Nothing could, therefore, be further from the truth than to say that Marx's conception of history is 'deterministic', if by this it is meant that socialism is, for him, inevitable. On the contrary, human activity, in the form of the 'revolutionary practice' of the class struggle, would be decisive in determining the fate of capitalist society.

Of course, this activity does not take place in a vacuum. Marx made this clear when he wrote at the beginning of *The Eighteenth Brumaire of Louis Bonaparte*: 'Men make their own history, but they do not make it just as they please; they do not make it under circumstances chosen by themselves, but under circumstances directly encountered, given and transmitted from the past' (**CW** xi 103). What human activity can achieve in a particular historical period depends upon the prevailing material and social conditions. His analysis of these conditions is the core of Marx's theory of history.

History and the class struggle

The most widely accepted view of history is also the most childish. History is seen as the doings of Great Men (and occasionally Great Women), of kings and politicians, generals and churchmen, artists and film stars. Such a conception of history can be traced back to the medieval chroniclers, who recorded the doings of monarchs and noblemen, their feasts, wars and adulteries. We are still served up with the same view, by courtesy of the most advanced technology, on the television screen and in the headlines of the daily tabloids.

There have always been those who were dissatisfied with this superficial view of history, who believed there was a more fundamental pattern at work beneath the play of events. In the Middle Ages, the ideological power of the church meant that this pattern was seen in primarily religious terms. The doings of men and women were interpreted as the workings of Divine Providence. Unconsciously human beings, while pursuing their own desires and interests, were fulfilling God's design for the universe. Hegel was the last great Christian philosopher, with his conception of history as the process through which Absolute

Spirit comes to self consciousness.

The scientific revolution of the 17th century led to a secular view of history, in which God no longer plays any role. But the Enlightenment still saw history as having a pattern, namely 'the progress of the human mind'. History was the story of the growing power of reason, of its constant battle with superstition, and of its inevitable but gradual victory. Such a view was both idealistic, since it conceived of ideas as the motor of historical change, and optimistic, since it involved the belief that society was steadily improving as people became more enlightened.

The Enlightenment conception of history was fairly credible in the 18th and 19th centuries, when the Western world, at least, experienced steady material and scientific progress. It is no longer plausible today. The 20th century has seen disaster heaped on disaster—two vastly destructive world wars, the horrors of the Nazi concentration camps and the prison camps of Stalinist Russia, the obscene juxtaposition of Western affluence and mass starvation in the Third World. Technical progress has accelerated so that our control over the natural environment has made astonishing leaps and bounds just in the past few decades. But the outcome of this progress may well be the destruction of humanity and of the earth itself as more and more resources are poured into producing ever more sophisticated nuclear weapons.

It is hardly surprising that many people have responded by denying that history has any pattern at all. History is for many a meaningless chaos of terrible events—'a succession of emergencies', as the liberal politician H A L Fisher put it. 'History is a nightmare from which I am trying to awake', wrote James Joyce, in words that speak for many people. It has been tempting in this terrible century to abandon any attempt to change the world, and to take refuge in personal relations or, in the case of those with the talents and the economic opportunities, personal achievement.

Marx's theory of history is a challenge thrown down both to the facile optimism of the Enlightenment and to the more modern view of history as mere chaos. For Marx, history does have a pattern. But not 'the progress of the human mind'. Marx's starting point is not thought but 'the real individuals, their activity and the material conditions of their life, both those which they find already existing and those produced by their activity' (**CW** v 31).

Production and society

As early as the *Economic and Philosophical Manuscripts of 1844* Marx had defined human beings as, first and foremost, producers. Their production has two aspects, material and social. Firstly it is the activity through which men and women seek to meet their needs by acting on and transforming nature. This implies a certain organisation of production, the possession of the appropriate tools, and so on. Secondly, production is a social process, in which people cooperate to produce the things they need. It always involves social relations between those taking part, relations which, crucially, concern the control of the process of production and the distribution of its products.

Marx calls the first, material aspect, the *forces of production*, and its second, social aspect, the *relations of production*.

The nature of the forces of production in a given society depends on what Marx calls the 'labour process', through which human beings act upon and transform nature. 'Labour', he writes, 'is first of all a process between man and nature, a process by which man, through his own actions, mediates, regulates and controls the metabolism between himself and nature' (**C** i 283).

Let us start with a sketch of the way human beings set out to meet their needs. The earliest human beings lived by hunting animals—for which they needed their own strength and hunting skills, and weapons, whether sharp sticks and stones that they found or spears and axes that they fashioned. Then people started tilling the land to grow food—again they needed their own strength and skills, plus more sophisticated tools. And more recently there is factory production—again nature provides the raw materials, human beings provide their labour, and we use yet more sophisticated tools: machines, electronic computers and so on.

In all three examples we can discern three things. Firstly there is 'nature', the animals that were hunted, the seeds to be sown and the land where they grew, and the raw materials to be processed in the factories. Secondly there is human labour. And thirdly there are the tools, whether hunting spears, ploughs or computers.

Marx puts these things under two headings. The labour process, he says, is composed of two basic elements, human *labour power* and the *means of production*. The means of production he divides again into two parts: the land and the raw materials which are to be transformed into the things we need—these he calls the 'object of labour'; and the tools we use—which he calls the 'instruments of labour'.

These tools, says Marx, form the decisive element in the labour process. What human labour can achieve depends on the instruments available to it:

> The use and construction of certain instruments of labour, although present in germ among certain species of animals, is characteristic of the specifically human labour process, and [Benjamin] Franklin therefore defines man as a 'tool-making animal'... It is not what is made, but how, and by what instruments of labour, that distinguishes different economic epochs (**C** i 286).

> The labour process...is an appropriation of what exists in nature for the requirements of man. It is...the everlasting nature-imposed condition of human existence, and it is therefore...common to all forms of society in which human beings live. We did not, therefore, have to present the worker in his relationship with other workers; it was enough to present man and his labour on one side, nature and its materials on the other. The taste of porridge does not tell us who grew the oats, and the process we have presented does not reveal the conditions under which it takes place, whether it is happening under the slave owner's brutal lash or the anxious eye of the capitalist (**C** i 290).

In other words, the organisation of the labour process, for example the division of labour which it may involve, does not in itself determine the nature of the society in question. There is a world of difference between the slash-and-burn agriculture of 'primitive' societies and modern assembly line production. The difference, in the first instance, is the outcome of the greater skill of human labour power today, of the development of scientific knowledge, and, as a result of this, of the much greater sophistication of the instruments of labour which we use.

These are material constraints on the labour process, which are there whatever the social relations between those who take part in that labour process. For example, to produce a car, we must have the technical skill and scientific knowledge necessary to construct an internal combustion engine; we need to be able to work metal in order to build the bodywork; to tap rubber and convert it into tyres; to extract the fuel which will power the car. These abilities are historical achievements which represent the growing power of human beings over nature. They will be needed as much under a future communist society as under capitalism.

The nature of the labour process is thus a reflection of the development of human technology, which in turn depends on our theoretical knowledge and practical skills. Improvements in the labour process mean that we can produce the same amount of things we need with a smaller quantity of labour. Potentially, therefore, they reduce the burden of material production on humanity. At the same time, they make us less dependent on the vicissitudes of our natural environment. They increase our control over nature. Today whether there is a shortage or plenty no longer depends on whether the summer has been a good one or not.

Marx believed that this development of the productive forces is cumulative. In other words, the technical and scientific achievements of one society provide a basis on which future societies can build. Changes in the labour process enable us to produce more efficiently, and thereby to expand our control over nature. This is a process, Marx argued, which has been going on throughout human history from the neolithic revolution, when human beings first began to sow crops and keep domestic animals, to the industrial revolution of the 18th and 19th centuries.

The development of the forces of production is a necessary condition for any improvement in our lives. Even under a future communist society, the labour process will be 'the everlasting nature-imposed condition of human existence'. But this development of the forces of production is not enough to explain historical change and development. The growth of our scientific knowledge and our practical skills does not occur in isolation from the way we organise to use the forces of production, from the social relations of production.

To understand what Marx meant by the relations of production we have to distinguish between two senses in which production is social. First, work is necessarily a social activity since it depends upon the cooperation of a number of individuals in order to achieve a common goal. In this respect, the relationships between individuals are determined by the material constraints of producing in a certain way. The allocation of tasks to the producers will reflect the nature of the labour process in question and the skills of the individuals.

But there is a second social aspect to production, one in which the *means of production*, the tools and raw materials, are again a decisive element. Marx writes:

> Whatever the social form of production, labourers and means of production always remain factors in it... For production to go on they must unite. The specific manner in which this union is accomplished distinguishes the different economic epochs of the structure of society from one another (**C** ii 36-7).

Marx argues that we cannot understand the nature of production, and therefore the nature of society, without examining who controls the means of production. For two reasons. First, once we have got beyond the most primitive forms of agriculture, no labour process can take place without means of production. Indeed, even slash-and-burn agriculture depends on having relatively free access to land.

Secondly, the distribution of the means of production provides the key to the division of society into classes. For there is no inherent necessity in the labour process which requires that the producers, those who do the actual work, should control the means of production, the tools and raw materials with which they work. Classes arise when the 'direct producers' have been separated from the means of production, which have become the monopoly of a minority.

This separation only takes place once the productive forces have developed to a certain level. Looking at the working day in a class society, Marx discerns two portions. During the first the direct producer performs necessary labour. In other words, he or she produces the means of subsistence needed to keep him or herself and dependents alive. (Under capitalism, the worker produces not the actual means of subsistence, but their equivalent in other goods for which he or she is paid in money, but the basic relationship is the same.)

During the second portion of the working day, the producer performs surplus labour. The product of these hours is taken, not by the person who did the actual work, but by the owner of the means of production. This is done in exchange for permitting the worker the privilege of using those means of production to do the labour without whose products he or she would perish. As Marx writes:

> Wherever a part of society possesses the monopoly of the means of production, the worker, free or unfree, must add to the labour time necessary for his own maintenance an extra quantity of labour time in order to produce the means of subsistence for the owner of the means of production, whether this proprietor be an Athenian aristocrat, an Etruscan theocrat, a Roman citizen, a Norman baron, an American slave owner, a Wallachian boyar, a modern landlord or a capitalist (**C** i 344-5).

Class society rests, therefore, on exploitation, that is, on the appropriation of surplus labour by a minority who control the means of production. However, in the early phases of human development, what Marx called 'primitive communism', in which the means of production were owned in common, there was little or no surplus labour. Almost all the working day was taken up with necessary labour to meet society's basic needs.

Only gradually, thanks to improvements in productive technique, do people become able to produce more than is necessary simply to keep them alive. This surplus product, however, is too small to improve everyone's standard of living significantly. Instead it is appropriated by a minority, who, for various reasons such as their greater efficiency or political power, gain control of the means of production. Thus do classes arise. As Engels puts it:

> All historical antagonisms between exploiting and exploited, ruling and oppressed classes to this very day find their explanation in this same relatively undeveloped productivity of human labour. So long as the really working population were so much occupied with their necessary labour that they had no time left for looking after the common affairs of society—the direction of labour,

affairs of state, legal matters, art, science, etc—so long was it necessary that there should constantly exist a special class, freed from actual labour, to manage those affairs; and this class never failed, for its own advantage, to impose a greater and greater burden of labour on the working masses (**AD** 217-18).

Control (or, more precisely, effective possession) of the means of production is not necessarily the same as their legal ownership. In this Marx set himself on the side of the materialist bourgeois philosophers such as Thomas Hobbes, 'who regarded *might* as the basis of right... If power is taken as the basis of right, as Hobbes etc do, then right, law etc, are merely the symptom, the expression of *other* relations upon which state power rests' (**CW** v 329).

The distinction between relations of production and legal property forms is important. Many people believe that capitalism depends upon there being individual capitalists who own and control the means of production. They therefore argue that the rise of the modern corporation, in which the business is actually run by top managers who are employees of the firm and own, at best, only a few shares, shows that we no longer live under capitalism. Nothing could be further from the truth. It is the effective possession of the means of production by a minority which defines class society, not the legal forms in which these relations of power are dressed up.

Modes of production and the class struggle

Relations of production are, in class society, 'not relations between individual and individual, but between worker and capitalist, between farmer and landlord etc' (**CW** vi 159). For Marx, these class relations based on exploitation are the key to understanding society:

The specific economic form, in which unpaid surplus labour is pumped out of the direct producers, determines the relationship between rulers and ruled... It is always the direct relationship of the owners of the conditions of production to the direct producers—a relation always naturally corresponding to a definite stage in the

103

development of the methods of labour and thereby its social productivity—which reveals the innermost secret of the entire social
structure... (**C** iii 791)

From these ideas follow the famous opening lines of the
Communist Manifesto:

The history of all hitherto existing society is the history of class
struggle.
    Freeman and slave, patrician and plebeian, lord and serf, guild-
master and journeyman, in a word, oppressor and oppressed, stood
in constant opposition to one another, carried on an uninterrupted,
now hidden, now open fight, a fight that each time ended, either
in a revolutionary reconstitution of society at large, or in the
common ruin of the contending classes...
    The modern bourgeois society that has sprouted from the ruins
of feudal society has not done away with class antagonisms. It
has but established new classes, new conditions of oppression,
new forms of struggle in place of the old ones (**CW** vi 483,485).

This idea is now to some degree accepted, even by bourgeois
historians, so it is difficult to grasp how revolutionary it was in
1848. Before that time history had been largely written only
about (and for) those at the top of society, or had traced the
noble march of reason through history. Now Marx brought to
light the decisive role which has been played by the mass of
working people in all the great historical transformations. Those
who today write history 'from below' are writing in the shadow
of Marx's declaration that 'history...is the history of class
struggle.'
    Marx himself did not regard the class struggle as his most im-
portant discovery. In a famous letter to Joseph Weydemeyer of
March 1852, he wrote:

And now as to myself, no credit is due to me for discovering the
existence of classes in modern society or the struggle between
them. Long before me bourgeois historians had described the historical development of this class struggle and bourgeois economists the economic anatomy of the classes. What I did that was
new was to prove: (1) that the *existence of classes* is only bound

up with *particular phases in the development of production*, (2) that the class struggle necessarily leads to the *dictatorship of the proletariat*, (3) that this dictatorship itself only constitutes the transition to the *abolition of all classes* and to a *classless society* (**SC** 69).

Marx was perhaps being too modest. Nevertheless, his basic point stands. The class struggle arises from certain historically specific relations of production, themselves 'always naturally corresponding to a definite stage in the development of the methods of labour and thereby its social productivity', in other words, to a certain level of development of the productive forces.

Marx called 'relations of production which correspond to a definite stage of development of the productive forces' a *mode of production*. He distinguished between four main types of class society: 'In broad outlines Asiatic, ancient, feudal, and modern bourgeois modes of production can be designated as progressive epochs in the economic formation of society' (**SW** i 504):

What distinguishes the various economic formations of society—the distinction between for example a society based on slave labour and a society based on wage labour—is the form in which this surplus labour is in each case extorted from the immediate producer, the worker (**C** i 325).

The form of exploitation itself depends on the distribution of the means of production. In the case of slavery, the labourer is an instrument of production, the property of the master in the same way as the land which the slave works, and the tools he or she uses. It actually seems that *all* the slave's labour is surplus labour, since he or she is entitled to none of its product—it all goes to the master. However, since the slave is a valuable investment for which the owner has spent money, she or he has to be kept alive. So a portion of the slave's product is set aside to feed, clothe, and house him or her.

In the case of feudalism, on the other hand, the peasant may actually control some of the means of production—tools, and animals, perhaps—but does not own the land on which he works. So he is compelled to divide his time between necessary labour, for himself and his family, and surplus labour, when he works for his lord. 'The one he does on his own field, the other on the seigneurial estate. Both parts of this labour time thus exist independently, side by side with each other' (C i 346).

In both these modes of production, exploitation is quite visible and depends on the physical power of the property owner over the direct producers. The slaveowner can, if he wishes, torture or kill a lazy or recalcitrant slave. Feudal lords possessed military power, in the form of their armed retainers. The landowner's power to squeeze surplus labour from his peasants depends on his monopoly of force. Indeed, on the surface it might even appear that this power relationship, the domination of ruler over ruled, is what really matters—as the superficial view of history implies—and not the economic relationship that it supports.

Under capitalism, however, the worker is legally free. He or she is not tied to the capitalist in the way the slave is to the master or the serf to the lord. Exploitation depends not on the physical subjection of producer to property owner, but on economic pressures, and above all the fact that the worker does not own the means of production. Marx wrote that workers are 'free in a double sense, free from the old relations of clientship, bondage and servitude, and secondly free of all belongings and possessions, and of every objective, material form of being, *free of all property*' (G 507).

In England the peasantry were separated from the land on which their livelihoods depended between the 15th and 18th centuries by means of various stratagems—evictions, the enclosure of the common land, and so on. It was only thus, through the creation of a working class owning nothing but their ability to work, their labour power, that the capitalist mode of production could develop.

The capitalist mode of production depends upon the separation of the direct producer from the means of production, which are controlled by a small group of capitalists. For the worker, the alternative to selling his or her labour power to the capitalist is ultimately starvation. The capitalist uses his control of the means of production to force people to work for him, and, once he has employed them, to work longer than is necessary to replace their wages, thus creating surplus labour. Exploitation in this case depends, in the first instance, on the property owner's economic power, and not on his monopoly of violence. Because there is no physical compulsion involved, because the worker is legally free, and his or her agreement to work for the capitalist is apparently quite voluntary, exploitation is here concealed. It is no less real for that.

Marx writes that the 'relations of production...correspond to a definite stage of development of their productive forces'. What precisely does 'correspond' mean here? Some commentators have thought that, for Marx, the productive forces were directly responsible for the rise and fall of modes of production. This view of history is sometimes called 'technological determinism', because it considers technological change the motor of social change.

There are passages in Marx's writings where he seems to support such a view. For example, he declares:

> ...that social relations are closely bound up with productive forces. In acquiring new productive forces men change their mode of production; and in changing their mode of production, in changing the way of earning their living, they change all their social relations. The handmill gives you society with the feudal lord: the steam mill, society with the industrial capitalist (**CW** vi 166).

Some later Marxists used remarks such as these to justify a perversion of Marx's theory of history, saying that, once the productive forces have reached a certain level, social revolution is inevitable. Karl Kautsky, the chief theoretician of the Second International (1889-1914), argued that the downfall of capitalism was fated, and would take place of 'natural necessity'. All that socialists had to do was to sit back and wait for this inevitable event.

This sort of do-nothing Marxism encouraged the parties of the Second International not to organise mass opposition to the First World War in 1914. Instead, they supported their own national governments, and the international labour movement disintegrated as workers went off to slaughter each other.

Fatalistic Marxism, which passively observes history rather than trying to influence its outcome, is a complete falsification of Marx's own views. To say that 'social relations are closely bound up with productive forces' is not to say that the former simply

107

responds to changes in the latter. The correspondence goes both ways. Each sets limits on the other.

The productive forces do set limits on the social relations of production. Marx and Engels argued vehemently that the abolition of classes could not take place under just any conditions. As Engels explained in a draft for the *Communist Manifesto*:

> Every change in the social order, every revolution in property relations, has been the necessary result of the creation of new productive forces which would no longer conform to the old property relations... So long as it is not possible to produce so much that not only is there enough for all, but also a surplus for the increase of social capital and the further development of the productive forces, so long must there always be a ruling class disposing of the productive forces of society, and a poor oppressed class. How these classes are composed will depend upon the stage of development of production...
>
> It is obvious that hitherto the productive forces had not yet been so far developed that enough could be produced for all or to make private property a fetter, a barrier, to these productive forces. Now, however, when the development of large scale industry has, *firstly*, created capital and productive forces on a scale hitherto unheard of and the means are available to increase these productive forces in a short time to an infinite extent; when, *secondly*, these productive forces are concentrated in the hands of a few bourgeois whilst the great mass of the people are more and more becoming proletarians, and their condition more wretched and unendurable in the same measure in which the riches of the bourgeois increase; when, *thirdly*, these powerful productive forces that can easily be increased have so enormously outgrown private property and the bourgeois that at every moment they provoke the most violent disturbances in the social order—only now has the abolition of private property become not only possible but even absolutely necessary (**CW** vi 348-9).

Socialism is thus not just a good idea, spun out of the minds of well-meaning dreamers. It is only possible once the productive forces have reached a level which will permit the abolition of classes. And its development to such a height can take place only under capitalism.

But correspondingly, it is equally true that the social relations of production set limits on the development of the productive forces. The extent to which improvements will be introduced into the labour process will depend on whether these improvements are in the interest of at least one of the main social classes.

Take the case of Europe in the Middle Ages. Historians have shown that feudal society suffered a succession of terrible crises, when the land could not support the existing population and living standards fell until war, famine and plague restored the balance. The people of Western Europe, most of them peasants scraping a bare living off the soil at the best of times, perished on a scale near to that of nuclear holocaust. The French Marxist historian Guy Bois has shown that half the population of eastern Normandy was wiped out in the mid-14th century, while even more died early the next century. On his estimate, in 1460 the population was less than a third of what it had been in 1300.

These were no mere natural disasters, examples of Malthus's law of population. They sprang from the prevailing feudal relations of production. The peasants had to hand over as much as half their product to the feudal lord, who used it to feed and arm his retainers, and to keep up his social position. The peasants had neither the incentive nor the resources to invest in improved methods of production.

This meant that farming techniques remained unchanged through most of the later Middle Ages (1300-1550). When population grew beyond a certain limit, there was not enough land or food to go round using these techniques. The lord would squeeze even harder to make sure that his income didn't suffer, even if his tenants starved. Unable to carry the burden, the peasant economy would collapse.

Even if the growth of scientific knowledge has given us the ability to raise the productivity of labour, whether this opportunity is actually used will depend on the prevailing social relations of production. Another example, this time from China, illustrates how social relations can halter technological progress.

Under the Sung dynasty (960-1259) China was several centuries ahead of Europe. Iron foundries built there in the 11th century were the largest in the world till the industrial revolution. Firearms, moveable type for printing, the magnetic compass, and mechanical clocks were all developed in China hundreds of years before they appeared in Europe. Yet these breakthroughs did not encourage the development of a modern industrial economy. Instead, the social structure, dominated by landowners and bureaucrats who had no interests in such advances, caused stagnation and decay, until in the 19th century the old Middle Kingdom fell prey to Western colonisers.

The social relations of production—the economic structure of society—and the productive forces—human skills and technology—thus interact with each other, rather than the one prevailing over the other. The level of skill and technology sets limits to, but may also stimulate social change; while the structure of society determines how far people will be able to alter the labour process and use new techniques.

Marx sees the relationship between them as one that changes over time. A given structure of society is only compatible with a certain level of development of human skill and technology. 'At a certain stage of their development, the material productive forces of society come into conflict with the existing relations of production... From forms of development of the productive forces, these relations turn into their fetters' (**SW** i 503-4). Society then enters a period of social crisis which can be ended only when new relations of production, relations which can promote the further development of the productive forces, have replaced the old.

The crisis of European feudalism referred to above may illustrate this process. The installation of feudal relations of production at the end of the Roman era undoubtedly led to considerable economic progress. Between the tenth and the 13th centuries agricultural output rose considerably, considerable amounts of land were brought into cultivation, the towns expanded, and population grew. Many scientific discoveries, made by the Greeks and Romans but ignored because the slave relations of production prevailing in the ancient world had discouraged their practical application, were now put to economic use.

But in the 13th century this economic growth ran into limits set by the feudal relations which had stimulated it. As we have already seen, neither lord nor peasant had much interest in making the agricultural improvements necessary to feed the rapidly growing population. The result was prolonged crisis.

Social crises, therefore, arise from the contradictions within the prevailing mode of production. At the same time they create the conditions from which a new mode of production can emerge. For example, in the case of feudalism, the scarcity of labour which followed the Black Death in the 14th century put the English peasantry in a strong enough position, despite the defeat of the great revolt of 1381, to force the abolition of serfdom. Peasants were no longer tied to the soil. They were not strong enough, however, unlike their French counterparts, to make themselves owners of the plots of land they worked. English landowners were able, from the 16th century onwards, to push the peasants off the soil, and enclose land into farms. These they then let to capitalist tenants employing wage labourers and producing goods for the market. The gradual undermining of feudal relations of production had given rise to the beginnings of capitalism .

The class struggle, argued Marx, has to be understood in the light of these contradictions. The replacement of one mode of production by another does not take place peacefully and gradually, but requires a violent revolution, in which the old ruling class is expropriated and a new class put in its place. 'The contradiction between the productive forces and the forms of intercourse...necessarily on each occasion burst out in a revolution, taking on at the same time various subsidiary forms, such as all-embracing collisions, collisions of various classes, contradictions of consciousness, battles of ideas etc' (**CW** v 74).

These famous lines from the Preface to *A Contribution to the Critique of Political Economy* sum up Marx's theory of history:

> In the social production of their life, men enter into definite relations that are indispensable and independent of their will, relations of production which correspond to a definite stage of development of their material productive forces. The sum total of these relations of production constitutes the economic structure of society, the real foundation, on which rises a legal and political superstructure and to which correspond definite forms of social consciousness. The mode of production of material life conditions the social, political and intellectual life process in general. It is not the consciousness of men that determines their being, but, on the contrary, their social being that determines their consciousness. At a certain stage of their development, the material

productive forces of society come into conflict with the existing relations of production, or—what is but a legal expression for the same thing—with the property relations within which they have been at work hitherto. From forms of development of the productive forces these relations turn into their fetters. Then begins an epoch of social revolution. With the change in economic foundation, the entire immense superstructure is more or less rapidly transformed (**SW** i 503-4).

Base and superstructure

'The history of all hitherto existing society is the history of class struggle.' And classes are, for Marx, fundamentally *economic* relations. He would undoubtedly have accepted Lenin's famous definition:

> Classes are large groups of people differing from each other by the places they occupy within a historically determined system of social production, by their relation (in most cases fixed and formulated in law) to the means of production, by their role in the social organisation of labour, and, consequently, by the dimensions of social wealth of which they dispose and the mode of acquiring it. Classes are groups of people one of which can appropriate the labour of another owing to the different places they occupy in a definite system of social economy.

Does not this conception of history, as many critics have argued since it was first formulated, crudely reduce the whole of social life to an expression of economic interests?

Marx's conception of the way in which the forces and relations of production shape the whole of the society was in fact a highly subtle and complex one. As many commentators have pointed out, his most important statement of the relationship between what has come to be known as the economic 'base' and the ideological and political superstructure is careful and qualified:

> The sum total of these relations of production constitutes the economic structure of society, the *real foundation,* on which rises a legal and political superstructure and to which *correspond* definite

forms of social consciousness. The mode of production of material life *conditions* the social, political and intellectual life process in general. It is not the consciousness of men that determines their being, but, on the contrary, their social being that *determines* their consciousness (**SW** i 503-4).

The picture of society outlined here is not one in which the superstructure—politics and ideology—merely passively reflects what happens in the economy. Rather, as the words I have italicised suggest, what happens is that the forces and relations of production set limits to developments in the superstructure. Now if this is so, then there is considerable scope for political and ideological factors to develop according to their own rhythms, and to react back onto the economy.

This at any rate is what Engels argued, in a letter he wrote a few years after Marx's death:

> According to the materialist conception of history the *ultimately* determining element in history is the production and reproduction of real life. More than this neither Marx nor I have ever asserted. Hence if somebody twists this into saying that the economic element is the *only* determining one, he transforms that proposition into a meaningless, abstract, senseless phrase. The economic situation is the basis, but the various elements of the superstructure—political forms of the class struggle and its results, to wit: constitutions established by the victorious class after a successful battle etc, juridical forms, and even the reflexes of all these actual struggles in the brains of the participants, political, juristic, philosophical theories, religious views and their further development into systems of dogma—also exercise their influence upon the course of the historical struggles and in many cases preponderate in determining their *form*. There is an interaction of all these elements, in which, amid all the endless *host* of accidents…the economic movement finally asserts itself as necessary (**SC** 417).

Establishing what relations of production prevail within a given society is, then, only the starting point for trying to understand that society. A proper understanding will involve grasping the way in which ideological and political factors interact with

113

the economy, always bearing in mind, however, that the relations of production are the 'real foundation' of society.

To arrive at a clear idea of what is involved in the relationship between base and superstructure, let us look at the two most important elements of the superstructure, namely, ideology and the state.

Talking of social revolutions, Marx writes that:

> ...a distinction must be made between the material transformation of the economic conditions of production...and the legal, political, religious, aesthetic or philosophic—in short, ideological forms in which men become conscious of this conflict and fight it out. Just as our opinion of an individual is not based on what he thinks of himself, so can we not judge of such a period of transformation by its own consciousness; on the contrary, this consciousness must be explained rather from the contradictions of material life, from the existing conflict between the social productive forces and the relations of production (**SW** i 504).

So, in the first place, Marx is denying that consciousness is independent of 'the contradictions of material life'. Social being determines consciousness, rather than the other way round. But what does it mean to say that 'social being determines consciousness'? Above all it means that the beliefs which people have will be formed under the pressure of the material and social circumstances in which they live. Human beings are not disembodied spirits living in some realm of pure reason. They are men and women struggling to survive in conditions which deny most of them more than a bare subsistence. The beliefs they have will be attempts to make sense of their situation, and to guide their everyday actions.

Moreover people have, since the end of primitive communism, lived in class societies. This means that it is important for the ruling class to persuade the direct producers to accept their situation. This acceptance can take a variety of forms. It can be simply resignation, based on the belief that the ruling class is too strong to overthrow. It can, however, be the positive belief that the present social order is a just and desirable one. In either case, the direct producers' beliefs play a crucial role in their acceptance of the status quo.

It follows that ideologies—the systematic beliefs which people have about the world—can only be understood from the standpoint of their role in the class struggle. In other words, they have to be analysed in terms of their contribution to sustaining or undermining the prevailing relations of production.

Now Marx believes that ideologies prop up class societies by misleading the exploited about their position in society. The effect is that the social relations of the class society in question are seen as *natural* relations which are inevitable and cannot be done away with, instead of being specific only to this period of human history. The result of this is that specific class interests are seen as universal human interests.

If capitalist relations of production represent the highest form of human development, then it is in everyone's interest that the capitalist should make a profit. He is not exploiting anyone: his role in social production is an essential one, and profits are a just reward of his contribution.

Ideologies in this way keep the existing mode of production going by persuading people to form mistaken views about the nature of society. It follows that, even during revolutionary periods, those who make history do not fully understand the nature of the roles that they are playing:

> Men make their own history, but they do not make it just as they please; they do not make it under circumstances chosen by themselves, but under circumstances directly encountered, given and transmitted from the past. The tradition of all the dead generations weighs like a nightmare on the brain of the living. And just when they seem engaged in revolutionising themselves and things, in creating something that has never yet existed, precisely in such periods of revolutionary crisis they anxiously conjure up the spirits of the past to their service and borrow from them names, battle cries and costumes in order to present the new scene of world history in this time-honoured disguise and this borrowed language. Thus Luther donned the mask of the Apostle Paul, the revolution of 1789 to 1814 draped itself alternately as the Roman Republic and the Roman Empire (**CW** xi 103-4).

This form of self deception was necessary in the great bourgeois revolutions because the leaders of these revolutions had to persuade themselves and their own supporters that the victory of their class was in the interests of humanity as a whole:

> Unheroic as bourgeois society is, it nevertheless took heroism, sacrifice, terror, civil war and battles of peoples to bring it into being. And in the classically austere traditions of the Roman Republic its gladiators found the ideals and the art forms, the self deceptions they needed in order to conceal from themselves the bourgeois limitations of the content of their struggles and to maintain their passion on the high plane of historical tragedy. Similarly, at another stage of development, a century earlier, Cromwell and the English people had borrowed speech, passions and illusions from the Old Testament for their bourgeois revolution (**CW** xi 104-5).

Marx believes that ruling class ideologies prevail among the masses thanks to the economic and political power of the ruling class. 'The ideas of the ruling class are in every epoch the ruling ideas: ie, the class which is the prevailing *material* force of society is at the same time its ruling *intellectual* force' (**CW** v 59). The ruling class uses its control of the means of production and of the state to create and sustain a variety of institutions through which people's beliefs are formed. In medieval times the most important of these institutions was the church. To this has now been added a variety of others, of which the education system and the mass media are the most important.

It is clear, however, that for Marx the ideological power of the ruling class was inseparable from their economic and political power. The economically dominant class was also the ruling class—that is, the class which controlled the means of production also controlled the state. The state was, for Marx, first and foremost a means through which the domination of a particular class could be maintained. 'The executive of the modern state is', in the celebrated words of the *Communist Manifesto*, 'but a committee for managing the common affairs of the whole bourgeoisie' (**CW** vi 486). 'Political power, properly so called, is merely the organised power of one class for oppressing another' (**CW** vi 505).

Marx never attempted to develop a systematic theory of the state. His views on the subject have to be gleaned from scattered remarks and specific analyses. Engels and Lenin took the matter much further. However, the main outlines of the theory they developed are already present in Marx.

Already in his 1843 *Critique of Hegel's Philosophy of Right* Marx had argued that the modern state was characterised by its separation from civil society, its separation from economic and social life. Later he and Engels showed that this separation could only be understood as the inevitable outcome of class antagonisms.

Engels argued that the emergence of the state is inseparable from the division of society into classes:

> The state…is a product of society at a certain stage of development; it is the admission that this society has become entangled in an insoluble contradiction with itself, that it has split into irreconcilable antagonisms which it is powerless to dispel. But in order that these antagonisms and classes with conflicting economic interests might not consume themselves and society in fruitless struggle, it became necessary to have a power seemingly standing above society that would alleviate the conflict, and keep it within the bounds of 'order'; and this power, arisen out of society but placing itself above it, and alienating itself more and more from it, is the state (**SW** iii 326-7).

The essence of this power is that the state controls the means of coercion; at its most basic, armed force. In pre-class societies, there was no distinction between the mass of the population and those who did whatever fighting was necessary. With the emergence of class antagonisms, however, this ceases to be the case. The use of force becomes the preserve of a specialised minority whose role is as much the repression of the mass of the population as fighting external enemies. Thus, the separation of the state from society is primarily the separation of the means of coercion from the direct producers on whose surplus labour the ruling class depends. The formation of the state, Engels explains, involves:

> …the establishment of a *public power* which no longer directly coincides with the population organising itself as an armed force. This special public power is necessary because a self-acting armed organisation of the population has become impossible with the split into classes… This public power exists in every state; it

117

consists not merely of armed men but also of material adjuncts, prisons and institutions of coercion of all kinds... It grows stronger...in proportion as class antagonisms within the state become more acute, and as adjacent states become larger and more populous. We have only to look at our present day Europe, where class struggle and rivalry in conquest have tuned up the public power to such a pitch that it threatens to swallow the whole of society and even the state (**SW** iii 327-8).

Engels thus recognises two main factors in the formation and evolution of states, the development and sharpening of class antagonisms, and struggles between rival stages for military domination. Marx developed this idea in a more historically concrete way in his writings on the Paris Commune, where he traced the origins of the modern capitalist state to the absolute monarchies which emerged in Europe at the end of the Middle Ages:

The centralised state machinery, which, with its ubiquitous and complicated military, bureaucratic, clerical and judiciary organs entoils (enmeshes) the living civil society like a boa constrictor, was first forged in the days of absolute monarchy as a weapon of nascent modern society in its struggle of emancipation from feudalism. The seignorial privileges of the medieval lords and cities and clergy were transformed into the attributes of a unitary state power, displacing the feudal dignitaries by salaried state functionaries, transferring the arms from medieval retainers of the landlords and the corporations of townish citizens to a standing army; substituting for the chequered (particoloured) anarchy of medieval powers the regulated plan of a state power, with a systematic and hierarchic division of labour. The first French revolution with its task to found national unity (to create a nation) had to break down all local, territorial, townish and provincial independence. It was, therefore, forced to develop what absolute monarchy had commenced, the centralisation and organisation of state power, and to expand the circumference and the attributes of the state power, the number of its tool[s], its independence, and its supernaturalist sway of real society (**CWF** I62-3).

The triumph of capitalism had thus led to an enormous strengthening of the power and efficiency of the state apparatus.

But was not this apparatus also more and more independent from the bourgeoisie as well as the exploited classes? This, at least, was what was suggested by the phenomenon of Bonapartism, the First and Second French Empires, of Napoleon I and Napoleon III respectively, when an individual adventurer whose power rested simply on military strength was able to win control of the state and to rule independently of capitalists as well as workers and peasants. The point could be made more strongly: does not the election since Marx's day of a number of governments controlled by parties whose political base is the working class contradict the idea that the state is an instrument of class domination?

To meet this challenge, we must remind ourselves that the state is, for Marx and Engels, the product of class antagonisms, as Marx put it, 'the official expression of antagonism in civil society' (**CW** vi 212). He writes of 'the concentration of the whole in the state' (**G** 227). In other words, all the contradictions of society are reflected and crystallised in the state. The continued domination of the ruling class may depend upon a series of compromises with other classes which will be reflected in the organisation of state power.

For example, Marx argued that the triumph of Napoleon III after the revolution of 1848 was the only way in which capitalist power could be preserved in France after several years of open civil war between bourgeoisie and proletariat:

> The empire, professing to rest upon the producing majority of the nation, the peasants, apparently out of the range of the class struggle between capital and labour (indifferent and hostile to both the contesting social powers), wielding the state power as a force superior to the ruling and ruled classes, imposing upon both an armistice (silencing the political, and therefore revolutionary form of the class struggle), divesting the state power from its direct form of class despotism by breaking the parliamentary and, therefore, directly political power of the appropriating classes, was the only possible state-form to secure the old order a respite of life (**CWF** 230-1).

Such an apparently paradoxical situation, in which the ruling class does not directly rule, in the sense of actually running the state apparatus, is possible under capitalism because exploitation does not depend on the day-to-day physical coercion of the direct producers. Instead economic pressures, ultimately the choice between working or starving, compel workers to submit to exploitation. 'The silent compulsion of economic relations sets the seal on the domination of the capitalist over the worker. Direct extra-economic force is still of course used, but only in exceptional cases' (C i 899).

It is, therefore, common in capitalist societies for economics and politics to appear as quite separate. The underlying reality is, however, different. On the one hand, capitalist control of an economy sets limits on what the state can do. If the bourgeoisie do not like what a government is doing, they can, for example, take their money out of the country. This sort of pressure has forced successive Labour governments in Britain to tone down or abandon the more radical of their policies. On the other hand, there is a division of labour within the state itself, between elected bodies such as parliament and the cabinet, and the permanent military and civil bureaucracy. The latter's close links with the capitalist class mean that they will sabotage, or, if pushed to it, simply rebel against a government committed to overthrowing bourgeois relations of production.

Nevertheless, the relative separation of politics and economics under capitalism does permit situations in which the bourgeoisie does not control the state apparatus. This enables them to enter into compromises with other classes, or fractions of classes, which will tone down social antagonisms and render their underlying domination more secure.

Marx believed that the Britain of his day illustrated such a situation:

> The British Constitution is…nothing but an antiquated, obsolete, out-of-date compromise between the bourgeoisie, which *rules not officially* but in fact [does rule] in all decisive spheres of civil society, and the landed aristocracy, which *governs officially*. Originally, after the 'glorious' revolution of 1688, only a section of the bourgeoisie, the *aristocracy of finance*, was included in the compromise. The Reform Bill of 1831 admitted another section, the *millocracy* as the English call it, ie, the high dignitaries of the *industrial* bourgeoisie…
>
> Even if the bourgeoisie…was on the whole acknowledged also

politically as the *ruling class*, this was only on the condition that the entire system of government in all its detail, even the executive department of the legislative power, ie, the actual making of laws in both Houses of Parliament, remained safely in the hands of the landed aristocracy (**CW** xiv 53-4).

The bourgeoisie can thus rule without governing. Engels argued that a similar division existed in Germany under Bismarck, where the industrial bourgeoisie were the chief beneficiaries of national unification, but the *Junker* classes of rural squires continued actually to govern. Some later Marxists have argued that it is a general feature of capitalism that the bourgeoisie rules but does not govern. Without going so far, we can see that Marx's theory of the state, like his general account of the relation between base and superstructure, was complex and subtle.

Marx thus developed a theory of history capable of accounting for the character of very different societies, and of explaining the variations in the political and ideological superstructures of societies that share the same relations of production. The emergence, especially since the Second World War, of a rich body of Marxist historical writing is a confirmation of the fertility of this theory. Nevertheless, Marx was not concerned primarily with formulating a more scientific theory of history than Condorcet's or Hegel's. The cutting edge of historical materialism lay in Marx's scientific analysis of capitalism, and his theory of revolutionary politics.

Capitalism

C	*apital* was Marx's crowning achievement, the centre-
	piece of his life's work. Its object was, as he put it in the
	Preface to Volume 1, 'to reveal the economic law of
motion of modern society' (C i 92). Previous economic
thinkers had grasped one or other aspect of capitalism's workings. Now Marx sought to understand it as a whole. In line
with the method of analysis and conception of history set out
in the two previous chapters, Marx analysed capitalism not as
the end of history, as the form of society corresponding to
human nature, but as a historically transitory mode of production whose internal contradictions would lead to its downfall.

It may be helpful to readers unfamiliar with the 'dismal science' of economics (as Thomas Carlyle called it) briefly to out-
line the subject matter of this chapter. It starts with the
cornerstone of *Capital*, the labour theory of value, according to
which commodities—products sold in the market place—
exchange in proportion to the socially necessary labour time
required for their production. We shall then see how this theory
underlies Marx's account of capitalist exploitation, for it is the
surplus value created by workers which is the source of the profits on which capitalism as an economic system rests. Competition
between capitals—whether individual capitalists, companies or
even nations—each out to grab the largest amount of surplus

value, leads to the formation of a general rate of profit, and therefore, as we shall see, to a modification of the labour theory of value. Competition also gives rise to a tendency for the rate of profit to fall, which is the fundamental cause of the crises which regularly afflict the capitalist system.

Labour and value

The basis of every human society is the labour process, human beings cooperating in order to make use of the forces of nature, and thus to meet their needs. The product of labour must, before anything else, answer some human need. It must, in other words, be useful. Marx therefore calls it a *use value*. Its value lies first and foremost in being of use to someone.

The need met by a use value does not have to be a physical need. A book is a use value, because people need to read. Equally, the needs that use values meet may be to achieve vile purposes. A murderer's gun or a policeman's truncheon is as much a use value as a can of baked beans or a surgeon's scalpel.

Under capitalism, however, the products of labour take the form of *commodities*. A commodity, as Adam Smith pointed out, does not merely have a use value. Commodities are made, not to be directly consumed, but to be sold on the market. They are produced in order to be exchanged. As such, each commodity has an *exchange value*, 'the quantitative relation, the proportion, in which use values of one kind exchange for use values of another kind' (**C** i 126). Thus, the exchange value of a shirt might be a hundred cans of baked beans.

Use value and exchange value are very different from each other. To take an example of Smith's, air is something of almost infinite use value to human beings, since without it we would die, yet it has no exchange value (if we ignore the ability of the rich to buy themselves less polluted surroundings). Diamonds, on the other hand, are of comparatively little use, but have a very high exchange value.

Moreover, a use value has to meet some *specific* human need. If you are hungry, a book is no good. By contrast, the exchange value of a commodity is simply the amount it will exchange for other commodities. Exchange values reflect what commodities have in common, rather than their specific qualities. A loaf of

123

LIVERPOOL JOHN MOORES UNIVERSITY
LEARNING SERVICES

bread can be exchanged for a tin opener, either directly or through the medium of money, even though their uses are very different. What is it that they have in common, that permits this exchange to take place?

Marx's answer is that all commodities have a *value*, of which exchange value is merely the reflection. This value represents the cost to society of producing that commodity. Because human labour power is the motive force of production, that cost can be measured only by the amount of labour devoted to the commodity.

But by labour Marx does not here mean the particular type of labour involved in, say, baking a loaf of bread or manufacturing a tin opener. This real, 'concrete' labour as Marx puts it, is too varied and complex to provide us with the measure of value that we need. To find our measure we must abstract labour from its concrete form. Writes Marx: 'A use value, or useful article, therefore has value only because *abstract human labour* is objectified or materialised in it (**C** i 129).

So labour has a 'dual character':

> On the one hand, all labour is an expenditure of human labour power in the physiological sense, and it is in this quality of being equal, or abstract, human labour that it forms the value of commodities. On the other hand, all labour is an expenditure of human labour power in a particular form and with a definite aim, and it is in this quality of being definite useful labour that it produces use values' (**C** i 137).

Marx described this *twofold character of labour* as one of 'the best points in my book' (**SC** 192). It was here that Marx's theory parted company with that of Ricardo and the political economists. Marx criticised Ricardo for focusing almost exclusively on trying to find a precise formula for determining the exchange value of commodities. They wanted, of course, to find ways of predicting market prices.

'Ricardo's mistake is that he is concerned only with the *magnitude of value*... What Ricardo does not investigate is the specific form in which labour manifests itself as the common element in commodities,' wrote Marx (**TSV** iii 131,138).

Marx was not specifically interested in market prices. His aim was to understand capitalism as a historically specific form of society, to find what made capitalism different from previous forms of society, and what contradictions would lead to its future transformation. Marx wanted to know, not *how much* labour formed the exchange value of commodities, but *in what form* labour performed this function and *why* under capitalism production was of commodities for the market rather than products for direct use as in previous societies.

The twofold character of labour is crucial in answering this question because labour is a social and cooperative activity. This is true not simply of particular sorts of work, but of society as a whole. The labour of each individual or group of individuals is social labour in the sense that it contributes to the needs of society. These needs require all sorts of different products — not simply various sorts of food, but also clothing, shelter, means of transport, the tools needed in production, and so on. This means that different sorts of useful labour have to be carried out. If everyone produced only one type of product, then society would soon collapse.

Every society therefore needs some means of distributing social labour among different productive activities. 'This *necessity* of the *distribution* of social labour in definite proportions cannot possibly be done away with by *a particular form* of social production', Marx writes (**SC** 209). But there is a fundamental difference between capitalism and other modes of production. Capitalism has no mechanism through which society can collectively decide how much of its labour will be devoted to particular tasks.

To understand why this is so, we must look at pre-capitalist modes of production, where the goal of economic activity was primarily the production of use values, and each community could meet all or most of its needs from the labour of its own members. Thus:

> ...in the patriarchal rural industry of a peasant family which produces corn, cattle, yarn, linen and clothing for its own use...the distribution of labour within the family and the labour time expended by the individual members of the family, are regulated by differences in sex and age as well as by seasonal variations in the natural conditions of labour (**C** i 171).

125

The distribution of labour is collectively regulated even in pre-capitalist societies where exploitation and classes exist. Thus, in feudalism:

> ...labour and its products...take the shape, in the transactions of society, of services in kind and payments in kind... Whatever we may think, then, of the different roles in which men confront each other in such a society, the social relationships between individuals appear in any event as their own personal relations, are not disguised as social relations between things, between the products of labour (**C** i 170).

In the case of slavery and feudalism, both modes of production based on class exploitation, the bulk of production is devoted entirely to meeting the needs of the producers and the exploiting class. The main issue is not *what* is produced, but rather the division of the social product between exploiter and exploited.

Under capitalism things are very different. The development of the division of labour means that production in each workplace is now highly specialised, and separate from other workplaces. Each producer cannot meet his needs out of his own production. A worker in a tin opener factory cannot eat tin openers. In order to live, he must sell them to others. The producers are thus interdependent in two senses: they need each other's products, but they also need each other as purchasers of their own products so that they can obtain the money with which to buy what they need.

This system Marx calls *generalised commodity production*. The producers are bound together only by the exchange of their products among one another:

> Objects of utility become commodities only because they are the products of the labour of private individuals who work independently of each other. The sum total of the labour of all these private individuals forms the aggregate labour of society. Since the producers do not come into social contact until they exchange the products of their labour, the specific social characteristics of their private labours appear only within this exchange. In other words, the labour of the private individual manifests itself as an element of the total labour of society only through the relations which the

act of exchange establishes between the products, and through their mediation, between the producers (**C** i 165-6).

Hitherto, concrete labour was directly social labour. Where production was for use, to meet some specific need, its social role was obvious, and there from the start. Where production is for exchange, however, there is no necessary connection between the useful labour carried out by a particular producer and the needs of society. Whether the products of a specific factory, for example, meet some social need can be discovered only *after* they have been manufactured, once they have been put on sale in the market. If no one wants to buy these goods, then the labour that produced them was not social labour.

There is a second respect in which there is a difference between social and private labour under capitalism. Makers of the same product will *compete* for the same market. Their relative success will depend on how cheaply they sell their products. This involves increasing the productivity of labour: 'in general, the greater the productivity of labour, the less the labour time required to produce an article, the less the mass of labour crystallised in that article, and the less its value,' writes Marx (**C** i 131).

The pressure of competition forces producers to adopt similar methods of production to their rivals, or find themselves undercut. Consequently, the value of commodities is determined not by the total amount of labour used to produce them, but rather by the *socially necessary* labour time, that is, by 'the labour time required to produce any use value under the conditions of production normal for a given society and with the average degree of skill and intensity of labour prevalent in that society' (**C** i 129). An inefficient producer who uses more than the socially necessary labour to produce something, will find that the price he gets for it will not compensate him for his extra labour. Only socially necessary labour is social labour.

Abstract social labour is thus not merely a concept, something that exists only in the mind. It dominates people's lives. Unless producers are able to meet the 'normal conditions of production', they will find themselves forced out of business.

But this is not all. We have seen that private useful labour only becomes social labour once its product has been sold. But

127

for exchange to take place, there must be some way of telling how much socially necessary labour each commodity contains. Society cannot do this collectively, because capitalism is a system in which the producers relate to each other only through their products.

The solution is for one commodity to take on the role of universal equivalent, against which the values of all the other commodities can then be measured. When one particular commodity becomes fixed in the role of universal equivalent, it becomes money. And, writes Marx, 'the representation of the commodity as money implies...that the different magnitudes of commodity values... are all expressed in a form in which they exist as the embodiment of *social labour*' (**TSV** iii 130).

So capitalism is an economic system in which individual producers do not know in advance whether their products meet a social need. They can find out only by trying to sell these products as commodities on the market. The competition between producers seeking to capture markets by underselling each other reduces their different labours to one measure, abstract social labour as embodied in money. Where the supply of a commodity exceeds the demand for it, its price will fall, and producers will shift to other more profitable economic activities. It is in this way, and only indirectly, that social labour is distributed among different branches of production.

Marx's analysis of value is therefore directed towards what makes capitalism unique as a form of social production. His focus is 'the real internal framework of bourgeois relations of production' (**C** i 175 n 34). His purpose is to show that 'as values, commodities are *social* magnitudes...relations of men in their productive activity... Where labour is communal, the relations of men in their social production do not manifest themselves as "values" of "things" ' (**TSV** iii 129).

Almost as soon as *Capital* was published, bourgeois economists objected that Marx's account of value at the beginning of Volume 1 does not prove that commodities actually exchange in proportion to the socially necessary labour time required to produce them. They have continued to do so to this very day. Marx commented on one such critic:

The unfortunate fellow does not see that, even if there were no chapter on 'value' in my book, the analysis of the real relations which I give would contain the proof and demonstration of the real value relation...

Science consists precisely in demonstrating *how* the law of value asserts itself. So that if one wanted at the very beginning to 'explain' all the phenomena which seemingly contradict that law, one would have to present the science *before* science (**SC** 209-210).

The whole of *Capital* is thus the proof of the labour theory of value. Marx considered the correct scientific method to be that of 'rising from the abstract to the concrete' (**G** 101). He starts off by setting out the labour theory of value in the very abstract form in which we have been so far considering it. But this is only the starting point of his analysis. He then proceeds, step by step, to show how the complex, and often chaotic behaviour of the capitalist economy can be understood on the basis of the labour theory of value, and only on that basis.

Surplus value and exploitation

The capitalist mode of production involves, according to Marx, two great separations. The first we have already discussed—the separation of the units of production. In other words, the capitalist economy is a system divided into separate, interdependent, and competing producers. Just as important, however, is the division *within* each unit of production, between the owner of the means of production and the direct producers, that is, between capital and wage labour.

Commodities can exist, Marx pointed out, without capitalism. Money and trade are to be found in pre-capitalist societies. However, the exchange of commodities in such societies is mainly a means of obtaining use values, the things people need. The circulation of commodities in such circumstances takes the form of C-M-C, where C stands for a commodity, and M for money. Each producer takes his commodity and sells it for money, using that money to buy another commodity from another producer. Money is only the intermediary in the transaction.

Where capitalist relations of production prevail, however, the circulation of commodities takes another, more complex form: M-C-M[1]. Money is invested in order to produce commodities

129

which are then exchanged for—more money.

What is more, the M^1, the money which the investor or capitalist holds after the transaction, is greater than M, the money invested in the first place. The extra money, or profit, Marx called 'surplus value'. Where does it come from?

Ricardo had effectively answered this question when he argued that the value created by labour was then divided into wages and profits. Labour was the source of surplus value. However, he was unable to grasp this clearly because he ran into an apparent contradiction. He defined *wages* as the value of labour. How can this be so when wages are less than the total value created by labour, which Ricardo argues is divided between wages and profits?

Ricardo did not confront this question because he took the existence of surplus value for granted. Marx's explanation of the existence of surplus value, however, rested on his analysis of the relationship between capital and wage labour. What the worker sells the capitalist in exchange for his or her wages is not labour, but labour *power*, as he explains:

> The use value which the worker has to offer to the capitalist…is not materialised in a product, does not exist apart from him at all, thus exists…only in potentiality, as his capacity. It becomes a reality only when…set in motion by capital (**G** 267).

Labour power is a commodity, and like all commodities it has a value and a use value. Its value is determined by the socially necessary labour time involved in keeping the worker alive, and in bringing up the children to replace him or her. 'Its value, like that of every other commodity, is already determined before it enters into circulation, for a definite quantity of social labour has been spent on the production of that labour power. But its use value consists in the subsequent exercise of that power' (**C** i 277).

Labour power's use value is labour, and once the worker has been employed, the capitalist sets him or her to work. But labour is the source of value, and moreover the worker will normally create during a working day more value than the daily wages with which the capitalist purchased his or her labour power. 'What was really decisive for him [the capitalist] was the specific use value which this commodity possesses of being a source not only of value, but of more value than itself' (**C** i 300-301).

For example, let us assume that in a working day of eight hours, four hours labour replaces the value of labour power advanced by the capitalist in the form of wages. The other four hours is pocketed by the capitalist. Surplus value, or profit, is merely the form of existence of surplus labour peculiar to the capitalist mode of production.

The significance of this analysis of the purchase and sale of labour power is that it enables Marx to trace the origins of surplus value to the exploitation of the worker by capital. Furthermore, it highlights the fact that the patterns traced by the classical economists are not natural and inevitable, but are historically specific relations of production.

Marx is able to do this while assuming that all commodities, including labour power, sell at their value. In other words, the capitalist does not gain his profit by cheating the worker and paying labour power less than the equivalent of the socially necessary labour time required to reproduce it. Exploitation is nothing abnormal, it is a typical outcome of the regular workings of the capitalist mode of production. It arises from the difference between the value created by labour power once it is put to work, and the value of labour power itself.

The purchase and sale of labour power depends upon the separation of the worker from the means of production so that 'the worker…[is] free in the double sense that as a free individual he can dispose of his labour power as his own commodity, and that, on the other hand…he is free of all the other commodities needed for the realisation of his labour power' (**C** i 272-3). The exchange between capital and wage labour presupposes 'the distribution of the elements of production itself, the material factors of which are concentrated on one side, and labour power, isolated, on the other' (**C** ii 33).

Marx shows in *Capital* Volume 1 Part Eight how this 'distribution' was the result of a historical process, in which the peasantry were deprived of their land, and the means of production—initially the land itself—became the monopoly of a class whose objective was profit.

Marx was thus able to explain the contrast between the

apparent political equality of all the citizens of capitalist society, and the real inequality of class exploitation. The exchange between capital and wage labour is an exchange of equivalents. Labour power is paid for at its value—the cost of reproducing it. Both worker and capitalist are commodity owners: the one of labour power, the other of money. Labour power is paid for at its value—the cost of reproducing it. So where's the exploitation?

As long as we stay in the 'realm of circulation', the market place where everyone is a commodity owner acting in accordance with his or her self interest, exploitation is invisible. It is only when we enter 'the hidden abode of production, on whose threshold there hangs the notice "no admittance except on business" ' (C i 279-280) that things change. Exploitation is possible because of the peculiar property of the commodity sold by the worker, namely the fact that its use value is labour, the source of value and surplus value. And in production that labour power is set to work.

Before we look at the process of production under capitalism, we need to pin down a little more accurately just what is meant by *capital*.

At its simplest, capital is an accumulation of value which acts to create and accumulate more value. Long before capitalism, of course, rich men accumulated wealth by expropriating the surplus labour of slaves and serfs. But this wealth was used for consumption, so that they and their retainers could have a greater share of the necessities and luxuries of life. This wealth was not capital, though it shares a common source—surplus labour.

The first sign that an accumulation of wealth has begun to act as capital is the formula $M\text{-}C\text{-}M^1$ which we came across earlier. The formula denotes a transaction in which money (M) is exchanged for commodities (C), which are then resold for a greater sum of money (M^1). At first such transactions were made by traders, who would, for example, import spices from the East and resell them in northern Europe, where the demand for spices to preserve meat meant they could get a higher price. But capital proper really only comes into existence when the commodity being bought and sold is labour power, for this wage labour then defines the relations of production that are particular to capitalism.

Capital, therefore, is defined by two things: what it *is* and how it *acts*. It *is* an accumulation of surplus value produced by labour, and this accumulation can take the form of money, commodities, or means of production—and usually a combination of all three. It *acts* to secure further accumulation: Marx described this as 'the self expansion of value'.

Capital is not necessarily identified with individual capitalists. In the early development of capitalism, wealthy individuals did play a major role, but this is far from the case today. It is in the nature of capitalism, in fact, that capital takes on a life of its own, operating according to an economic logic that transcends any individuals. Individual units of capital, which are usually termed 'capitals', can be anything from a small company to a major corporation, a financial institution to a nation state.

In order to grasp the peculiar nature of the capitalist production process, Marx formulated a number of new concepts. We saw in the previous chapter that there are two main elements of any labour process—labour power and the means of production. Under the capitalist mode of production both elements take the form of capital. The capitalist has to invest money in purchasing both labour power and the means of production before he can hope to increase his initial investment. The money used to buy labour power Marx called variable capital; that advanced to obtain plant, equipment, raw materials, and other means of production he called constant capital.

The reason for these names should be obvious in the light of the labour theory of value. *Variable* capital expands in value, because it is invested in labour power, the commodity which is the source of value. *Constant* capital does not. Capitalist production thus involves both living labour—the labour of the worker which replaces the value of labour power and at the same time creates surplus value, and dead labour accumulated in the means of production. This dead labour is the labour of the workers who made the means of production in the first place. As the machinery gradually deteriorates through its use to make new commodities, its value is transferred to these commodities.

The rate of surplus value was the name Marx gave to the ratio between surplus value and variable capital, the capital invested in labour power. This measured the rate of exploitation, in other words the degree to which the capitalist was successful in pumping surplus labour out of the worker. To go back to our previous example, if necessary labour is four hours, and surplus labour is

133

four hours, then the rate of surplus value is 4:4, or 100 percent.

There were two ways, Marx argued, in which capitalists could increase the rate of surplus value, one common to all modes of production, the other specific to capitalism. These were the production of, respectively, absolute and relative surplus value. Absolute surplus value is created by lengthening the working day. Thus, if workers spend ten instead of eight hours a day at work, while necessary labour is still only four hours, then another two hours of surplus labour have been added. The rate of surplus value has risen from 4:4 to 6:4, or from 100 to 150 percent.

Some of the most brilliant and powerful pages in *Capital* are those in which Marx describes how, especially in the early phases of the industrial revolution, capitalists sought to extend the working day as long as possible, forcing even nine year old boys to work three twelve hour shifts running in the hellish conditions of the iron foundries. 'Capital', he writes, 'is dead labour which, vampire-like, lives only by sucking living labour, and lives the more, the more labour it sucks' (C i 342).

There are, however, objective limits to the extension of the working day. Pushed too far, it 'not only produces a deterioration of human labour power by robbing it of its normal moral and physical conditions of development and activity, but also produces the premature exhaustion and death of this labour power itself' (C i 376). Capital, which depends on labour power as the source of value, thus acts against its own interests. At the same time, the remorseless extension of the working day engenders organised resistance by its victims. Marx chronicles the role played by collective working class action in forcing British capitalists to accept the Factory Acts limiting the hours of work. 'Hence, in the history of capitalist production, the establishment of a norm for the working day presents itself as a struggle over the limits of that day, a struggle between collective capital, ie the class of capitalists, and collective labour, ie the working class' (C i 344).

Capital can nonetheless raise the rate of surplus value also by the production of relative surplus value. An increase in the productivity of labour will lead to a fall in the value of the commodities it produces. If some technical improvement in the conditions of production thus cheapens the consumer goods which workers buy with their wages, then the value of labour power has fallen. Less social labour will now be needed to re-produce labour power, and the portion of the working day devoted to necessary labour will fall, leaving more time spent creating surplus value.

Let us say that higher productivity in consumer industries leads to a halving of the value of consumer goods. To go back to our original example, necessary labour will now take up only two hours out of an eight hour day. So the rate of surplus value is now 6:2. It has risen from 100 to 300 percent.

Marx argues that although both absolute and relative surplus value will be found in all phases of capitalist development, there tends to be a historical shift in their importance. When capitalist relations of production are first introduced, they do so on the basis of methods of production inherited from the artisan industries of feudal society. These handicraft methods are not at first fundamentally altered: workers are simply grouped together into larger units of production, and subjected to a more complex division of labour. New relations of production are grafted on to an old labour process:

> Given a pre-existing mode of labour...surplus value can be created only by lengthening the working day, ie by increasing *absolute surplus value* (C i 1021).

In a mode of production such as feudalism, where neither exploiter nor exploited necessarily has a strong interest in expanding the productive forces, more surplus labour can only be extracted from the direct producers by making them work longer hours. Capitalism, however, introduces a new way of increasing the rate of exploitation, by getting the producers to work more efficiently.

'With the production of relative surplus value the entire form of production is altered and a *specifically capitalist form of production* comes into being' (C i 1024). What Marx calls manufacture, based on 'the broad foundation of the town handicrafts and the domestic industries of the countryside' (C i 490) is supplanted by modern large scale industry, or 'machinofacture', in which production is organised around systems of machines, and the labour process is constantly altered in the light of technological innovations. 'There now arises a technologically and   135 otherwise *specific mode of production—capitalist production—* which transforms *the labour process and its actual conditions'* (**C** i 1034-5).

The most important consequence is that the labour process is increasingly socialised. Production now takes place in large units organised around machines, and involving a highly complex division of labour. 'The *real lever* of the overall labour process is increasingly not the individual worker' but '*labour power socially combined*' (**C** i 1039-40). Capitalism thus creates what Marx calls the 'collective worker', of which individuals are limbs, bound together by their joint effort in producing commodities.

Marx emphasises that the purpose of the constant transformations of the labour process under capitalism is that of increasing the rate of exploitation by producing relative surplus value:

> Like every other instrument for increasing the productivity of labour, machinery is intended to cheapen commodities and, by shortening the part of the working day in which the worker works for himself, to lengthen the other part, the part he gives the capitalist for nothing. The machine is a means for producing surplus value (**C** i 492).

This highlights what we saw in the last chapter, that the productive forces develop to the extent that they are permitted to do so by the prevailing relations of production. The peculiarity of capitalism is that these relations *require* continual improvements in the productivity of labour.

Competition, prices and profits

Marx's analysis of the capitalist production process in the first volume of *Capital* takes place at quite a high level of abstraction. Most important is the fact that he assumes that commodities exchange at their values, that is, in proportion to the socially necessary labour time involved in their production. In particular, he excludes the effects of competition, and of fluctuations in the supply of commodities and the demand for them.

This procedure was justified because Marx was concerned at this point to grasp the essential features of the capitalist economy, and to trace them to their source in the extraction of surplus value from the workers within the process of production. Marx's object in analysing the capitalist process of production was what he called 'capital in general, as distinct from the particular capitals'. This, he conceded, was an abstraction, not:

> ...an arbitrary abstraction, but an abstraction which grasps the specific characteristics which distinguish capital from all other forms of wealth—or modes in which social production develops. These are the aspects common to every capital as such, or which make every specific sum of values into capital (**G** 449).

The 'aspects common to every capital as such' come down to the fact that capital is the self expansion of value, which arises from the exploitation of the worker in production. Thus, what distinguishes capital from other 'modes in which social production develops' is surplus value as 'the specific economic form in which unpaid surplus labour is pumped out of the direct producers' (**C** iii 791). The analysis of 'capital in general' is intended to uncover the basis of capitalist relations of production.

There is, however, another stage in Marx's examination of capitalism. We saw that this mode of production involves two separations: one between labour power and the means of production, which underlies the exchange between wage labour and capital and thus makes possible the extraction of surplus value; the other between the units of production, which arises from the fact that there is no collective way under capitalism for social labour to be distributed among different activities, and so individual producers relate to each other only through the exchange of their products.

It is an essential feature of capitalism that no single producer controls the economy. 'Capital exists and can only exist as many capitals,' writes Marx (**G** 414).

The sphere of 'many capitals' is that of competition. Individual capitals struggle with each other over markets, seeking to win control of particular sectors. The behaviour of these capitals can only be understood in the light of Marx's analysis of 'capital in general', and especially of the process of production. What makes them *capitals* is the self expansion of value in production. But in a very important sense Marx's analysis of competition

137

completes that of the process of production.

To appreciate this point fully, we must first take a look at the three volumes of *Capital*. Volume 1, as we have seen, is concerned with the analysis of the process of production. But because capitalism is a system of generalised commodity production, the capitalist will actually obtain the surplus value he has extracted from the worker only if he succeeds in selling the commodities which embody this value. What Marx calls the realisation of the value created in production—its transformation into money—depends on the circulation of commodities on the market.

Volume 2 of *Capital* is concerned with this process of circulation, examining its implications in two ways. First, Marx considers the different circuits of capital, the successive transformations of, for example, money capital into the labour power and means of production which are used to produce commodities, and then into a larger sum of money if these commodities are sold at their value. Marx then considers the way in which the circuits of individual capitals interweave to bring about the reproduction of the entire economy. Much of what he says in Volume 2 is brilliant and innovative, but in this book we shall only touch on it when discussing crises in the following section.

It is in *Capital* Volume 3 that the analysis of competition becomes relevant. Here Marx is concerned with capitalist production as a whole. Because the realisation of the value generated in production depends on the circulation of commodities:

> ...the capitalist process of production taken as a whole represents a synthesis of the processes of production and of circulation... The various forms of capital as evolved in this book...approach step by step the form which they assume on the surface of society, in the action of different capitals on one another, in competition, and in the ordinary consciousness of the agents of production themselves (**C** iii 26).

The central importance of competition is that through *its* pressure individual producers are forced to behave as capitals. 'The influence of individual capitals on one another has the effect precisely that they must conduct themselves as *capital*' (**G** 657).

The law of value—the exchange of commodities in

proportion to the socially necessary labour time involved in their production—depends upon competition in two ways. Marx distinguishes between the value of a commodity, and its market price. Value is the social labour expended on it; the market price is the amount of money which it will fetch at any one time. The two will often differ, because the market price will fluctuate in response to oscillations in supply and demand. Marx argues that these fluctuations cancel each other out over time.

A commodity's value, however, as we saw in the opening section of this chapter, is the *socially necessary* labour involved in its production. This may well differ from the actual amount of labour used to produce it. Marx therefore distinguishes between a commodity's individual value, the labour time it embodies, and its social or market value, which reflects the prevailing conditions of production in that industry.

The market value of the commodity is determined by the competition between the capitals in that industry, each trying to win a larger share of the market than its rivals, each seeking to do so by improving its conditions of production and thus reducing the value of its commodities. Usually the resulting market value will be the value of goods produced in the average conditions of production in the industry. An individual capital's products will, as a result of this competition, sell at the market value, even if the actual labour used to produce these commodities, their individual value, is more or less than the market value.

There is, moreover, a second way in which competition enters into the workings of the law of value. This arises from the fact that commodities are the '*product of capital*' (C i 949 ff). In other words, the capitalist invests his capital in the production of commodities, not for its own sake, but in order to produce surplus value. Now, as we saw in the previous section, the source of surplus value is variable capital—in other words, the workers that the capitalist employs in exchange for their wages. However, the capitalist does not simply advance the money to pay these wages; he also has to fork out for the machinery, buildings, raw materials and so on, which are necessary if the workers are actually to produce commodities. What counts for the capitalist is not simply the return he makes on the variable capital, but rather that on his total investment, variable capital plus the constant capital tied up in the means of production.

nition of this fact led Marx to distinguish between the
rplus value and the *rate of profit*. The rate of surplus
imply the ratio of surplus value to variable capital. As
we saw in the previous section, this measures the degree of exploitation of labour power. The rate of profit, on the other hand,
is the ratio between surplus value and total capital, variable capital *plus* constant capital. From the point of view of understanding capitalism, the rate of surplus value is more basic, because
labour power is the source of value. But what matters to the capitalist is the rate of *profit* because he needs to make an adequate
return on his total investment, not just on what he spends on
wages.

Obviously, the two rates will differ. Take a capitalist who employs 100 workers at a wage of £50 a week. His total wage bill—
his variable capital—is £5,000 a week. If the rate of surplus value
is 100 percent, then the surplus value produced every week will
also be £5,000. This is his profit. (The capitalist also gets back his
original £5,000, making £10,000 in all.) But suppose the capitalist also has to advance £2,500 a week to pay for the plant, buildings and so on. This is his constant capital. The total capital
invested each week will be £7,500, and the rate of profit, the
return on this total investment, is the ratio of the profit received
to the total capital, or £5,000:£7,500—66 percent.

The existence of a rate of profit is an illustration of how, according to Marx, competition conceals the real relations of production. For it is the rate of profit that capitalists use in their
everyday calculations. Because this concept relates surplus value
to the total capital, the fact that labour power is the source of surplus value is concealed. It appears as if the constant capital invested in the means of production is also responsible for creating
value and surplus value. This is an example of what Marx calls
commodity fetishism, the way the working of the capitalist economy leads people to believe that their social relationships are in
some mystical way governed by physical objects—use values
and the machinery used to produce them. The effect is to justify
the existence of profits, since the capitalist, as the owner of the
means of production, seems just as entitled as the worker to a
share of the product they have supposedly cooperated in making.

There is more to the rate of profit, however, than this mystifi-
cation. Marx argues that the rate of profit will differ from industry

to industry depending on the prevailing conditions of production. To explain this he uses another concept, that of the *organic composition of capital*. This is the ratio of constant capital to variable capital. In other words, it reflects (in value terms) the amount of machinery, raw materials and so on that are needed to produce a given commodity relative to the labour power needed.

It is in fact a measure of the productivity of labour. For the more efficient labour power is, the more machinery will an individual worker set to work, the more raw materials will he or she use and so on. So the higher the productivity of labour, the higher the organic composition of capital will be too.

What does this mean for the rate of profit?

Let us examine the case of two capitalists, A and B. Let us assume that each has the same weekly wage bill—£5,000—and, as Marx does, that each has the same rate of surplus value, 100 percent . So each receives a weekly profit of £5,000. But while A invests constant capital each week of £5,000, B, in a different sector of industry, has to invest £10,000.

For A, then, the organic composition of his capital, the ratio of constant to variable capital, is £5,000:£5,000, or 1:1. His profit of £5,000 is made with a total capital of £10,000, so his rate of profit is £5,000:£10,000 or 50 percent. The organic composition of B's capital, on the other hand, is £10,000:£5,000, or 2:1—twice that of A. B's rate of profit is £5,000:£15,000, or only 33 percent.

So the higher the organic composition of capital, the more machinery and raw materials used by each worker, the lower the rate of profit—because only labour power produces surplus value.

Now capitalists are concerned to gain the largest possible return for their investment, the highest possible rate of profit. Since the amount of machinery, buildings and so on needed for production varies from industry to industry, in other words, some industries have higher organic composition of capital than others, capital will tend to flow to where the rate of profit is highest—in other words, to where the organic composition of capital is low. Why, after all, should capitalist B continue investing all his money where it gives him a return of only 33 percent when he could get 50 percent if he put his capital in industry A?

This leads to what Marx calls the equalisation of the rate of profit. The flow of capital from one industry to another will tend   141 to even out the differences in the rate of profit. The result is that a general rate of profit is formed which reflects the relationship between the total surplus value produced in the entire economy, and the total social capital invested. Individual capitals will receive a share of the total surplus value extracted, in proportion, not to the variable capital they have advanced, but to the total capital they have invested.

To see what this means, let's go back to A and B, and assume that they are the only two capitals in the economy. The total surplus value is then £10,000 and the total social capital £25,000. The *general* rate of profit is £10,000:£25,000, or 40 percent. It is higher than B's original 33 percent, but lower than A's 50 percent. Each will receive a return of 40 percent on their total capital. On his £10,000 A will get £4,000, while B, with £15,000, will get £6,000. Since each enterprise extracts £5,000 in surplus value from its workers, £1,000 has been transferred between them.

How does this happen? Unfortunately, our model above, with capitalists A and B, is too simplified to demonstrate the mechanism that causes this transfer of surplus value, but we can still use it to show how this mechanism is set in motion.

Capitalist B, seeing A making a higher rate of profit than he is, is naturally going to want a piece of the action. He's going to shift some of his capital into industry A. This will lead to an increase in production, and this increase will continue until the supply of these goods exceeds the demand. Once there are more of these goods for sale than there are buyers, their price will fall. So these commodities will end up being sold below their value, and industry A will become less profitable.

Conversely, since capitalist B has removed some of his money from his own industry, production of B goods will fall. When the supply of these goods is lower than demand, the price of these commodities will rise, and they will sell at prices above their value. The profit rate of industry B, initially low, will rise.

So as capital continually searches for the highest return, the increase of investment in industries with low use of plant, machinery and raw materials relative to labour power, in other words low organic composition of capital and therefore high rate of profit, will tend to bring prices down and reduce that rate of profit. The opposite will happen in industries with high organic composition of capital.

As Marx writes: 'This incessant outflow and influx', through which capital is constantly redistributed among the different spheres of production depending on their relative profitability, will continue until 'it creates such a ratio of supply and demand that the average profit in the spheres of production becomes the same, and values are, therefore, converted into prices of production' (C iii 195-6). Equilibrium is reached when the prices of different goods are set at levels which earn every capital the same rate of profit.

It is as if all the surplus value pumped out of workers, wherever they may be employed, flows into a single pool from which capitalists draw profits in proportion to the sums they have invested. The origin of surplus value is thus further mystified, since the profits a capitalist gains no longer seem to bear any relation to the amount of labour his workers have performed. 'All these phenomena', Marx comments, '*seem* to contradict the determination of value by labour time... *Thus everything appears reversed in competition*' (C iii 209).

This appearance is dissolved once we consider the overall relationship between the capitalist class and the working class:

> In each particular sphere of production, the individual capitalist, as well as the capitalists as a whole, take part in the exploitation of the total working class by the totality of capital... For, assuming all other conditions...to be given, the average rate of profit depends on the intensity of exploitation of the sum total of labour by the sum total of capital (C iii 196-7).

> The capitalists strive (and this striving is competition) to divide among themselves the quantity of unpaid labour...which they squeeze out of the working class, not according to the surplus labour produced directly by a *particular* capital, but corresponding *firstly* to the relative portion of the aggregate capital which a particular capital represents, and *secondly* according to the amount of surplus labour produced by the aggregate capital. The capitalists, like hostile brothers, divide among themselves the loot of other people's labour so that on average one receives the same amount of unpaid labour as the other (TSV ii 29).

Here, then, we have a mathematically precise proof why capitalists

143

form a veritable freemason society *vis-à-vis* the whole working class, while there is little love lost between them in competition among themselves (**C** iii 198).

One consequence of the equalisation of the rate of profit is that the law of value must be modified. 'It is evident that the emergence...of the *general rate of profit* necessitates the *transformation of values* into *cost prices* that are *different* from these values' (**TSV** ii 434).

To see why this is so, let's go back to our old friends the capitalists A and B. To arrive at the value of their weekly products, let us assume that the value of all the constant capital they advance each week is transferred to the commodities they produce. The total value of their weekly product is then equal to variable capital + surplus value + constant capital. In A's case this is £5,000 + £5,000 + £5,000 = £15,000. In B's case it is £5,000 + £5,000 + £10,000 = £20,000. But the equalisation of the rate of profit means that £1,000 of surplus value has been transferred from A to B. So the values produced must be modified to take account of this redistribution. For A, we then get £5,000 + £4,000 + £5,000 = £14,000, and for B, £5,000 + £6,000 + £10,000 = £21,000.

Marx calls these converted values which reflect the formation of the general rate of profit *prices of production*. Their formation is an inevitable consequence of the fact that 'capital exists, and can only exist as many capitals'. 'What competition, first in a single sphere [of production], achieves is a single market value and market price derived from the various individual values of commodities. And it is competition of capitals in different spheres, which first brings out the price of production, equalising the rates of profit in the different spheres' (**C** iii 180). The conversion of values into prices of production is part of the same process as the formation of values themselves. For it is competition in particular industries which leads to commodities being sold at their socially necessary labour time in the first place.

The transformation of values into prices of production thus completes the labour theory of value rather than undermining it. Marx points out that the deviations of prices of production from values 'always resolves itself into one commodity receiving too little of the surplus value while another receives too much, so that the deviations from the values which are embodied in the prices of production compensate one another' (**C** iii 161). 'The sum of the prices of production of all commodities produced in society...is equal to the sum of their values' (**C** iii 159-60). If we turn back to the case of A and B two paragraphs ago, we see that the total value of their products, £35,000, remains the same before and after the conversion of values into prices of production.

The so called 'transformation problem' has nevertheless caused an enormous controversy, which began when *Capital* Volume 3 was published in 1894 and shows no sign of abating today. Some of the criticisms are simple matters of ignorance. For example, the Austrian economist Eugen von Boehm-Bawerk, author of one of the first discussions of the transformation problem, argued that Marx had changed his mind after writing *Capital* Volume 1, and decided that commodities did not after all exchange at their values. This ignores the fact, as Engels pointed out when he published *Capital* Volume 3 after Marx's death, that the manuscripts on which it is based were written by Marx in 1864 and 1865, before he completed the final draft of Volume 1! In any case, *Theories of Surplus Value*, taken from the even earlier 1861/63 manuscripts, shows that Marx, like Ricardo before him, was perfectly well aware that the existence of the general rate of profit implied that the law of value must be modified.

There are some more valid technical criticisms. Marx, in his examples of the transformation, ignored the fact that the value of the commodities represented by variable and constant capital must themselves be converted into prices of production. It will not do, therefore, as I did in my own illustration, to leave A's capital at £10,000 and B's at £15,000 both before and after the transformation. The goods consumed by workers, and the plant, machinery and so on which they use to produce commodities, will themselves have been affected by the formation of a general rate of profit, and will also have had their values transformed into prices of production. Marx was not unconscious of this problem, but felt that it was not important enough to worry about (see **C** iii 164-5). Later research suggests that he is wrong, and that a complete transformation of values into prices of production has more far-reaching implications than Marx thought. However, those mathematical solutions to the problem which have been

145

reached do not invalidate Marx's basic account of the conversion of values into prices of production.

Some economists, including a number of Marxists, still insist that the 'transformation problem' proves that the labour theory of value must be rejected. Their main argument for this is that there are techniques for determining the prices of commodities that do not involve starting from their values. This is perfectly true, but mistakes the point of the labour theory of value. Its main purpose is not to provide us with a formula for determining the ratio in which commodities will exchange for each other (although it does do that, once we have corrected Marx's version of the transformation). Marx's intention is 'to reveal the economic law of motion of modern society'—to uncover the tendencies of historical development contained in the capitalist mode of production. The labour theory of value is an instrument towards this end.

Marx's procedure in *Capital* reflects his general method of 'rising from the abstract to the concrete'. In Volumes 1 and 2, where he is analysing 'capital in general', the basic characteristics of capitalist relations of production, he assumes that commodities exchange at their values. This is a perfectly valid assumption to make, because the transformation problem arises only when we start considering the *differences* between capitals. It is only when Marx comes to consider the sphere of 'many capitals', and the competition which takes place between them, as in *Capital* Volume 3, that he is obliged to drop the assumption that commodities exchange at their values. This is necessary if we are to 'locate and describe the concrete forms which grow out of the movements of capital *as a whole*' (**C** iii 26).

However, we can do this successfully only if we *have* made the initial abstraction, that of assuming that commodities exchange at their values, which was necessary to analyse 'capital in general'. Marx's chief criticism of Ricardo was that he simply assumed the existence of the general rate of profit, failing to consider value and surplus value in isolation from competition. His error was 'lack of the power of abstraction, inability when dealing with the values of commodities, to forget profits, a factor which confronts him as a result of competition' (**TSV** ii 191).

So far we have considered the relationship between 'capital in general' and 'many capitals' statically, merely looking at how it affects the formation of value. Let's now take a more dynamic view, and examine the role played by competition between capitals in the development of the bourgeois economy.

Accumulation and crises

One of the main features of capitalism which sets it off from other modes of production, is the accumulation of capital. In slave or feudal societies, the exploiter will consume the bulk of the surplus product which he has seized from the direct producers. Production is still dominated by use value: its objective is consumption.

This changes once the capitalist mode of production prevails. Most of the surplus value squeezed out of the workers is not consumed. Rather, it is reinvested in further production. It is this process, through which surplus value is constantly ploughed back into the production of yet more surplus value, that Marx calls the accumulation of capital.

In a famous passage in *Capital* Volume 1, Marx shows how this gives rise in the capitalist class to an ideology of 'abstinence', in which the bourgeoisie are encouraged to deny even their own consumption, and to save as much surplus value as possible so that it may be reinvested:

> Accumulate, accumulate! That is Moses and the prophets! 'Industry furnishes the material which saving accumulates' [says Adam Smith]. Therefore save, save, ie reconvert the greatest possible portion of surplus value or surplus product into capital! Accumulation for the sake of accumulation, production for the sake of production: this was the formula in which classical economics expressed the historical mission of the bourgeoisie in the period of its domination (C i 742).

But, says Marx, the motive for this is not greed (though as an individual the capitalist might be greedy). We don't need to look for some 'natural propensity to truck and barter' in human nature. The system itself provides the capitalist's motive:

> ...in so far as he is capital personified, his motivating force is not the acquisition and enjoyment of use values, but the acquisition and augmentation of exchange values... As such, he shares

147

with the miser an absolute drive towards self enrichment. But what appears in the miser as the mania of an individual is in the capitalist the effect of a social mechanism in which he is merely a cog (C i 739).

This 'social mechanism' is competition between 'many capitals'. We have seen that Marx believed 'the influence of individual capitals on one another has the effect precisely that they must conduct themselves as *capital*'. This is especially true of accumulation itself. A capital which does not reinvest surplus value will soon find itself outstripped by its rivals. Those who have invested in improved methods of production are able to produce more cheaply and can undercut the price of the first capital's goods. A capital which fails to accumulate will soon find itself driven into bankruptcy.

The accumulation process, just because it is inseparable from competition between capitals, is not a smooth or even affair. Marx argues that the accumulation process is also the reproduction of capitalist relations of production. What he means is that society cannot go on existing unless production is constantly renewed and this depends on capitalists ploughing the value they have realised on the market back into production.

Marx distinguishes between two forms of reproduction. *Simple* reproduction takes place when production is renewed at the same level as previously—and the economy stagnates rather than grows. *Extended* reproduction, however, involves surplus product being used to increase production. This latter case is the norm under capitalism.

In Volume 2 of *Capital* Marx analyses the conditions under which simple or extended reproduction takes place. He shows that here use value plays a very important role. For reproduction to happen, it is not enough for there to be the money to buy labour power and the instruments of production. There must also be enough consumer goods to feed the workers, and enough machinery, raw materials and so on for them to put to work.

Marx divides the economy into two broad sectors, Departments I and II. Department I of the economy produces the means of production: for instance, mining for raw materials and factories producing machinery. Department II produces consumer goods: food, clothing and so on. Marx shows that for either simple or extended reproduction to happen, both Departments must produce goods in certain proportions.

But whether these proportions between the different sectors of the economy actually hold is a matter largely of accident. Capitalists produce, not for themselves, but for the market. There is no guarantee whatsoever that what is produced will be consumed. Whether this happens depends on there being effective demand for the commodity. In other words, not only must someone want to buy it, but they must have the money to do so. Often this demand does not exist. The result is an economic crisis.

For example, let us say that capitalists in Department I (means of production) cut the wages of their workers in order to increase the rate of surplus value. These workers will then be able to buy fewer of the products of Department II (consumer goods). Capitalists in Department II may react to this decline in their markets by cutting back on their orders for new plant and equipment. Department I capitalists, hit in turn by this fall in demand for their products, may lay off workers, which then causes their Department II counterparts to do the same...and so on. This process, only really understood by bourgeois economists since the appearance of J M Keynes's *General Theory of Employment, Interest and Money* in 1936, was analysed by Marx in *Capital* Volume 2 some 70 years earlier.

The possibility of economic crises is inherent in the very nature of the commodity. Let us recall that the simple circulation of commodities takes the form of C-M-C. A commodity is sold, and the money used to buy another commodity. But there is no reason why a sale must necessarily be followed by another purchase. Having sold his commodity, the seller may decide to hoard the money he has received. There are often conditions in which capitalists decide to do precisely this, because the rate of profit is too low for it to be worth their while to invest.

The source of crises is thus ultimately the unplanned character of capitalist production, where 'a balance is itself an accident owing to the spontaneous nature of this production,' as Marx writes (**C** ii 499). However, this merely shows that crises are *possible*. To understand why they actually happen we have to dig deeper into the nature of the accumulation process.

Marx's explanation of economic crises is based on what he called the law of the tendency of the rate of profit to fall, 'in every respect the most important law of modern political economy, and the most essential for understanding the most difficult relations', he wrote (**G** 748).

The rate of profit has a *general* tendency to fall under capitalism, says Marx. Not just in specific areas of the economy nor just in particular periods but generally, and the reason, he says, is the continual increase in the productivity of labour. To use his own words: 'The progressive tendency of the rate of profit to fall is just *an expression, peculiar to the capitalist mode of production*, of the progressive development of the social productivity of labour' (**C** iii 212).

The higher the productivity of labour, the more machinery and raw materials an individual worker is responsible for. In other words, the amount of constant capital invested in plant, equipment and raw materials grows relative to the variable capital used to pay the worker's wages. In value terms, this means that the organic composition of capital is higher. And we have already seen how, because labour power is the source of surplus value, the higher the organic composition of capital, the lower the rate of profit. So as productivity increases, the rate of profit falls.

But if this is so, then why should any capitalist ever invest for higher productivity? The answer is that, in the short term, he benefits from doing so, and in the long term he is *forced* to do so by competition.

Let us recall that the individual value of a commodity, the actual labour embodied in it, may differ from the social or market value, which is determined by the average conditions of production in that industry. Now take the case of an individual capitalist using these average conditions of production. Suppose that he introduces a new technique, which raises the productivity of his workers above the average. The individual value of his commodities will fall below their social value because they have been produced more efficiently than is normal in that sector. The capitalist can now fix their prices at a level that is lower than the social value thus undercutting his competitors, but still higher than their individual value, thus realising an extra profit.

But this situation will not last indefinitely. Other capitalists will adopt the new technique to prevent themselves being undercut and driven out of business. Once this innovation becomes the norm in the industry the social value of its products will fall to match the individual value of the innovator's commodities, wiping out his advantage.

Through the pressure of competition capitals are therefore compelled to adopt new techniques and raise the productivity of labour. 'The law of determination of value by labour time' thus acts as 'a coercive law of competition,' writes Marx (**C** i 436). For the individual capitalist, 'the determination of value as such…interests him only in so far as it raises or lowers the cost of production of commodities for himself, thus only in so far as it makes his position exceptional' (**C** iii 873). Each capitalist is concerned to raise the productivity of labour only as a means of outstripping his competitors. The effect is to force all the 'many capitals' to conform to the law of value, and constantly to increase the productivity of labour.

However, the outcome of all these self seeking actions by capitalists out to increase the amount of surplus value they can seize from their workers and their competitors is to bring down the general rate of profit:

> No capitalist ever voluntarily introduces a new method of production no matter how much more productive it may be, and how much it may increase the rate of surplus value, so long as it reduces the rate of profit. Yet every such new method of production cheapens the commodities. Hence, the capitalist sells them originally above their prices of production, or, perhaps, above their value. He pockets the difference between their costs of production and the market prices of the same commodities produced at higher costs of production. He can do this…because his method of production stands above the social average. But competition makes it general and subject to the general law. There follows a fall in the rate of profit—perhaps first in this sphere of production and eventually it achieves a balance with the rest, which is, therefore, wholly independent of the will of the capitalist (**C** iii 264-5).

This tendency of the rate of profit to fall is a reflection of the fact that 'beyond a certain point, the development of the powers of production becomes a barrier for capital; hence the capital relation a barrier for the development of the productive powers of labour' (**G** 749). The greater productivity of labour, which reflects humanity's growing power over nature, takes the form,

151

within capitalist relations of production, of a rising organic composition of capital, and hence a falling rate of profit. It is this process which underlies economic crises. 'The growing incompatibility between the productive development of society and its hitherto existing relations of production expresses itself in bitter contradictions, crises, spasms' (**G** 749).

The falling rate of profit is, however, only the starting point of Marx's analysis of capitalist crises. He stresses that there are 'counteracting influences at work, which cross and annul the effect of the general law, and which give it merely the characteristic of a tendency', 'a law whose absolute action is checked, retarded and weakened' (**C** iii 232, 235). Indeed, 'the same influences which produce a tendency in the general rate of profit to fall, also call forth counter-effects, which hamper, retard and partly paralyse this fall' (**C** iii 239).

For example, the rising organic composition of capital means that a smaller number of workers can produce a given amount of commodities. The capitalist may well react by sacking the surplus workers—this may indeed have been his aim in introducing the new technique in the first place. The result is that the accumulation of capital involves the constant expulsion of workers from production. What Marx calls 'relative over-population' is created. It is not, as Malthus and his followers claimed, that there are more people than there is food to keep them alive. Rather, there are more people than capitalism needs, and so the surplus is deprived of the wages on which workers depend for their existence.

The capitalist economy consequently generates an 'industrial reserve army' of unemployed workers, which plays a crucial role in the accumulation process. Not only do the unemployed provide a pool of workers that can be flung into new branches of production. They also help to prevent wages from rising too high.

Labour power, like every commodity, has a value—the labour time involved in its production, and a price—the amount of money paid for it. The price of labour power is wages, and like all market prices wages fluctuate in response to rises and falls in the supply and demand of labour power. The existence of the industrial reserve army keeps the supply of labour power large enough to prevent the price of labour power from rising above its value. Writes Marx: 'The general movements of wages are exclusively regulated by the expansion and contraction of the industrial reserve army' (**C** i 790).

This does *not* mean that Marx believed in the 'iron law of wages', according to which wages cannot rise above the bare physical minimum necessary for subsistence. As he pointed out in the *Critique of the Gotha Programme*, this so called 'law' is based on Malthus's theory of population, and is therefore utterly false. Capitalism, as we have seen, involves constant increases in the productivity of labour. These lead, of necessity, to a steady reduction in the value of commodities, including labour power. The falling value of consumer goods means that the purchasing power of workers' wages can stay the same or even rise although the value of labour power has fallen. So in *absolute* terms, workers' living standards may well rise. In *relative* terms, however, their position has deteriorated, because the rate of surplus value has risen, and so their share of the total value they have created has fallen.

The existence of an industrial reserve army strengthens the position of the capitalist, and makes it easier for him to increase the rate of surplus value. If the total amount of capital remains the same, then the rate of profit will rise. So a greater intensity of exploitation is one counteracting influence on the falling rate of profit.

Increasing the rate of exploitation is double-edged, however. If it is achieved through increasing the productivity of labour, then the organic composition of capital will rise, and so a higher rate of surplus value will in this case mean a lower rate of profit. Marx believed that such a situation was typical of the tendency of the rate of profit. He rejected any attempt to explain economic crises through workers winning higher wage increases:

> The tendency of the rate of profit to fall is bound up with a tendency for the rate of surplus value to rise... Nothing is more absurd, for this reason, than to explain the fall in the rate of profit by a rise in the rate of wages, although this may be the case by way of an exception... The rate of profit does not fall because labour becomes less productive, but because it becomes more productive. Both the rise in the rate of surplus value and the fall in the rate of profit are but specific forms through which growing productivity of labour is expressed under capitalism (**C** iii 240).

153

The same was true, Marx argued, of another counteracting influence, the cheapening of the elements of constant capital. Rising productivity in Department I, the production of the means of production, means that the value of the plant, machinery and so on which make up the constant capital falls:

> With the growth in the proportion of constant to variable capital, grows also the productivity of labour, the productive forces brought into being, with which social labour operates. As a result of this increasing productivity of labour, however, a part of the existing constant capital is continuously depreciated in value, for its value depends, not on the labour time it cost originally, but on the labour time with which it can be reproduced, and this is continually diminishing as the productivity of labour grows (**TSV** ii 415-16).

Many critics of Marx (some of them Marxists) have argued that the fact that rising labour productivity cheapens the elements of constant capital means that the organic composition does not rise and so the rate of profit does not fall. Even though the technical composition of capital, in other words the physical ratio between means of production and labour power, grows enormously, they contend, in value terms this relationship stays the same because the cost of producing the means of production has fallen. What they ignore is that what matters for the capitalist is the return he makes on his *original* investment. The money he laid out on plant, equipment and so on will have been to buy these means of production at their original values, not the labour time it would now cost to replace them. He must make an adequate profit on this investment, not on what it might now cost him to make it.

But let us now look at crises themselves.

It is indeed mainly through crises that the value of constant capital is brought in line, not with 'the labour time it cost originally', but with 'the labour time with which it can be reproduced'. Economic crises may be precipitated by a variety of factors. For example, one may be brought on by a sudden rise in the price of some important raw material—such as the fourfold rise in the price of oil in 1973-4. Often crises start through some disruption of the financial system—for example, a major bank going bankrupt, or a stock market crash. A large portion of *Capital* Volume 3 is devoted to explaining how development of the credit system, as a result of which more and more money is created by the banks themselves, plays a vital role in both preventing and bringing about crises. However, the underlying cause of crises is always the tendency of the rate of profit to fall, and the counteracting influences which it brings into play.

We have seen that the nature of the commodity is such that C-M does not necessarily lead to M-C. Money gained by selling a commodity may be hoarded rather than used to buy another commodity. This takes place on a massive scale during economic crises. Vast numbers of commodities go unsold.

This sets capitalism apart from earlier modes of production. In slave and feudal societies crises were those of underproduction, of shortage, in which there was not enough to feed everyone. Capitalist crises, however, are those of *over*production. This does not mean, Marx emphasises, 'that the amount of products is excessive in relation to the need for them...the limits to production are set by the profit of the capitalist and in no way by the needs of the producers' (**TSV** ii 527). Too many commodities have been produced to realise an adequate profit for the capitalist. If we want an example, we need look no further than the butter mountains and wine lakes created to keep the price of agricultural goods high, while more than 700 million people starve in the Third World.

At the same time as crises are produced by the internal contradictions of capital accumulation, they 'are always momentary and forcible solutions of the existing contradictions' (**C** iii 249). This takes place through what Marx called the depreciation or devaluation of capital. The collapse of the markets for their goods forces many capitals out of business. Effectively, large amounts of capital are destroyed.

The destruction of capital is sometimes literal—machinery rusts, stocks of goods rot or are destroyed. But falling prices also wipe out a large part of the value of the means of production. 'The *destruction of capital* through crises means the depreciation of *values* which prevents them from renewing their reproduction process as capital on the same scale' (**TSV** ii 496). It is in this way, through economic crises, that the value of constant capital is brought in line, not with the labour time originally used

155

to produce it, but with what it would now cost to reproduce it. In this manner the organic composition of capital is reduced and the rate of profit recovers.

So crises serve to restore capital to a condition in which it can be profitably employed:

> The periodical depreciation of existing capital—one of the means immanent in capitalist production to check the fall of the rate of profit and hasten accumulation of capital value through the formation of new capital—disturbs the given conditions within which the process of circulation and reproduction of capital takes place, and is therefore accompanied by stoppages and crises in the production process (C iii 249).

There are other ways in which crises serve to offset the tendency of the rate of profit to fall. Marx writes that 'crises are always prepared by...a period in which wages rise generally and the working class actually gets a larger share of that part of the annual product which is intended for consumption' (C ii 414-15).

This reflects the fact that at the height of economic booms many commodities become scarce because they are in demand by so many capitals eager to get as large a share of the market as possible. This is true of labour power: as the pace of economic growth quickens, so the industrial reserve army is run down, and workers, especially skilled ones, become scarce. The workers' improved bargaining position then enables them to bid up the price of labour power, and so the rate of wages rises. An economic recession, by forcing up unemployment, makes it easier for the employers to drive down wages, and to compel those workers still with jobs to accept worse conditions of production.

Crises, then, are periods when the capitalist system is reorganised and reshaped in order to restore the rate of profit to a level at which investment will take place. Not all capitals benefit equally from this process. The weaker and less efficient firms, and those with an especially large burden of out-of-date machinery, will be driven out of business. The stronger and more efficient capitals survive, and emerge from the recession stronger. They are able to buy up land and instruments of production at bargain-basement prices, and to force on workers changes in the labour process which will increase the rate of surplus value.

Crises therefore contribute to the process which Marx called the centralisation and concentration of capital. Concentration takes place when capitals grow in size through the accumulation of surplus value. Centralisation, on the other hand, involves the absorption of smaller by bigger capitals. The process of competition itself encourages this trend, because the more efficient firms are able to undercut their rivals and then to take them over. But economic recessions speed up the process by enabling the surviving capitals to buy up the means of production cheap. A constant increase in the size of individual capitals is therefore an inevitable part of the accumulation process.

'The path characteristically described by modern industry', Marx writes, 'takes the form of a...cycle (interrupted by smaller oscillations) of periods of average activity, production at high pressure, crisis, and stagnation' (C i 785). The alternation of boom and slump is an essential feature of the capitalist economy. As Trotsky put it, 'Capitalism does live by crises and booms, just as a human being lives by inhaling and exhaling... Crises and booms were inherent in capitalism from its birth; they will accompany it to its grave.'

The analysis of the way in which crises are built into the accumulation of capital, which Marx develops in *Capital*, is conducted at quite a high level of abstraction. It needs to be elaborated, as we shall see in the final chapter, by an account of how, as the system grows older, the centralisation and concentration of capital makes it more difficult for crises to perform their role of restoring the conditions of profitable accumulation. Nevertheless, *Capital* provides the basis of any attempt to understand the capitalist economy.

Conclusion

The capitalist mode of production illustrates Marx's general thesis that reality is dialectical, that it contains contradictions within it. For, on the one hand, technological change, the introduction of new methods of production, is part and parcel of capitalism's very existence. The pressure of competition forces capitalists constantly to innovate, and thereby to increase the forces of production. On the other hand, the development of the

157

productive forces under capitalism leads inevitably to crises. As Marx puts it in the *Communisto Manifesto*:

> The bourgeoisie cannot exist without constantly revolutionising the instruments of production, and thereby the relations of production, and with them the whole relations of society. Conservation of the old modes of production in unaltered form, was...the first condition of existence for all earlier industrial classes. Constant revolutionising of production, uninterrupted disturbance of all social conditions, everlasting uncertainty and agitation distinguish the bourgeois epoch from all earlier ones (**CW** vi 487).

The difference between capitalism and its precursors arises from the relations of production:

> It is clear that in any economic formation of society where the use value rather than the exchange value of product predominates, surplus labour will be restricted to a more or less confined set of needs, and that no boundless thirst for surplus labour will arise from the character of production itself (**C** i 345).

The feudal lord, for example, was content so long as he received enough rent from his peasants to support himself, his family, and his retainers in the style to which they were accustomed. The capitalist, however, has a 'voracious appetite', a 'werewolf-like hunger for surplus labour' (**C** i 349, 355) which springs from the need to match the technical improvements of his competitors or be driven out of business.

Marx was a firm defender of what he called 'the great civilising influence of capital' (**G** 409) against those, such as the Romantics, who looked back nostalgically to pre-capitalist societies. He praised Ricardo for 'having his eye solely for the development of the productive forces' (**C** iii 259). 'To assert, as sentimental opponents of Ricardo's did, that production as such is not the object, is to forget that production for its own sake means nothing but the development of human productive forces, in other words the *development of the richness of human nature as an end in itself*' (**TSV** iii 117-18).

So capitalism was historically progressive:

[It] drives beyond national barriers and prejudices...as well as al traditional, confined, complacent, encrusted satisfactions of human needs, and reproductions of old ways of life. It is destructive to all this, and constantly revolutionises it, tearing down all the barriers which hem in the development of the forces of production, the expansion of needs, the all-sided development of production, and the exploitation and exchange of natural and mental forces (**G** 410).

At the same time, however, the tendency of the rate of profit to fall shows that capitalism is not, as the political economists believed, the most rational form of society, but is rather a historically limited, and contradictory mode of production, which fetters the forces of production at the same time as it develops them. 'The *real barrier* of capitalist production is *capital itself*,' writes Marx (**C** iii 250). 'The violent destruction of capital, not by relations external to it, but rather as a condition of its self preservation, is the most striking form in which it is given it to be gone and to give room to a higher state of social production' (**G** 749-50).

Contrary to what many commentators, some of them Marxists, have said, Marx did not believe that the economic collapse of capitalism is inevitable. 'Permanent crises do not exist', he insisted (**TSV** ii 497 n). As we have seen, 'the crises are always momentary and forcible *solutions* of the existing contradictions.' There is no economic crisis so deep that the capitalist system cannot recover from it, provided that the working class is prepared to pay the price in unemployment, falling living standards, deteriorating working conditions. Whether any crisis leads to 'a higher state of social production' depends upon the consciousness and action of the working class.

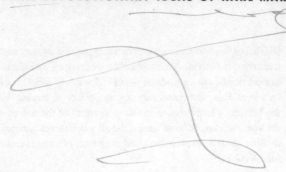

Workers' power

The most basic proposition of Marxism is that capitalism creates the material and social conditions of communism. The abolition of classes is possible only where capitalist relations of production have lifted the productivity of labour to a level where scarcity can be abolished. We have seen how these relations come to act as a fetter on the productive forces, giving rise to a regular, cyclical succession of boom and slump.

Another way of putting this is to say that capitalism makes communism both historically possible and historically necessary. But there is more to it than that. Capitalism brings into being the social force which will overthrow it and abolish classes. This force is the working class.

As Marx and Engels put it in the *Communist Manifesto*:

> The essential condition for the existence, and for the sway of the bourgeois class, is the formation and augmentation of capital; the condition for capital is wage labour...The advance of industry, whose involuntary promoter is the bourgeoisie, replaces the isolation of the labourers, due to competition, by their revolutionary combination, due to association. The development of modern industry, therefore, cuts from under its feet the very foundation on which the bourgeoisie produces and appropriates products. What

result of the material interests and struggles of workers within the process of production. 'We call communism the *real* movement which abolishes the present stage of things' (**CW** v 49).

The pressure of capitalist exploitation forces workers to organise and act collectively. Only thus can they tap the source of their real power, which springs from their position within capitalist relations of production. The self expansion of value depends on their labour, and they have, therefore, the capacity to paralyse the whole system of production. To use that capacity, however, they must band together. Solidarity is the very basic principle of every working class action. Without it, every strike would fail.

So it is the place that the working class occupies within the capitalist system of exploitation which gives it the power to abolish classes. Capitalism socialises the labour process, vastly increasing the size of the means of production, making them dependent on the combined labour of the collective worker. These instruments of production cannot be operated by individuals. Equally, the working class can only seize the means of production collectively, as a class. It doesn't make any sense to talk about sharing a factory out among the workers, breaking it up into little bits—if that was done, it would cease to be a factory, and all its benefits would be lost.

The decisive role which workers play in the struggle against capitalism does not arise from their being the most oppressed section of society. On the contrary, there may be others in a worse position. For example, Marx points out that there are sections of the industrial reserve army, what he calls the 'stagnant element', 'vagabonds, criminals, prostitutes, in short the actual lumpenproletariat', 'the demoralised, the ragged, and those unable to work', who are permanently excluded from the process of production, and are worse off than the rest of the working class (**C** i 797). It does not follow that they are more revolutionary. On the contrary, just because they are never subject to the discipline of capitalist production they are more liable to be picked up by reactionary movements able to exploit their misery. The lumpenproletariat's 'conditions of life', Marx predicted in the *Manifesto*, 'prepare it...for the part of a bribed tool of reactionary intrigue' (**CW** vi 494).

Thus Louis Bonaparte formed in the aftermath of the 1848   163 revolution the Society of 10 December, a private army which was to help him to power as Napoleon III. Similarly, the unemployed are always fertile recruiting grounds for fascist movements because they are no longer subject to the pressure of capitalist exploitation which leads workers to band together against the boss.

But if misery is not enough to make a social group the motive force for communism, neither is exploitation. The peasantry, as a class, are exploited. Surplus labour is extracted from them in the form of rent to landowners, interest to moneylenders, and taxes to the state. However, Marx argues that this does not make them a revolutionary class. In *The Eighteenth Brumaire of Louis Bonaparte*, he shows how the French peasantry provided Napoleon III with the passive support which enabled him to present himself as an arbiter between the bourgeoisie and the proletariat:

The smallholding peasants form a vast mass, the members of which live in similar conditions but without entering into manifold relations with one another. Their mode of production isolates them from one another instead of bringing them into mutual intercourse... Their field of production, the smallholding, admits of no division of labour in its cultivation, no application of science and, therefore, no diversity of development, no variety of talent, no wealth of social relationships. Each individual peasant family is almost self sufficient; it itself directly produces the major part of its consumption and thus acquires its means of life more through exchange with nature than in intercourse with society. A smallholding, a peasant and his family; alongside them another smallholding, another peasant and another family. A few score of these make up a village, and a few score of villages make up a *departement*. In this way, the great mass of the French nation is formed by simple addition of homologous magnitudes, much as potatoes in a sack form a sack of potatoes. In so far as millions of families live under economic conditions of existence that separate their mode of life, their interests and their culture from those of other classes, and put them in hostile opposition to the latter, they form a class. In so far as there is merely a local interconnection among these smallholding peasants and the identity of their interests begets no community, no national bond and no political organisation among them, they do not form a class (**CW** xi 187).

Marx is not arguing that the peasantry can never play a positive role in social and political struggles. The three great revolutions of modern times, France 1789, Russia 1917, and China 1949, all saw the smallholding peasantry make a decisive contribution to their victory. But because the relations of production confine peasants' horizons to the limits of their smallholding, their village, at best their province, their uprisings have a parochial character. The local landlord is lynched, his manor house burned down, and his estate divided among the peasants. And things improve, until the army arrives, executes a few ringleaders, and restores the landowner's son to his inheritance.

It is only when peasant risings coincide with a confrontation between the ruling class and another class which is challenging their power that they can play a part in transforming society. Peasants can become a national political force when they are led by another class. In France in 1789 that class had been the bourgeoisie. Marx believed that, with the advent of capitalism, the working class could weld the discontent of the peasantry into a national movement against bourgeois society. The conclusion of his analysis of the French peasantry in the *Eighteenth Brumaire* was that 'the peasants find their natural ally and leader in the urban proletariat, whose task is the overthrow of the bourgeois order' (**CW** xi 191).

Again, in *The Civil War in France*, Marx declared that 'the Commune was perfectly right in telling the peasants that "its victory was their only hope" ', and asked how the peasants' traditional loyalty to Bonapartism, which had been betrayed completely by Napoleon III, could 'have withstood the appeal of the Commune to the living interests and urgent wants of the peasantry?' (**CWF** 75, 77). Marx was, therefore, in favour of the workers' movement seeking to win the peasantry to their side by appealing to their material interests. But only the working class itself could overthrow capitalism, and, in liberating itself, also free all the other exploited and oppressed sections of society.

Marx and Engels learned from the Utopian Socialists, and especially from Fourier, a bitter and unremitting hatred of sexual oppression, the subjection of women to men. The *Communist Manifesto* contains a savage attack on the bourgeois family, and Engels sought to show in *The Origin of the Family, Private Property and the State* that the oppression of women was bound up

165

with the emergence of the monogamous family, of classes, and of the 'special bodies of armed men' whose duty it is to defend the interests of property. The emancipation of women, he concluded, was inseparable from that of the working class.

There are a number of defects in Engels' analysis. It is now clear that sexual inequality predates the emergence of class antagonisms, and its origins may have had more to do with factors such as wars between tribal societies than Engels had thought. Moreover, he and Marx were wrong to predict that the development of capitalism would lead to the disappearance of the working class family.

Nevertheless, their conclusion still stands. The family, in the form in which it has existed since the triumph of industrial capitalism, is based on the isolation and confinement of married women to the home. The condition of the housewife is one of the most alienated in bourgeois society. The separation of women in the home makes it difficult for them to organise and act collectively. One of the most important developments of capitalism this century has been the way in which it has drawn women into the workforce, so that two workers in every five in Britain today are women, and most working class women spend a considerable portion of their lives at work. In the workplace women can acquire the collective organisation and power to liberate themselves, in conjunction with the men with whom they work, who are subject, like them, to capitalist exploitation.

Party and class

The working class, by virtue of its position within capitalist relations of production, is the only class capable of installing a classless society. The obvious difficulty, in Marx's day as in our own, is that the mass of workers accept the continued existence of capitalism as inevitable. It is daily instilled into them, from childhood onwards, that working people are incapable of running society. This task, they are told at school, in the press, and on television and radio, must be left to the experts—to managers, civil servants, members of parliament and trade union officials. The workers' role is to accept orders from above. How can this lack of workers' confidence in their ability to transform society be broken down?

As Marx put it: how does the working class become a class 'for itself', that is, a class conscious of its position and interests in capitalist society, and of its historical role in overthrowing it? His answer was that workers become aware of their interests as a class through the class struggle itself. Through their daily battles with capital in the process of production workers acquire the consciousness, confidence and organisation necessary if they are to play a revolutionary role .

This takes us back to the notion which we found in the *Theses on Feuerbach* and *The German Ideology* that 'in revolutionary activity the changing of oneself coincides with the changing of circumstances' (**CW** v 214). Driven to engage in the class struggle by the exploitation they experience in the process of production, workers begin to transform both themselves and society.

This conception of revolutionary change meant that Marx had a very positive attitude towards strikes, and generally to the economic class struggle through which workers organised in trade unions to seek to improve their conditions within the framework of capitalism. This again set Marx apart from the other socialists of his day. He wrote of them that, when confronted with 'strikes, combinations and other forms in which the proletarians carry out before our eyes their organisation as a class, some are seized with real fear and others display a *transcendental* disdain' (**CW** vi 211). Such an attitude is still to be found among socialists today, some of whom are contemptuous of workers who go on strike for higher wages, and dismiss them for acting with self interested and 'economistic' motives.

Marx was profoundly hostile to this disdain of workers struggles. In *Wages, Price and Profit* he challenged the widespread belief, advanced in this case by the British socialist John Weston, a follower of Robert Owen, that the trade union struggle was at best irrelevant and at worst harmful to workers' living standards. This claim was based on the 'iron law of wages', according to which wages cannot rise above bare physical subsistence levels because of population pressures.

Marx used the labour theory of value to refute this 'law'. He showed that while subsistence forms an 'ultimate limit' below which wages cannot fall without endangering the reproduction of labour power, 'the value of labour is in every country determined by a *traditional standard of life*...the satisfaction of certain wants springing from the social conditions in which people are placed and reared up' (**SW** ii 71-2).

Furthermore, 'as to *profits*, there exists no law which determines their *minimum*.' The maximum rate of profit is 'limited by the physical minimum of wages and the physical maximum of the working day... The fixation of its actual degree is only settled by the continuous struggle between capital and labour... The matter resolves itself into a question of the respective powers of the combatants' (**SW** ii 72-3).

But it was not primarily the role of strikes in maintaining or raising workers' living standards which led Marx to attribute such great importance to them. The decisive factor was their contribution in raising the consciousness and organisation of the working class. Commenting in 1853 on a wave of strikes in Lancashire and the Midlands which derived their impetus from unskilled and unorganised workers, Marx wrote:

> There exists a class of philanthropists, and even of socialists, who consider strikes as very mischievous to the interests of the 'working man himself', and whose great aim consists of finding out a method of securing permanent average wages. Besides, the fact of the industrial cyclus, with its various phases, putting every such average wages out of the question [Marx's own words—he was writing in English]. I am, on the very contrary, convinced that the alternative rise and fall of wages, and the continual conflicts between masters and men resulting therefrom, are, in the present organisation of industry, the indispensable means of holding up the spirit of the labouring classes, of combining them into one great association against the encroachments of the ruling class, and of preventing them from becoming apathetic, thoughtless, more or less well-fed instruments of production. In a state of society founded upon the antagonism of classes, if we want to prevent slavery in fact as well as in name, we must accept war. In order to rightly appreciate the value of strikes and combinations, we must not allow themselves to be blinded by the apparent insignificance of their economical results, but hold, above all things, in view their moral and political consequences. Without the great alternative phases of dullness, prosperity, over-excitement, crisis and distress, which modern industry traverses in periodically recurring cycles, with the up and down of wages resulting from them, as

with the constant warfare between masters and men closely corresponding with those variations of wages and profits, the working classes of Great Britain, and of all Europe, would be a
heart-broken, a weak-minded, a worn-out unresisting mass, whose
self emancipation would prove as impossible as that of the slaves
of ancient Greece and Rome (**CW** xii 169).

Engels was speaking for Marx too when, more than 20 years
later, he criticised the Gotha programme adopted by the German
Social Democratic Party in 1875 because, among other errors
and omissions:

> …there is not a word about the organisation of the working class
> as a class by means of the trade unions. And that is a very essen-
> tial point, for this is the real class organisation of the proletariat,
> in which it carries on its daily struggles with capital, in which it
> trains itself, and which nowadays even amid the worst reac-
> tion…can simply no longer be smashed (**SC** 293).

The trade union struggle is not, however, an end in itself. Marx
had argued that the level of the rate of profit depends on the 'respective powers of the combatants'. But these powers are un-
equal. Capital, because it controls the means of production, can
reorganise the labour process so as to reduce the size of the workforce, and force up unemployment, thereby weakening labour's
position within the process of production. 'In its merely economic action capital is the stronger side' (**SW** ii 73):

> Trade unions work well as centres of resistance against the en-
> croachments of capital. They fail, generally, from limiting them-
> selves to a guerrilla war against the effects of the existing system,
> instead of simultaneously trying to change it, instead of using their
> organised forces as a lever for the final emancipation of the work-
> ing class, that is to say, the ultimate abolition of the wages system
> (**SW** ii 75-6).

Trade unions take the existence of the relationship between
capital and wage labour for granted. They seek simply to improve the workers' position within that relationship. But wage
labour is merely the form through which surplus labour is

pumped out of the workers. The capitalists' superior power within the process of production means that any victory over them can only be temporary, liable to be undermined once the balance of forces shifts in capital's favour. The only lasting security lies in overthrowing the capitalist system, which means eradicating the capital-wage labour relationship. 'Instead of the *conservative* motto, *"A fair day's wage for a fair day's work!"* ' said Marx, workers 'ought to inscribe on their banner the *revolutionary* watchword, *"Abolition of the wages system!"*' (**SW** ii 75).

So the class struggle of the working class can succeed only if it is transformed from an economic into a political struggle, that is, into the 'struggle of class against class' in which workers become aware of their historic interests and seek to wrest political power from the capitalists. Marx believed that the economic class struggle in fact had an inherent tendency to become political.

The struggle to secure legislation limiting the working day was an example of this. It was 'the product of a protracted and more or less concealed civil war between the capitalist class and the working class' (**C** i 412-13). However, 'the result was not to be attained by private settlement between the working men and the capitalists. It was achieved by legislative interference', by the state passing a law, even though 'without the working men's continuous pressure from without that interference would never have taken place' (**SW** ii 73).

The class struggle would develop, Marx believed, from being a battle between capital and labour in specific workplaces or industries into a global confrontation between the two classes in which the state would play an increasingly prominent role. Marx welcomed this development. He was highly contemptuous of those, such as Bakunin and Proudhon, who opposed the class struggle taking a political form. He believed that the working class could emancipate themselves only by seizing power, destroying the capitalist state machine, and setting up a new form of state controlled by the workers. 'To conquer political power', Marx declared in the First International's inaugural address, is 'the great duty of the working classes' (**SW** ii 17).

The two forms of struggle interacted with each other:

The political movement of the working class has as its object, of course, the conquest of political power for this class, and this naturally requires a previous organisation of the working class developed up to a certain point and arising precisely from their economic struggles.

On the other hand, however, every movement in which the working class comes out as *as a class* against the ruling classes and tries to coerce them by pressure from without is a political movement. For instance, the attempt in a particular factory or even in a particular trade to force a shorter working day out of individual capitalists by strikes etc is a purely economic movement. On the other hand, the movement to force through an eight hour day etc *law*, is a *political* movement. And in this way out of the separate economic movements of the workers there grows up everywhere a *political* movement, that is to say, a movement of the *class*, with the object of enforcing its interests in a general form, in a form possessing a general socially coercive force. While these movements presuppose a certain degree of previous organisation, they are in turn equally a means of developing this organisation.

Where the working class is not yet far enough advanced in its organisation to undertake a decisive campaign against the collective power, ie the political power of the ruling classes, it must at any rate be trained for this by continual agitation against this power and by a hostile attitude toward the policies of the ruling classes. Otherwise it remains a plaything in their hands (**SC** 270-1).

As long as the working class confines itself to a purely economic struggle it remains subject to the political and ideological domination of capital. For the trade union struggle does not challenge the existence of capitalist relations of production, 'fighting with effects, but not with the causes of those effects' (**SW** ii 75). The political organisation of the working class, the formation of a workers' *party*, was necessary to achieve the complete independence of the proletariat from the bourgeoisie, said Marx.

Following the defeat of the revolution of 1848, Marx and Engels warned against the danger of the German workers' movement being submerged in a broader class alliance embracing the petty bourgeoisie, or lower middle class, and even sections of the bourgeoisie. In doing so, they were reflecting critically on their own experience during 1848-9 when they themselves allowed

171

the Communist League to wither away, working instead as the extreme left wing of the bourgeois democratic movement.

> At the present moment [March 1850], when the democratic petty bourgeoisie is everywhere oppressed, they preach in general unity and reconciliation with the proletariat, they offer it their hand and strive for the establishment of a large opposition party which will embrace all shades of opinion in the democratic party, that is, they strive to entangle the workers in a party organisation where social democratic phrases predominate, and serve to conceal their special interests, and in which the definite demands of the proletariat are not brought up for the sake of beloved peace. Such a union would turn out solely to their advantage and altogether to the disadvantage of the proletariat. The proletariat would lose its whole independent laboriously achieved position and once more be reduced to an appendage of official bourgeois democracy. This union must, therefore, be most decisively rejected. Instead of once again stooping to serve as the applauding chorus of the bourgeois democrats, the workers, and above all the [Communist] League, must exert themselves to establish an independent secret and public organisation of the workers' party alongside the official democrats and make each community [League branch] the central point and nucleus of workers' associations in which the attitudes and interests of the proletariat will be discussed independently of bourgeois influences (**CW** x 281-2).

To avoid becoming the 'applauding chorus', the 'appendage' of the bourgeoisie, the working class must form their own party. Some commentators have argued that the March 1850 'Address of the Central Committee to the Communist League', from which the above passage is quoted, was written at a time when Marx and Engels were close to the ideas of Auguste Blanqui, who, as we have seen, believed that a secret conspiratorial organisation could seize power on behalf of the working class.

Marx and Engels, however, never wavered from their 'battle cry: the emancipation of the working class must be achieved by the working class itself.' At much the same time as they wrote the March 1850 'Address', they penned a brilliant portrait of the Blanquist professional conspirator, unemployed, hanging around taverns, enjoying an ambiguous relationship with the secret police who were quite happy to use him for their own ends, belonging to the lumpenproletariat rather than the working class:

> It need scarcely be added that these conspirators do not confine themselves to the general organising of the revolutionary proletariat. It is precisely their business to anticipate the process of revolutionary development, to bring it artificially to crisis point, to launch a revolution on the spur of the moment, without the conditions for a revolution. For them the only condition for revolution is the adequate preparation of their conspiracy. They are the alchemists of revolution and are characterised by exactly the same chaotic thinking and blinkered obsessions as the alchemists of old. They leap at inventions which are supposed to work revolutionary miracles: incendiary bombs, destructive devices of magic effect, revolts which are expected to be all the more miraculous and astonishing in effect as their basis is less rational. Occupied with such scheming, they have no other purpose than the most immediate one of overthrowing the existing government and have the profoundest contempt for the more theoretical enlightenment of the proletariat about their class interests (**CW** x 318).

The task of communists, then, is not to substitute themselves for the working class, 'to anticipate the process of revolutionary development' by attempting to seize power as an enlightened and conspiratorial minority. Rather, communists must involve themselves in 'the general organising of the revolutionary proletariat', and in its 'theoretical enlightenment'.

It is in this light that we are to understand these famous lines of the *Communist Manifesto*:

> The communists do not form a separate party opposed to other working class parties.
>
> They have no interests separate and apart from those of the proletariat as a whole.
>
> They do not set up any sectarian principles of their own, by which to shape and mould the proletarian movement.
>
> The communists are distinguished from other working class parties by this only: (1) In the national struggles of the proletarians of the different countries they point out and bring to the front the common interests of the entire proletariat, independently of all

173

nationality. (2) In the various stages of development which the struggle of the working class against the bourgeoisie has to pass through, they always and everywhere represent the interests of the movement as a whole.

The communists, therefore, are on the one hand, practically the most advanced and resolute section of the working class parties of every country, that section which pushes forward all the others; on the other hand, theoretically, they have over the great mass of the proletariat the advantage of clearly understanding the line of march, the conditions, and the ultimate general results of the proletarian movement (**CW** vi 497).

The revolutionary party is not, therefore, an institution separate from the working class which acts in its name. It is, rather, *part*, 'the most advanced and resolute section', of the class, which possesses a clear and scientific understanding of the conditions under which the workers' movement can succeed. It fights, therefore, for the broadest possible unity of workers, seeking to combat the national and racial divisions fostered by capitalism.

In all this, the task of the communists is to act as a stimulus to the self education of the working class. We have seen how, for Marx, workers learn in struggle. When workers are involved in strikes, and so confronting the employers and the state, their direct experience clashes most sharply with the view of the world instilled in them by the institutions of capitalist society. The revolutionary party must orient itself on these struggles, says Marx, because it is here that workers are most open to communism.

This stress on the class struggle as the school of revolutionary politics was made by Marx and Engels throughout their lives. When they split from the Communist League in September 1850, Marx denounced the 'left', by whom 'the revolution is seen not as the product of realities of the situation but as the result of an effort of *will*.' By contrast, 'We say to the workers: You have 15, 20, 50 years of civil war to go through in order to alter the situation and to train yourselves for the exercise of power' (**CW** x 626). (Marx does not literally mean 50 years of continuous armed struggle; he often uses 'civil war' as a metaphor for the class struggle.)

Similarly, Engels was highly critical in the 1880s and 1890s of the first Marxist groups in Britain and America, who reduce 'the

Marxist theory of development to a rigid orthodoxy which work-ers are not to reach as a result of their class consciousness, but which, like an article of faith, is to be forced down their throats at once and without development' (**SC** 474). Writing about America, he argued:

> The masses must have time and opportunity to develop, and they can have the opportunity only when they have a movement of their own—no matter in what form so long as it is *their* movement—in which they are driven further by their mistakes and learn to profit by them...
>
> What the Germans [most American Marxists until as late as the 1930s were of German or Russian origin] ought to do is to act up to their own theory—if they understand it, as we did in 1845 and 1848—to go in for any real general working class movement, accept its actual starting point as such, and work it gradually up to the theoretical level by pointing out how every mistake made, every reverse suffered, was a necessary consequence of mistaken theoretical views in the original programme (**SC** 396, 399).

Within this broad conception of how the working class would become a 'class for itself', Marx and Engels took a fairly matter of fact approach towards how to organise. In the 1840s they struggled to build a separate communist party which would aim to stimulate the general development of the working class move-ment rather than to run secret conspiracies. After breaking with the League, they abstained from systematic practical activity till 1864. Even then, although Marx exercised enormous influence on the First International, this was a coalition of disparate group-ings which inevitably fell apart under its internal strains. Marx and Engels had a tendency to refer to 'our party' even when no communist organisation, however rudimentary, existed.

This approach was connected with a sometimes rather fatalist attitude, which treated the formation of revolutionary class con-sciousness as the inevitable outcome of a process of natural de-velopment. For example, Engels wrote in 1886 that 'the great thing is to get the working class to move as a class; that once ob-tained, they will soon find out the right direction, and all who resist...will be left out in the cold with small sects of their own' (**SC** 398). This passage, and others like it, suggest that Marx and

175

Engels believed that the logic of the historical process somehow guaranteed the attainment of socialist consciousness by the working class. Pushed to the limit, this conception leads to the claim that the workers' revolution is itself inevitable. Marx writes in *Capital* of it happening 'with the inexorability of a natural process' (**C** i 929).

These views cut across the main thrust of Marx's conception of history, that 'men make their own history, but they do not make it just as they please' (**CW** xi 103). Instead, it seems as if history is a juggernaut, pursuing its own ends independent of the beliefs and actions of human beings. The *Communist Manifesto* had warned that the class struggle had two possible outcomes: 'a revolutionary reconstitution of society at large, or…the common ruin of the contending classes' (**CW** vi 483). But if the triumph of the working class is inevitable, why bother to struggle and fight?

The stress placed by Marx and Engels on the development of class consciousness as an objective process is understandable when we remember that most 19th century revolutionaries regarded the fall of capitalism as 'the result of an effort of *will*', the product of an elitist conspiracy. Moreover, their political life took place largely at a time when trade unions organised only a very small, and usually highly privileged section of skilled workers. Only towards the end of Engels' life, and especially after the foundation of the Second International in 1889, did there emerge in Europe a mass working class movement, organising millions of workers in trade unions, and winning their votes in elections to bourgeois parliaments chosen increasingly on the basis of universal suffrage.

It was then that the dangers of Marx's and Engels' conception of the party came to the fore. For the new mass labour movement spawned a conservative bureaucracy based in both party and trade unions which saw its role as negotiating the improvement of workers' conditions within the framework of capitalism. These 'labour lieutenants of capital', as the American revolutionary Daniel de Leon called them, could quite happily live with a formal commitment to Marxism. The German Social Democratic Party (SPD), which adopted a Marxist programme in 1891, was presided over by Karl Kautsky, theoretical 'pope' of the Second International, who preached the inevitability of the proletarian revolution, while the party and trade union leaders gradually accommodated themselves to German capital and the state. Engels in his last years warned a number of times against this development, which culminated in the SPD's support for the First World War in 1914.

It was left to Lenin and the Bolsheviks in Russia to develop a different conception of the workers' party, one closer to the spirit, if not the letter of Marx's and Engels' thought. Just as the latter had argued in March 1850 that the political independence of the working class required a separate communist party, so Lenin urged that such a party should combine a firm commitment to revolutionary principles, excluding all those who did not accept these principles in word and deed, with constant and active involvement in the life and struggles of the working class. In this way Marx's basic idea that the working class would become a revolutionary 'class for itself' as a result of a continual interaction between the party and the rest of the class was preserved.

The dictatorship of the proletariat

Marx, as we have seen, believed that the struggle of the working class would increasingly transform itself into a political movement whose objective would be the conquest of state power. The state, he believed, was a product of class antagonisms and an instrument of class domination: 'political power, properly so called, is merely the organised power of one class for oppressing another' (**CW** vi 505). The working class could, therefore, triumph only by overthrowing the capitalist state. The *Communist Manifesto* declares that 'the first step in the revolution by the working class must be to raise the proletariat to the position of ruling class' (**CW** vi 504).

Marx made it clear from the start that this change could not take place peacefully, but would require the destruction of the existing state apparatus. In the *Eighteenth Brumaire*, he traced the evolution of the modern capitalist state in France 'with its enormous bureaucratic and military organisation, with its extensive and artificial state machinery, with a host of officials numbering half a million, besides an army of another half a million, this appalling parasitic body' whose triumph Napoleon III embodied (**CW** xi 185). Marx noted that 'all revolutions perfected this machine instead of breaking it. The parties that contended in

177

turn for domination regarded the possession of this huge state edifice as the principal spoils of the victor' (**CW** xi 186). The workers' revolution would 'concentrate all its forces of destruction against it' (**CW** xi 185).

During the Paris Commune of 1871, Marx wrote to one of his supporters, Ludwig Kugelmann:

> If you look at the last chapter of my *Eighteenth Brumaire* you will find that I declare that the next attempt of the French Revolution will be no longer, as before, to transfer the bureaucratic-military machine from one hand to another, but to *smash* it, and this is the preliminary condition for every real people's revolution on the Continent (**SC** 262-3).

On the ruins of the capitalist state, Marx wrote in *The Class Struggles in France*, there would be established 'the *class dictatorship* of the proletariat as the necessary transit point to the *abolition of class distinctions generally*' (**CW** x 127). This famous phrase, 'the dictatorship of the proletariat', naturally makes many people uneasy. In a century that has seen Stalin's bloody despotism, it is easy to believe that the 'dictatorship of the proletariat' would be a dictatorship over the working class by a small minority. And that is, indeed, how Blanqui, who coined the phrase, saw it.

We should remember, however, that in the 19th century the term 'dictatorship' was not so strongly associated with images of secret police and concentration camps. Educated people would have been aware that the dictator was originally an official of the ancient Roman republic, appointed to rule for a limited period of six months in times of emergency. Marx indeed saw the dictatorship of the proletariat as *temporary*, the 'necessary transit point' between capitalism and a classless communist society.

Moreover, as we have seen, Marx and Engels believed that the state was first and foremost an instrument of coercion, 'special bodies of armed men' as Lenin succinctly put it. In this respect, the dictatorship of the proletariat would be no different from any previous form of state, since all were based on coercion, and would not necessarily be any more arbitrary or repressive than its predecessors.

The main distinguishing feature of the dictatorship of the

proletariat was that it was precisely 'the *proletariat* organised as the ruling class' (**CW** vi 504, italics added). For the first time in history the direct producers, the mass of ordinary working people, would control the state. Indeed, they would be the state. The state would have ceased to be the means through which an exploiting minority dominated the exploited majority. It would be the dictatorship of the majority over the minority.

While Marx had already developed the main outlines of this conception of the dictatorship of the proletariat after the revolution of 1848, it was still, in the form so far set out, rather abstract. It was not theoretical analysis which gave definite and concrete shape to Marx's conception of workers' power but the deeds of the Parisian workers in 1871. Engels wrote 20 years later:

> Of late, the social democratic philistine has once more been filled with wholesome terror at the words: dictatorship of the proletariat. Well and good, gentlemen, do you want to know what this dictatorship looks like? Look at the Paris Commune. That was the dictatorship of the proletariat (**CWF** 17-18).

Shortly after the Commune's defeat, Marx wrote in *The Civil War in France*:

> It was a thoroughly expansive political form, while all previous forms of government had been emphatically repressive. Its true secret was this. It was essentially a working class government, the produce of the struggle of the producing against the appropriating class, the political form at last discovered under which to work out the economic emancipation of labour (**CWF** 72).

What were the main features of this 'political form'?

The first decree of the Commune...was the suppression of the standing army, and the substitution for it of the armed people.

The Commune was formed of the municipal councillors, chosen by universal suffrage in the various wards of the town, responsible and revocable at short terms. The majority of its members were naturally working men, or acknowledged representatives of the working class. The Commune was to be a working, not a parliamentary body, executive and legislative at

179

LIVERPOOL JOHN MOORES UNIVERSITY
LEARNING SERVICES

the same time. Instead of continuing to be the agent of the central government, the police was at once stripped of its political attributes, and turned into the responsible and at all times revocable agent of the Commune. So were the officials of all other branches of the administration. From the members of the Commune downwards, the public service was to be done at *workmen's wages*...

The judicial functionaries were to be divested of that sham independence which had but served to mask their abject subserviency to all succeeding governments to which, in turn, they had taken, and broken, the oaths of allegiance. Like the rest of public servants, magistrates and judges were to be elective, responsible and revocable (**CWF** 67-8).

Marx and Engels believed, as we have already seen, that the state involved 'the establishment of a *public power* which no longer directly coincides with the population organising itself as an armed force' (**SW** iii 327). The whole thrust of the measures taken by the Commune was to break down this separation of the state from the mass of the population, and to make it subject to their control. In this sense, the dictatorship of the proletariat is a higher form of democracy than that found in bourgeois society. 'Freedom', Marx wrote, 'consists in converting the state from an organ superimposed on society into one completely subordinate to it' (**SW** ii 25).

The Commune did not do away with representative government, that is, with the election of those empowered to make and enforce laws. However, under bourgeois democracy representative government means 'deciding once in three or six years which member of the ruling class was to misrepresent the people in parliament' (**CWF** 69). The electorate has no control over what their representatives do once elected, and when the parties come up for re-election, the choice is usually between the lesser of two evils. Moreover, parliament itself has little control over the real source of political power, the permanent civil and military bureaucracy.

Under the Commune, however, all public officials were not only elected, but were subject to immediate recall by those who had chosen them. In this way:

...universal suffrage was to serve the people...as individual suffrage serves every other employer in the search for the workmen and managers in his business. And it is well known that companies, like individuals, in matters of real business generally know how to put the right man in the right place, and, if they for once make a mistake, to redress it promptly (**CWF** 70).

The power to recall unsatisfactory representatives would obviously vastly increase popular control over the government. At the same time, the abolition of the standing army would mean that the means of coercion were in the hands of 'the population organising itself as an armed force'. The state would cease to be a 'unity independent of, and superior to, the nation itself, from which it was but a parasitical excrescence' (**CWF** 69).

The experience of the Paris Commune thus confirmed, and developed Marx's basic insight that 'the working class cannot simply lay hold of the ready-made state machinery, and wield it for its own purposes' (**CWF** 64). There are, however, two important qualifications that must be made about this experience. One of these Marx noted, which was what he called the 'good nature' of the Commune, their unwillingness to take the offensive against their bourgeois enemies at Versailles, and to act ruthlessly against the threatened counter-revolution (see, for example, **SC** 263).

The experience of 1848 had taught Marx and Engels that revolution is a form of war, and that like any war it must be fought with ruthlessness and determination. In the wake of 1848 Engels wrote, in words that could be applied to the Commune and to many later revolutions:

> Insurrection is an art quite as much as war or any other, and subject to certain rules of proceeding, which, when neglected, will produce the ruin of the party neglecting them… Firstly, never play with insurrection unless you are fully prepared to face up to the consequences of your play. Insurrection is a calculus with very indefinite magnitudes, the value of which may change every day; the forces opposed to you have all the advantage of organisation, discipline and habitual authority; unless you bring strong odds against them, you are defeated and ruined. Secondly, the insurrectionary career once entered upon, act with the greatest determination, and on the offensive. The defensive is the death of every armed rising; it is lost before it measures itself with its enemies.

181

Surprise your antagonists while their forces are scattering, prepare new successes, however small, but daily; keep up the moral ascendant which the first successful rising has given to you; rally thus those vacillating elements to your side which always follow the strongest impulse, and which always look for the safer side; force your enemies to a retreat before they can collect their strength against you; in the words of Danton, the greatest master of revolutionary policy yet known; *de l'audace, de l'audace, encore de l'audace!* [boldness, boldness, yet more boldness!] (**CW** xi 85-6)

Historical experience since that of Marx and Engels has shown that these rules of insurrection can only be successfully applied where there exists a revolutionary party whose eyes are firmly fixed on the seizure of political power. The victory of the Russian working class in October 1917 would have been impossible without the Bolsheviks under the leadership of two 'masters of revolutionary policy' greater than Danton, Lenin and Trotsky. To this extent, Marx and his successors agreed with Blanqui: the conquest of power by the working class requires a party which is prepared to practise the art of insurrection. Where they parted course with Blanqui was in their insistence that such a party could contemplate taking power only with the active support of a majority of workers.

Marx did not recognise the second weakness of the Commune. It was elected by all the male citizens of Paris, divided into separate wards. The exclusion of women, which is especially striking in the light of the magnificent role played by the working women of Paris under the Commune, was a reflection of the influence of Jacobinism on the French labour movement. Moreover, the election of representatives on a territorial basis meant that the Commune was chosen by members of all classes. Just as in bourgeois elections, all citizens were treated as equal irrespective of their class position. Normally, this formal equality conceals the real inequalities of wealth and power which undermine bourgeois democracy. In Paris under the Commune, this method of election did not have such harmful effects because most of the bourgeoisie had fled the city. The use by the Commune of the same way of electing representatives as is found in bourgeois democracies reflected the fact that in 1871 most French workers were still artisans working in small workshops. So the workplace was not the main focus of working class organisation and action. Workers could exercise collective power only on the streets, not within the process of production.

Only after the emergence of the modern industrial working class, organised in large factories using machine production, did the specific form of workers' rule appear, the 'soviet' or workers' council. Thrown up first during the Russian revolution of 1905, the soviet has appeared many times since. Arising from the struggle within the process of production as a body of workplace delegates, the soviet develops into an institution uniting the whole of the working class and challenging the bourgeoisie's monopoly of political power. Here, unlike the Commune, its representatives are chosen in the workplace, where the ability of the working class to organise and act collectively is formed.

The emergence of soviets has thus completed Marx's theory of the dictatorship of the proletariat by creating a form of political rule which directly reflected workers' power in the process of production. Marx could not have anticipated this development: as we have seen, he learned from the experience of the revolutions of 1848 and 1871, as we must continue to learn from future revolutions.

There is, however, sometimes a hesitancy in Marx's writings about how generally he wished to extend the lessons of the class struggle in France. For example, he told the Hague congress of the First International that 'there are countries such as America, England and...Holland...where the working people may achieve their goal by peaceful means' (**SW** ii 293). Similarly, in the letter to Kugelmann quoted earlier, Marx says that it is essential for 'every real people's revolution *on the Continent*', in other words excluding Britain, to '*smash*' the 'bureaucratic-military machine'. In other words, Marx seems to think that bourgeois democracies, where workers possess the vote, are different from other forms of capitalist state.

This did *not* mean that Marx had changed his view that the bourgeois democratic state was a means of class domination based on 'special bodies of armed men'. Engels wrote in his preface to the English edition of *Capital* Volume 1 that Marx had:

> [come] to the conclusion that, at least in Europe, England is the only country where the inevitable social revolution might be effected

183

entirely by peaceful means. He certainly never forgot to add that he hardly expected the English ruling classes to submit, without a 'pro-slavery rebellion', to this peaceful and legal revolution (C i 113).

The bourgeoisie could thus be expected to react to any attempt to expropriate them with violent resistance, just as the Southern states of America unleashed civil war in 1861 to prevent the abolition of slavery.

This prediction was entirely realistic. Experience since Marx's and Engels' time has shown that attempts to introduce socialism peacefully are invariably met with armed resistance. The military coup in Chile of September 1973 is but the latest example of this. The capitalist class can always call on the armed forces, whose first loyalty is not to parliament, but to the existing social order.

So why did Marx attempt to exclude Britain (and, in principle, other bourgeois democracies) from his general conclusion? Lenin tried to get Marx out of this hash by arguing in *The State and Revolution* that Britain in 1871 was 'without a military clique and, to a considerable degree, without a bureaucracy' but that she had subsequently 'sunk into the all-European filthy, bloody morass of bureaucratic-military institutions'. This is, unfortunately, false. Throughout the 19th century the British state had a military machine which was used, not only in the 'filthy, bloody morass' of endless colonial wars of conquest, but also to keep Ireland under British rule, and used, especially during the first half of the century, against workers in Britain itself. Marx was, quite simply, wrong. Bourgeois democracies depend, like other capitalist states, on 'special bodies of armed men' which the armed proletariat must crush if it is to take and hold power.

Marx was led into this mistake by a lifelong tendency to overestimate the effects of universal suffrage. Before he became a communist, in his 1843 *Critique of Hegel's Philosophy of Right*, Marx had argued that the introduction of universal suffrage would involve the abolition of the separation between the state and civil society which he then regarded as a form of human alienation.

Even after developing the materialist conception of history, Marx and Engels continued to believe that the introduction of universal suffrage would undermine bourgeois rule. This is a major theme of *The Class Struggles in France* and the *Eighteenth Brumaire*, which analyse the contradictions produced under the Second French Republic of 1848-51 by the granting of the vote to all male citizens. Discussing the British class struggle in 1850, Engels wrote, in words Marx would have endorsed, that 'universal suffrage in an England two-thirds of whose inhabitants are industrial proletarians means the exclusive political rule of the working class with all the revolutionary changes in social conditions which are inseparable from it' (**CW** x 298).

We know now that universal suffrage means no such thing. But even universal male suffrage was rare in the 19th century. Demanded by the Chartists in Britain, it was bitterly resisted by the ruling class, Liberals and Tories alike. Only in 1867 was the vote extended to some workers. All men got the vote only in 1918; all women only ten years later. Those countries where male suffrage was introduced, such as France and Germany after 1870, had a majority of peasants, who provided a popular base for bourgeois or aristocratic parties. It was easy, therefore, for Marx to overestimate the impact of universal suffrage in a country with a predominantly working class population.

Later experience has shown that capitalism can live with universal suffrage, as Engels acknowledged in his later years. The method of election, as we have seen, treats all citizens as equal, despite the real differences between their wealth and power. Moreover, popularly elected parliaments rule in name rather than in fact. Even the emergence of mass working class organisations has not undermined capitalist domination. These organisations are normally controlled by a conservative labour bureaucracy committed to class conciliation rather than class struggle. In these circumstances, the stability of bourgeois democracy depends on capitalism being sufficiently prosperous to concede improvements in workers' living standards, which is why this political form has flourished mainly in the richer imperialist states.

These criticisms do not amount to a rejection of Marx's concept of the dictatorship of the proletariat. If anything, they reinforce it by showing that even in bourgeois democracies 'the working class cannot simply lay hold of the ready-made state machinery' but must smash it.

185

World revolution

Capitalism, Marx emphasised, is a *world* system. 'Competition on the world market', he wrote, is 'the basis and the vital element of capitalist production' (**C** iii 110). Indeed, the formation of an international economy is, in a real sense, the outcome of the development of capitalist relations of production. 'The tendency to create the *world market* is directly given in the concept of capital itself' (**G** 408).

The development of capitalism involved the formation of a world system in which large portions of Asia and the whole of the Americas were subordinated to the European powers. Africa too was involved, providing the black slaves on whose sweated labour the plantation economies of the West Indies and the American South depended. The plunder of the world provided the wealth necessary for the 'primitive accumulation of capital', the concentration of money in the hands of European capitalists which could then be used to purchase the labour power 'freed' from the means of production by the expropriation of the peasantry:

> The discovery of gold and silver in America, the extirpation, enslavement and entombment in mines of the indigenous population of that continent, the beginnings of the conquest and plunder of India, and the conversion of Africa into a preserve for the commercial hunting of blackskins, are all things which characterise the dawn of the era of capitalist production. These idyllic proceedings are the chief moments of primitive accumulation. Hard on their heels follows the commercial war of the European nations, which has the globe as its battlefield. It begins with the revolt of the Netherlands from Spain, assumes gigantic dimensions in England's anti-Jacobin war [against revolutionary and Napoleonic France], and is still going on in the shape of the Opium Wars against China etc (**C** i 915).

The result of this process is to draw the entire world into a unified economic system. Different countries participate in an international division of labour. The slave plantations of the Southern United States provided cotton for the textile factories of Lancashire. India's own native textile industry was destroyed to provide a larger market for British goods. The emergence towards the end of Marx's life of other industrial powers to challenge Britain's economic dominance—Germany, the United States, France—merely intensified the competitive struggle of 'many capitals', making this genuinely international.

Marx argued that as a consequence of the emergence of the capitalist world system, the proletarian revolution could succeed only on an international scale. In a farsighted passage of *The German Ideology*, he wrote that world revolution was essential:

> ...because without it privation, *want* is merely made general and with *want* the struggle for necessities would begin again, and the whole filthy business would necessarily be restored... Empirically, communism is only possible as the act of the dominant peoples 'all at once' and simultaneously, which presupposes the universal development of the productive forces and the world intercourse bound up with them (**CW** v 49).

This argument is an extension of Marx's general thesis that communism is only possible once the productive forces have developed to the appropriate level. Now he is saying that this development takes place on a *world* scale, not simply within individual countries. As a result, revolutions confined to individual countries will fail, because they will not be able to tap the resources necessary to abolish classes, which are available only internationally. The pressure of the world system, still intact despite the victory of the working class in one country, will mean that '*want* is merely made general...and the whole filthy business would necessarily be restored'. The productive forces of the country concerned would not be sufficient to abolish classes, so the class struggle would continue.

Engels, in *Principles of Communism*, a draft programme of the Communist League written in 1847, answered the question 'Will it be possible for this revolution to take place in one country alone?' with an emphatic:

> No. Large scale industry, already by creating the world market, has so linked up all the peoples of the earth, and especially the civilised peoples, that each people is dependent on what happens to one another. Further, in all civilised countries large scale

industry has so levelled social development that in all these countries the bourgeoisie and the proletariat have become the two decisive classes of society and the struggle between them the main struggle of the day. The communist revolution will therefore be no merely national one; it will be a revolution taking place simultaneously in all civilised countries, that is, at least in England, America, France and Germany (**CW** vi 351-2).

Stalin, when trying to justify the idea of 'socialism in one country' in the 1920s, poked fun at the idea of simultaneous revolutions, dismissing it as a youthful excess on the part of Marx and Engels. But such a vista of international upheavals had been confirmed hardly before the ink had dried on *Principles of Communism*. 1848 *did* see uprisings in different countries, each following rapidly on the others. In that respect, the notion of simultaneous revolutions wasn't at all silly.

Nevertheless, matters are undoubtedly more complex than Marx and Engels believed in the 1840s. Lenin laid great stress on the problem of uneven development, the way in which societies evolve at different rates, and in different forms, so that even those sharing the same relations of production may have very different social and political structures. America today is very different from 18th century Britain, or from Nazi Germany, yet all are capitalist social formations. In his writings on the Russian revolution of February 1917, Lenin stressed how each revolution is the outcome of a combination of different factors, economic, political, social and cultural, unique to the country concerned. Marx, in his writings on individual countries, whether France, Spain, Britain or the United States, was similarly sensitive to the specific characteristics of different social formations.

It was Trotsky who drew attention to the phenomenon of what he called combined development. All these different societies are part of a single world system, and subject to its pressures, which forces states and capitals to compete with each other. Therefore, even if the revolution may start in an individual country, it can only be completed on a world scale. So although simultaneous revolutions are improbable because of uneven development, world revolution is essential, because of combined development.

The famous concluding words of the *Communist Manifesto*—

'WORKING MEN OF ALL COUNTRIES, UNITE!'

(**CW** vi 519)—are thus no mere flourish of the pen, no mere ethical or emotional commitment to the brotherhood of man. The international victory of the working class is an absolute practical necessity if communism is to be built. The conquest of power by the working class in one country could only be the prelude to such a victory, and the first task of the dictatorship of the proletariat in that country would be to spread the revolution internationally.

Internationalism was at the heart of the socialism of Marx and Engels. Marx was, as we have already seen, the dominating figure in the First International, while Engels devoted the last 25 years of his life to the development of the international working class movement, engaging in an enormous correspondence in a variety of languages in order to give advice and encouragement to socialists all over the world.

How, then, did Marx and Engels, committed revolutionary internationalists, cope with a Europe dominated by rival nationalisms, whether they were those of the great powers, or of the various independence movements within the multinational empires of Russia, Austria and Turkey? The 19th century was the epoch when nations which had been absorbed into larger European states—Poles, Irish, Czechs, Serbs, Hungarians and many others—claimed their right to self determination.

Marx's and Engels' starting point was that no serious revolutionary could ignore the existence of national differences. Often, as Marx pointed out at a meeting of the general council of the First International in June 1866, when Proudhon's followers 'came out with the announcement that all nationalities and even nations were "antiquated prejudices",' such an attitude can strengthen national chauvinism. He told Engels afterwards:

> The English laughed very much when I began my speech by saying that our friend Lafargue and others, who had done away with nationalities, had spoken '*French*' to us, ie a language which nine-tenths of the audience did not understand. I also suggested that by the negation of nationalities he appeared, quite unconsciously, to understand their absorption into the model French nation (**SC** 179).

Abstract internationalism, which ignores the existence of national oppression, could conceal nationalism.

However, neither were Marx and Engels supporters of the   189 abstract 'principle of nationality'. They believed that any specific national movement should be supported or opposed only to the extent that it favoured or undermined the interests of the revolution. But how to judge these interests?

It is important here to bear in mind the general nature of the epoch in which Marx spent the bulk of his life. Lenin characterised this period as beginning in 1789 and ending in 1871, that is, from the Great French Revolution to the Franco-Prussian War and the Commune:

> The general feature of the epoch...was the progressiveness of the bourgeoisie, ie its unresolved and uncompleted struggle against feudalism. It was perfectly natural for the elements of present-day democracy, and for Marx as their representative, to have been guided at the time by the unquestionable principle of support for the progressive bourgeoisie (ie capable of waging a struggle) against feudalism... It is quite natural that *no other* question could have been posed at this time except the following: the success of *which* bourgeoisie, the success of which combination of forces, the failure of which reactionary forces (the feudal-absolutist forces which were hampering the rise of the bourgeoisie) promised contemporary democracy more 'elbow room'?

In Europe until 1871 the central question was that of the uncompleted bourgeois democratic revolution. Marx and Engels believed that the most radical solution of this question, that is, the establishment of revolutionary democratic republics on the model of the First French Republic in the 1790s, would favour the interests of the working class, since it would provide the clearest expression of the class struggle between capital and labour, unencumbered by feudal survivals. The country where this issue was most sharply posed was their own country, Germany, which lacked even the most essential condition of bourgeois statehood, national unity. The principal obstacle to the bourgeois democratic revolution in Germany and in Europe generally was provided by Tsarist Russia, whose vast peasant armies were used with such deadly effect against the revolutions of 1848.

Marx and Engels therefore judged national movements from the standpoint of how they fitted into this European alignment of forces, by their relationship to those nations which were in the vanguard of the bourgeois democratic revolution against Russia and her allies. Engels advocated in 1849 'an alliance of the revolutionary peoples against the counter-revolutionary peoples, an alliance which comes into being not on *paper*, but only on the *battlefield*' (**CW** viii 363).

Engels identified three chief 'revolutionary peoples'—the Germans, the Poles and the Hungarians. The main plank of the *Neue Rheinische Zeitung* in 1848-9 was a call for a united German republic to wage revolutionary war, in alliance with Poland and Hungary, against Russia, just as the Jacobins had launched a Europe-wide revolutionary war against the monarchies of the *ancien régime* in the 1790s. Marx and Engels consistently supported Polish independence throughout their long political career, never wavering from the belief stated by Marx in 1848 that Poland's 'emancipation has become the point of honour for all the democrats of Europe' (**CW** vi 549).

The other side of the coin, however, was that there were counter-revolutionary peoples. Marx and Engels were especially hostile to the doctrine of pan-Slavism espoused by both supporters of the Tsarist monarchy and some of its opponents, notably Bakunin. According to this theory the Russians and Poles should unite with their fellow Slavs ruled by Austria and Turkey—the Czechs, Slovaks and Southern Slavs (Serbs, Croats, Bulgarians and others)—to form a single nation.

The political reasons for rejecting this programme were obvious in the light of Marx's and Engels' general strategy. Pan-Slavism could too easily become a stalking horse for Tsarist expansionism. 'Behind this ludicrous theory', Engels wrote, 'stood the terrible reality of the *Russian Empire*, that empire which by every movement proclaims the pretension of considering all Europe as the domain of the Slavonic race and especially of the only energetic part of this race, of the Russians' (**CW** xi 47). He pointed to the way in which the Austrian monarchy used its Southern Slav subjects to crush the Hungarian revolution in 1849.

Engels toyed with the concept, borrowed from Hegel, of 'peoples which have never had a history of their own', of which the Southern Slavs were an example (**CW** viii 367). Such a notion of 'historyless nations' is a dubious one, based as it is on Hegel's assumption that 'in the history of the world, only those peoples can

191

come under our notice which form a state.' The thrust of Engels' analysis was, however, a materialist one. The peasants who then made up the bulk of the population of Europe could play a revolutionary role only under the leadership of an urban class, in this case the bourgeoisie. In the Austrian Empire, 'the class that was the driving force and standard bearer of the movement, the bourgeoisie, was everywhere German or Magyar. The Slavs could only with difficulty give rise to a national bourgeoisie, and the Southern Slavs only in quite isolated cases' (**CW** viii 232).

So the general approach made by Marx and Engels to the national question in 1848-9 was intelligible in the light of the state of Europe at the time. It had ceased, however, to have much relevance by the end of the 1860s. The bourgeois democratic revolution was by then completed in Germany, but in a form and through an agency quite unanticipated by Marx and Engels. It was Bismarck, a representative of the reactionary *Junker* agrarian class, who united Germany. This was what Gramsci called a 'passive revolution', a revolution from above, based on an alliance of the *Junkers* and the industrial bourgeoisie. The latter were happy to allow the former to control the state apparatus, in exchange for national unification and pro-capitalist economic policies.

The new epoch ushered in by the Franco-Prussian War was one in which both Europe and the world fell increasingly under the domination of a handful of capitalist powers competing with each other for territories and peoples. The national question was no longer primarily that of the struggle between revolutionary and counter-revolutionary peoples. It now took two, closely connected forms—on the one hand, the nationalism which bound the workers of the imperialist countries to their exploiters, and, on the other, the nationalism of oppressed peoples struggling against their foreign rulers.

Marx confronted this problem in the concrete form it took in Britain—namely, the age old struggle of the Irish for national independence, which in the 1860s and 1870s took the spectacular form of the armed actions of the Fenians. While condemning their terrorist excesses, Marx firmly endorsed the demand for Irish national independence, and persuaded the International to adopt this position. He had two main reasons. The first is of less interest now. Marx regarded Ireland as the main bulwark of the

English landed aristocracy, many of whom had estates there, and therefore believed that the victory of the Irish independence movement and the consequent expropriation of these estates would bring down the ruling class in Britain.

This analysis was simply wrong. The late 19th century was a time when the British landowning class was in steep economic and political decline. Their diminishing importance was reflected in the policies of the Gladstone and Balfour administrations in the 1880s and early 1900s, which together organised the peaceful transfer of the bulk of the Anglo-Irish estates to the Catholic peasantry.

Much more interesting was Marx's second argument for supporting the Irish national movement, namely that the oppression of Ireland helped to cement British workers to their exploiters:

> Every industrial and commercial centre in England now possesses a working class *divided* into two *hostile* camps, English proletarians and Irish proletarians. The ordinary English worker hates the Irish worker as a competitor who lowers his standard of life. In relation to the Irish worker he feels himself a member of the *ruling* nation and so turns himself into a tool of the aristocrats and capitalists *against Ireland* thus strengthening their domination *over himself*. He cherishes religious, social, and national prejudices against the Irish worker. His attitude towards him is much the same as that of the 'poor whites' to the 'niggers' in the former slave states of the USA...
>
> This antagonism is artificially kept alive and intensified by the press, the pulpit, the comic papers, in short by all the means at the disposal of the ruling classes. This *antagonism* is the *secret of the impotence of the English working class*, despite its organisation. It is the secret by which the capitalist class maintains its power. And that class is fully aware of it (**SC** 236-7).

This analysis is obviously of general relevance. Nationalism in the imperialist countries is a means by which workers are divided from each other and united with their exploiters. 'After all, we're all British,' they say. Lenin generalised Marx's argument, insisting that workers in the imperialist countries should support the right of self determination of oppressed nations as a means of breaking the links which bound them to their ruling classes. Here   193 again, we see that the question is one of whether national movements contribute to the general interests of the revolution, only now it is the workers' revolution, and movements are to be judged by whether they cement or undermine the international unity of the working class.

Communism

The dictatorship of the proletariat, established first on a national and then on an international level, 'only constitutes the transition to the *abolition of all classes* and to a classless society' (**SC** 69). The overthrow of capitalism was thus a beginning, not an end. 'This social formation', Marx wrote of capitalism, 'brings...the pre-history of human society to a close' (**SW** i 504).

Marx did not believe there could be an instant leap from class society into communism. Doing away with the remnants of capitalism would take time. 'Between capitalist and communist society lies the period of the revolutionary transformation of the one into the other. Corresponding to this is also a political transition period in which the state can be nothing but the *revolutionary dictatorship of the proletariat*' (**SW** iii 26).

Marx did not try to anticipate in any detail the nature of this transition, or of communism. He was highly critical of the Utopian Socialists' attempts to lay down, often in obsessive detail, how the future society would be run. In the *Communist Manifesto* he insisted:

> [that] the theoretical conclusions of the communists are in no way based on the ideas or principles that have been invented, or discovered by this or that would-be universal reformer.
>
> They merely express, in general terms, actual relations springing from an existing class struggle, from a historical movement going on under our very eyes (**CW** vi 498).

This does not mean that Marx and Engels dismissed everything the Utopians had to say. On the contrary, it is clear that they learned a great deal from them, and agreed with many of their practical proposals. Both, and especially Engels, greatly admired Fourier. They took much of their vision of what communism would be like from the Utopian Socialists. However, they believed that the most important current task was to understand the historical forces which would bring this society into being.

Marx's most extended discussion of the phases of the transition to communism is in the *Critique of the Gotha Programme*. Earlier he had defined the tasks of the dictatorship of the proletariat as 'the appropriation of the means of production, their subjection to the associated working class and, therefore, the abolition of wage labour, of capital and of their mutual relations' (**CW** x 78).

These tasks were interconnected. Marx envisaged the state taking control of the most important means of production. Since the state would be 'the proletariat organised as the ruling class', this measure would abolish the separation of labour power from the means of production, a separation on which the existence of capital and wage labour depended. (Of course, this doesn't mean that *any* nationalisation abolishes wage labour; only when the working class controls the state will this happen.)

These steps would involve the introduction of a planned economy. Marx believed that labour was 'the everlasting nature-imposed condition of human existence'. 'After the abolition of the capitalist mode of production…the determination of value continues to prevail in the sense that the regulation of labour time and the distribution of social labour among the various production groups…becomes more essential than ever' (**C** iii 851). Except that now the decisions about how much social labour would depend, not on the blind workings of competition, but on a collective and democratic assessment by the associated producers in the light of the needs of society.

Surplus labour would continue to exist in the sense that a portion of the social product would be set aside and not consumed, in order to replace existing means of production as they wore out, to allocate resources to long term projects, and to provide an emergency reserve. But, 'apart from surplus labour for those who on account of age are not yet, or no longer, able to take part in production, all labour to support those who do not work would cease' (**C** iii 847).

Part of the social product actually consumed would be done so collectively, through the provision of schools, health services and so on. The rest would be divided up among the individual producers. Marx believed that the principles according to which this distribution would take place were likely to change as society progressed towards communism.

In 'the first phase of communist society as it is when it has just emerged after prolonged birth pangs from capitalist society', it would be 'in every respect, economically, morally and intellectually, still stamped with the birth marks of the old society from whose womb it emerges' (**SW** iii 19). People would still be shaped by their experience of wage labour under capitalism, where they could expect to be materially rewarded in proportion to the amount of work they did:

> Accordingly, the individual producer receives back from society— after the deductions have been made—exactly what he gives to it... He receives a certificate from society that he has furnished such and such an amount of labour...and with this certificate he draws from the social stock of means of consumption as much as costs the same amount of labour (**SW** iii 17-18).

This principle, 'from each according to his capacity, to each according to his works', is an example, Marx emphasises, of 'bourgeois right'. For it takes no account of the differences between individuals, of the fact that one person is stronger than another, or more intelligent, or with more dependants. Yet these are all factors which will affect the individual's ability to work, and thus his or her ability to be rewarded by society, or will mean that he or she has to spread the proceeds of his or her labour over more people.

> This *equal* right is an unequal right for unequal labour. It recognises no class differences, because everyone is only a worker like everyone else; but it tacitly recognises unequal individual endowment and thus productive capacity as natural privileges. *It is, therefore, a right of inequality, in its content, like every right* (**SW** iii 18).

This undesirable way of going about things is forced on the associated producers by the fact that they have only recently escaped from capitalism, and so neither the development of the productive forces, nor social attitudes, permit a more radical approach. However:

In a higher phase of communist society, after the enslaving

subordination of the individual to the division of labour, and therewith also the antithesis between mental and physical labour, has vanished; after labour has become not only a means of life but life's prime want; after the productive forces have also increased with the all-round development of the individual, and all the springs of cooperative wealth flow more abundantly—only then can the narrow horizon of bourgeois right be crossed in its entirety and society inscribe on its banners: From each according to his ability, to each according to his needs! (**SW** iii 19)

At a higher stage of development, then, communist society will be able to take account of individuals' particular needs and abilities, rather than applying a common standard insensitive to the differences between people. We can see that the usual criticism of Marxism, that it ignores and suppresses individuality, treating people as all the same, is nonsense. Genuine equality requires paying close attention to people's individual needs and capacities. The higher stage of communism will be 'an association in which the free development of each is the condition for the free development of all' (**CW** vi 506). A communist society would be, in the words of the Marxist philosopher Theodor Adorno, 'one in which people could be different without fear.'

The transition to communism will also lead, Marx argues, to the disappearance of the state as a distinct institution:

When, in the course of development, class distinctions have disappeared, and production has been concentrated in the hands of a vast association of the whole nation, the public power will lose its political character. Political power, properly so called, is merely the organised power of one class for oppressing another. If the proletariat during its contest with the bourgeoisie is compelled, by the force of circumstances, to organise itself as a class, if, by means of a revolution, it makes itself the ruling class, and, as such, sweeps away by force the old conditions of production, then it will, along with these conditions, have swept away the conditions for the existence of class antagonisms and of classes generally, and will thereby have abolished its own supremacy as a class (**CW** vi 505-6).

The state is a product of class antagonisms, and, therefore, will vanish along with them. The possibility of such a 'withering away of the state' is present in the dictatorship of the proletariat from the start. Engels analyses the consequences of socialist revolution for the state as follows:

> *The proletariat seizes political power and turns the means of production in the first instance into state property.*
>
> But, in doing this, it abolishes itself as proletariat, abolishes all class distinctions and class antagonisms, abolishes also the state as state. Society thus far, based upon class antagonisms, had need of the state, that is, of an organisation of the particular class, which was *pro tempore* [for the time being] the exploiting class, for the maintenance of its external conditions of production, and, therefore, especially, for the purpose of forcibly keeping the exploited classes in the condition of oppression corresponding with the given mode of production (slavery, serfdom, wage labour)... As soon as there is no longer any social class to be held in subjection; as soon as class rule, and the individual struggle for existence based upon our present anarchy in production, with the collisions and excesses arising from these, are removed, nothing more remains to be repressed, and a special repressive force, a state, is no longer necessary. The first act by virtue of which the state really constitutes itself the representative of the whole of society—the taking possession of the means of production in the name of society—this is, at the same time, its last independent act as a state. State interference in social relations becomes, in one domain after another, superfluous, and then withers away of itself; the government of persons is replaced by the administration of things, and by the conduct of processes of production. The state is not 'abolished'. *It withers away* (**AD** 332-3).

The dictatorship of the proletariat is thus, to use Lenin's words, 'no longer a state in the proper sense of the word'. It is important to note, however, that the withering away of the state does not take place instantly, but over time. It is a process, and one which depends upon other factors, such as rising labour productivity, and a consequent reduction in the working day, which would free workers for participation in running society.

Socialist democracy in some respects would mirror the democracy of ancient Athens. Slave labour permitted the citizens of Athens to devote the bulk of their time to public affairs—to discussion in the marketplace, to decision making in the sovereign assembly of all citizens, and to involvement in administration (most public offices were undertaken by ordinary citizens by rotation). With communism, on the other hand, thanks to the enormous development of the productive forces in the past two and a half millenia, citizens would enjoy their free time thanks to the work, not of wretched slaves, but of inanimate machines produced by human ingenuity.

The replacement of the 'government of persons' by the 'administration of things', a notion developed originally by Saint-Simon, does not involve the utopian belief that communism would involve no coercion. It suggests, rather, that with the abolition of classes the main source of social conflict would be removed, so there would be no need for 'a special repressive force'. Obviously, there would be many issues on which the associated producers might disagree—over sources of energy, styles of architecture, methods of child rearing. But without the grinding material pressures produced by class exploitation, these conflicts could be solved democratically, through debate and majority decision. Where individuals rejected the outcome of these procedures, any necessary compulsion would be the action of the associated producers themselves, not that of a special military-police apparatus.

Far from advocating a strengthening of the state, Marx and Engels looked forward to its abolition. The notion, for example, of 'state socialism' was for them a contradiction in terms. They consistently combatted the belief, influential in the German workers' movement thanks to Lassalle, that the existing state was a potentially benevolent institution which could be won over to the workers' interests. To refute this doctrine was the main purpose of Marx's *Critique of the Gotha Programme*, aimed at the shabby and confused compromise produced by the fusion of his own and Lassalle's followers. The attribution to him of a totalitarian desire to dissolve the individual into the state is a result of liberal misrepresentation, and of Stalin's terrible corruption of Marxism.

Closely connected with the claim that the transition to communism would involve the withering away of the state was Marx's belief that it would also require the abolition of the distinction between mental and manual labour. From the *Economic and Philosophic Manuscripts of 1844* onwards Marx had denounced this division as one of the main ways in which human beings were stunted, distorted, turned into something less than human, under capitalism. People, he believed, could live happy and fulfilled lives only if they used all their capacities, mental and physical alike, rather than being restricted to one narrow type of work.

In a famous passage of *The German Ideology*, Marx writes:

> …in communist society, where nobody has one exclusive sphere of activity but each can become accomplished in any branch he wishes, society regulates the general production and thus makes it possible for me to do one thing today and another tomorrow, to hunt in the morning, fish in the afternoon, rear cattle in the evening, criticise after dinner, just as I have a mind, without ever becomii hunter, fisherman, shepherd or critic (**CW** v 47).

Commentators have often denounced this picture as utopian. One can indeed wonder how literally Marx meant it to be taken, and it is worth noting that all the pursuits he lists are ones to be found in a traditional pre-industrial society. Nevertheless, there is a serious point underlying the passage, which is that the development of the productive forces under communism will be such as to free people from their existing role as cogs of the economic machine.

Marx pursues this point in one of the most brilliant passages of the *Grundrisse*. He argues that the tendency under capitalism to increase the productivity of labour, and therefore the organic composition of capital, the share of the means of production in total investment, will lead to the transformation of the labour process into 'an *automatic system of machinery*', which the worker merely 'supervises…and guards against interruptions' (**G** 692).

The result is to reduce the role of manual labour in production:

> To the degree that labour time—the mere quantity of labour—is posited by capital as the sole determinant element, to that degree, does direct labour and its quantity disappear as the determinant principle of production—of the creation of use values—and is reduced both quantitatively, to a smaller proportion, and qualitatively, as

an of course indispensable but subordinate moment, compared to general scientific labour, technological application of the natural sciences, on the one side, and to the general productive force arising from social combination on the other side (**G** 700).

This passage is a brilliant anticipation of developments in capitalism this century—the introduction of mass assembly line production during its first half, and the increasing automation of the labour process during its second half.

Within the framework of capitalist relations of production these changes take an antagonistic form—unemployment for many workers, speed-up for those left on the job, the 'deskilling' of craft labour. But they create the potential for a society in which the drudgery of heavy, repetitive manual labour has been abolished, in which people are no longer tied daily to many hours of backbreaking and boring physical work. The resulting reduction of the working week to a fraction of its present length—hotly resisted by capitalists because it would reduce their profits—would free people to develop their intellectual powers and physical skills.

In communist society, thanks to the development of the productive forces and their subjection to common social control, many of the Utopian Socialists' dreams would become reality. As Fourier had anticipated, the barrier between 'work' and 'play' could be broken down—labour for the sake of physical survival and labour for sheer enjoyment's sake would no longer be separated from, and opposed to each other. Engels argued that the antithesis between town and country would also be abolished, with the establishment of communes like those advocated by Fourier and Robert Owen in which both agriculture and industry would be carried on. The development of new forms of technology in recent years requiring decentralised units of production linked together by advanced communications systems has made such arrangements more feasible.

Marx emphasised that all this depended on the development of the productive forces:

The realm of freedom actually begins only where labour which is determined by necessity and mundane considerations ceases; thus in the very nature of things it lies beyond the sphere of actual material production… Freedom in this field can only consist in socialised man, the associated producers, rationally regulating their interchange with nature, bringing it under their common control, instead of being ruled by it as by the blind forces of nature; and achieving this with the least expenditure of energy and under conditions most favourable to, and worthy of, their human nature. But it nonetheless remains a realm of necessity. Beyond it begins that development of human energy which is an end in itself, the true end of freedom, which can blossom forth only with this realm of necessity as its basis. The shortening of the working day is its basic prerequisite (C iii 820).

Communism thus both drastically reduces the burden of extracting a living from nature, freeing us for other pursuits, and subjects the labour process, 'the realm of necessity', to rational and collective control. In Engels' words, 'it is humanity's leap from the kingdom of necessity to the kingdom of freedom' (AD 336).

Marx today

No discussion of Marx's life and thought can ignore developments since his death. Marx had set out, after all, to lay the basis of a scientific theory of history, and, in particular, of the capitalist mode of production. Now the only way in which we can establish even the approximate truth of a scientific theory is by comparing its predictions with what actually happened.

Many would argue that by this criterion Marxism must be judged false. The course of history, they claim, has completely refuted Marx's thought. Most of his predictions have allegedly been contradicted by later developments, while even where his ideas have triumphed it is supposedly in a form quite contrary to his hopes and expectations. Indeed, within the labour movement itself, there has been a succession of 'crises of Marxism', the first within a few years of Engels' death in 1895, in each of which the irrelevance of Marx's ideas to contemporary society has been proclaimed.

A book such as this obviously cannot discuss these criticisms at any length. Here I wish merely to confront, briefly, the three most important arguments against Marx. The first concerns the origins and nature of the so called 'socialist' countries today, the second the condition of capitalism today, and the third the position of the working class within it.

203

'Really existing socialism'

The Russian Revolution of October 1917 was undoubtedly the most important event of the 20th century. A working class under avowedly Marxist leadership seized power. Yet innumerable critics have argued that the revolution and its aftermath completely refute Marx.

There are two main strands of this argument. First, it is claimed that Marx expected revolutions to happen first in the advanced industrial countries. How then could he account for the fact that the first successful socialist revolution took place in a backward, largely rural country?

Further support is lent to this point by the emergence of so called 'Marxist-Leninist' regimes in various underdeveloped countries—China, Vietnam, Cuba and so on. Secondly, the subsequent degeneration of the Russian Revolution into Stalin's bloody despotism supposedly proves that Marx was wrong again: the dictatorship of the proletariat does not lead to an extension of democracy and to the eventual abolition of classes, but to a tyranny even more vile than the one it replaced.

The first part of the argument is comparatively easy to deal with. It attributes to Marx a picture of history in which humanity necessarily passes through certain stages, so that modes of production succeed each other according to the iron laws of historical necessity. Such a version of Marxism was indeed accepted by some Russian socialists, such as Georgi Plekhanov and the Mensheviks, who believed that socialism would not be possible in Russia until the development of capitalism had turned her into an industrialised country like Britain or Germany.

This was not, however, Marx's own view. Russia was one of the first countries where his ideas were taken up. He was highly critical of attempts to treat his analysis, in *Capital* Volume 1 Part Eight, of the evolution of capitalism as applicable to all societies. Marx attacked one Russian writer for having transformed 'my historical sketch of the genesis of capitalism in Western Europe into an historico-philosophic theory of the general path every people is fated to tread, whatever the historical circumstances in which it finds itself.' Such an approach treated Marxism as 'a general historico-philosophical theory, the supreme virtue of which consists in being super-historical' (**SC** 313).

Marx was careful not to rule out the possibility that a social revolution might enable Russia to arrive at socialism without passing through a capitalist phase, provided that 'the Russian Revolution becomes the signal for a proletarian revolution in the West' (**SW** i 100).

We saw in the previous chapter that revolutions take place as a result of a process of 'uneven and combined development'. They arise, in other words, from the unique class structure and state of economic development of the society in question, which in turn is bound up with its position in the capitalist world system. Precisely this is true of the Russian Revolution.

A backward, primarily rural society, Russia experienced a phase of rapid industrialisation at the turn of the 19th century. This was brought about by a government keen to catch up economically with the West for fear it would otherwise become militarily vulnerable, and by foreign capitalists eager to exploit cheap Russian labour. The result was to create a small, highly concentrated industrial working class possessing a social and political weight far greater than its numbers. The contradiction between capital and labour was added to the age-old struggle between lord and peasant.

The explosive nature of the combination was first made plain by the revolution of 1905. The Tsarist state survived this upheaval, only to have its back broken by defeat in the First World War. The revolution of February 1917 then swept it aside, giving rise to a situation of 'dual power' between the bourgeois Provisional Government and the soviets or workers' and soldiers' councils. In October 1917 the soviets seized power, under the leadership of the Bolsheviks, a party firmly based in the urban working class, and benefiting from the benevolent neutrality of the peasants, to whom they had promised the estates of the gentry.

A much more serious challenge to Marxism than the fact of a revolution in a backward country is what happened in Russia *after* October 1917, the transformation of a democratic workers' state into the bureaucratic monstrosity which rules Russia today. The answer is to be found in Marx's insistence that socialism could succeed only on a world scale. The Bolsheviks, like him, believed that the Soviet regime could survive only if it became 'the signal for a proletarian revolution in the West'.

But despite the revolutionary wave which did shake Europe at the end of the First World War, the new Soviet republic remained isolated. Furthermore, the bloody war unleashed on Russia by the Western powers and by counter-revolutionary forces caused enormous destruction. The industrial economy collapsed, and workers streamed back to the villages that they had only lately left. The end of the civil war in 1921 found the country exhausted, the working class disintegrated, the soviets a shell of workers' power, and the Bolsheviks effectively the dictatorship of a minority suspended above a largely hostile smallholding peasantry.

As Marx had predicted, the confinement of the revolution to a single country meant that 'the whole filthy business' of exploitation and class struggle was restored. The low level of development of the productive forces within Russia were not sufficient to provide a basis for moving towards communism. Only the resources existing on a *world* scale could have done so.

The Bolshevik leadership, especially after Lenin's active political life ceased with his first stroke in 1922, increasingly adapted themselves to the situation. They came to see the interests of the Soviet state as more important than those of the world working class. So again and again in the years between 1923 and 1939 revolutionary possibilities—in China, France and Spain—were squandered because they conflicted with the current objectives of Russian foreign policy. The doctrine of 'socialism in one country' was formulated to justify this approach. Critics within the regime, such as Trotsky and the Left Opposition, were excluded, imprisoned, exiled and murdered. The repression inside the party favoured the development of Stalin's personal dictatorship, which crystallised the domination of Russia by a layer of privileged bureaucrats.

The defeats suffered by the working class abroad increased the isolation of the Russian regime, and the danger of foreign invasion. To counter this threat Russia required the latest weapons, which could only be produced by an advanced industrial economy. But the resources necessary to industrialise the country could come only from the surplus labour of the workers and peasants. In 1928-9 Stalin flung the regime on to a new course of forced industrialisation.

The land was 'collectivised'—in other words, it was placed under state control. Millions of peasants perished in the process.

This move provided the regime with the grain necessary to feed the towns, and to sell abroad, where it would earn the foreign exchange necessary to buy advanced Western machinery. At the same time, an enormous range of heavy industries was built from scratch. Peasants were driven off the land—and sucked into the new factories on an enormous scale. It was their surplus labour which made industrialisation possible: one Russian economist has calculated that the economic expansion of the 1930s was financed by an enormous rise in the extraction of both relative and absolute surplus value.

Marx had written that the 'primitive accumulation' of capital in Western Europe involved the massive use of coercion—to drive the peasants off the land, to force artisans to work longer hours and thus to produce absolute surplus value, to loot the world of its wealth and to keep unemployed 'vagabonds', deprived of their livelihood, from threatening society. 'These methods...all employ the power of the state, the concentrated and organised force of society, to hasten, as in a hothouse, the process of transformation of the feudal mode of production, and to shorten the transition' (C i 915-16).

This bloody work, which took centuries in Western Europe, was packed into a decade in Russia. The effect was the same. The peasants were separated from the means of production, and what was left of the gains made by workers thanks to the 1917 revolution were eliminated. The effect was, as surely as the process of 'primitive accumulation' analysed by Marx, to separate the direct producers from the means of production, and compel them to sell their labour power.

It is true that this situation was concealed by what Marx would call the 'metaphysical or juridical illusion' (CW xviii 99) created by the fact that, legally, the state owned the means of production, and the workers controlled the state. This appearance, like the formal equality of capitalists and workers described by Marx, concealed an underlying reality of class exploitation. The workers did not control the state; rather, the party-state bureaucracy headed by Stalin had political power, and through it enjoyed effective possession of the means of production.

We have seen that capitalism involves two separations. The first, that of the direct producers from the means of production, was brought about in Russia by the forced collectivisation and industrialisation

207

of the 1930s. But what of the second separation, the division of the economy into competing capitals? It is natural to believe that such a state of affairs does not exist in the Soviet Union, since within the country the market for goods other than labour power itself has largely been replaced by state planning and control.

Here again, however, the reality is different from how it appears. Once we set Russia in its context, that of the capitalist world system, matters change. For it is clear that the Soviet state is subject to the pressures of the world system. This is reflected in the priority within the Russian economy given to military production, which takes an enormous 12-14 percent of the gross national product. The initial decision in the 1920s to collectivise and industrialise was not the result of Stalin's malevolence and power-lust, but of the pressure of objective circumstances—the need to match Western military might. The same pressure continues to bind Russia to the world system today, and to ensure that surplus labour is not used to benefit the associated producers, but instead is ploughed back into further production.

The result is a situation in principle identical to that analysed by Marx in *Capital*. The aim of production under capitalism is not consumption but accumulation, production for production's sake. And this aim is not the result of a voluntary decision on the capitalist's part. Rather he is compelled as a result of competition to reinvest his profits, or be driven out of business by his rivals. 'The influence of individual capitals on one another has the effect precisely that they must conduct themselves as *capitals*' (**G** 657). The position is the same when we look at the relationship between Russia and the West, only now we are dealing with state capitals, rather than private firms, and they compete militarily as well as economically.

The prevailing relations of production in the Soviet Union are thus not socialist, but rather are those of *bureaucratic state capitalism*. The working class is exploited collectively by a state bureaucracy which competes with its Western counterparts. The fate of the Russian Revolution therefore does not refute Marx: rather, it can be explained only on the basis of his theory, as the inevitable consequence of the failure of the revolution to spread, and of the pressures of the capitalist world system.

The emergence of 'socialist' regimes elsewhere in the world can be understood in this light. In Eastern Europe they are an extension of Soviet military power, created as a chain of buffer states against invasion from the West. Events in Poland since August 1980 have revealed how little these are workers' states. We have seen a working class organise against 'their' state only to be crushed by the military.

The appearance of 'socialist' regimes in the Third World reflects the difficulties faced by bourgeois democratic revolutions in backward countries. Marx had noted in 1848 that 'the German bourgeoisie developed so sluggishly, timidly and slowly that at the moment when it menacingly confronted feudalism and absolutism, it saw menacingly confronting it the proletariat' (**CW** viii 162). So it was unwilling to act in the decisive and revolutionary fashion of its English and French forebears.

Marx argued that the resulting vacuum could only be filled by the working class:

> It is our interest and our task to make the revolution permanent, until all more or less possessing classes have been forced out of their position of dominance, the proletariat has conquered state power, and the association of proletarians, not only in one country but in all the dominant countries of the world, has advanced so far that competition among the proletarians has ceased and that at least the decisive productive forces are concentrated in the hands of the proletarians (**CW** x 281).

Just such a process of 'permanent revolution' took place in Russia in 1917. The bourgeoisie there, as in Germany, was too weak and afraid of the working class to do anything but ally itself with the Tsarist regime in the hope of achieving a 'passive revolution' like Bismarck's in Germany. Only the working class were prepared to back the peasants in their struggle with the feudal gentry. So in Russia the bourgeois democratic revolution against feudalism merged with the proletarian socialist revolution against capitalism into a single process under working class leadership. Unfortunately, because the revolution did not spread to other countries, it was, in the end, defeated.

In other backward countries, while the bourgeoisie has played a similarly passive and feeble part, the working class was itself, whether because of economic underdevelopment, because of the influence of non-revolutionary parties or because of the privileges enjoyed by some workers in the Third World, unable to play the revolutionary role of the Russian workers in 1917. So when movements for national independence developed in the colonial and semi-colonial countries they fell under the leadership of other social forces.

These were mainly middle class intellectuals, who, while hostile to the West and to local capitalists, had no interest in the emancipation of the working masses. They were before anything nationalists, who wished to build strong and independent nation states. Stalinist Russia was an attractive model for many of them, as a backward country which had industrialised under state control, so they described themselves as 'Marxist-Leninists'. But their socialism had nothing to do with the self emancipation of the working class. When they succeeded in expelling their foreign masters, most notably in China, Vietnam and Cuba, they reproduced all the main features of bureaucratic state capitalism as it existed in Russia.

'Really existing socialism' in the Eastern bloc is thus the negation of socialism as Marx conceived it. It rests, not on the self emancipation of the working class but its exploitation. Anyone who remains true to Marx's thought must work wholeheartedly for the downfall of these regimes.

Capitalism today

The second major criticism often made of Marx concerns the fact that capitalism has changed since his day. However accurate a picture *Capital* may give of Marx's own world, it is argued, it is only a very imperfect guide to our own. The most cogent arguments to this effect were made in two books, both published in 1956 by Labour Party intellectuals, Anthony Crosland's *The Future of Socialism* and John Strachey's *Contemporary Capitalism*. Strachey had been an enormously influential Marxist publicist in the 1930s; Crosland was a dominant figure in a generation of Labour politicians who believed that the class struggle and nationalisation were no longer relevant to socialist politics, some of whom have now gone on to found the Social Democratic Party.

Both Crosland and Strachey argued that the structure of capitalism had fundamentally changed. The growth of monopolies has led to a convergence between the state and big business which makes economic planning possible as it was not in earlier phases of capitalist development. Power has also shifted within companies. What has come to be known as the 'separation of ownership and control' means that they are run, not by the shareholders, but by managers with little personal stake in the company, oriented on long term growth rather than short term profit. Finally, the techniques of demand management, provided with intellectual justification by J M Keynes, mean that governments can manage the economy so as to avoid the extremes of boom and slump.

Crosland, less cautious than Strachey, who retained some of his old Marxist training, concluded that 'it...seems misleading to continue talking about "capitalism" in Britain'. 'We stand...on the threshold of mass abundance', he announced. The thrust of socialist activity, he said, should be towards the gradual elimination of surviving inequality and poverty. The class struggle had gone for good: 'One cannot imagine today a deliberate offensive alliance between government and employers...with all the brutal paraphernalia of wage cuts, national lockouts, and anti-union legislation'.

It is easy in 1983, during the deepest slump for half a century and under a highly reactionary Tory government, to deride Crosland's optimism. Nevertheless, it is clear that capitalism *has* changed since Marx's day. Furthermore, for a quarter of a century after the Second World War the world economy did enjoy a sustained boom—world gross national product grew by three and a half times between 1948 and 1973. Can Marx's theory explain these developments?

The emergence of monopoly capital, far from contradicting Marx's analysis in *Capital*, is central to it. As we have seen, Marx argued that competition between capitals would lead to the growth in size of the units of production. This process takes two connected forms—the concentration of capital through the accumulation of surplus value, and the centralisation of capital, the absorption of smaller and less efficient firms by their larger and more efficient rivals.

At the same time as this 'constant decrease in the number of capitalist magnates' (C i 929), legal property forms were changing. Marx described the emergence of joint-stock companies as 'the abolition of capital as private property within the framework

211

of capitalist production itself', involving the 'transformation of the actually functioning capitalist into a mere manager of other people's capital, and of the owner of capital into a mere owner, a mere money capitalist' (C iii 436-7). The famous 'separation of ownership and control' would thus have come as no surprise to Marx.

⚡ The growth of monopoly capital has continued apace during the 20th century. For example, the 100 largest companies in Britain in 1970 accounted for 46 percent of net manufacturing output. Since the Second World War the big corporations have increasingly operated on an international scale, spreading their operations across the globe.

These changes have not made the behaviour of industrialists any less capitalist. Claims to the contrary tend to rely on businessmen's psychology—on the differences between the Victorian *laisser faire* capitalist out to grab the most for himself, and the smooth 'socially aware' mid-20th century executive, concerned more about the company than about his own personal interests.

Even if we ignore the question of how accurate these pictures are, they are irrelevant to the central issue of the nature of contemporary capitalism. For, as we have seen, Marx stressed that the dynamic that leads capitalists to extract and accumulate surplus value has nothing to do with their personal desires, but rather arises from the impersonal pressures of the competitive system of which they are part. And competition between capitals continues as ferociously as ever, even if the struggle is now between multinational firms rather than individual capitalists.

In such a competitive environment, profits remain the only adequate measure of success or failure—above all because they are the source of the funds for reinvestment. The shift from short term profit to long term growth, even if it has happened, simply reflects a change in the means of maximising profits, not an abandonment of the goal of profitability.

The other major alteration in the structure of capitalism has been the growth in the role of the state. Although even in the 19th century the state never played the 'nightwatchman' role to which liberal ideologists sought to confine it, its activities were then largely concerned with providing what Engels called the 'external conditions' of capital accumulation—army, police, the courts, the Poor Law. Today, however, the state is itself a large scale capitalist, producing commodities through the nationalised firms that it owns. At the same time, it employs a large portion of the workforce, namely the providers of services such as health, education and welfare. Finally, the government has overall responsibility for the management of the economy.

These developments were hailed by Strachey in particular as the triumph of 'controlled capitalism', in which workers could use their political power through the vote to direct the economy in their interests. Once again, such claims seem much less credible in the 1980s than they did in the 1950s. Then it was believed that the state, through Keynesian demand management techniques, could keep the economy on an even keel. Now national states seem impotent in the face of world recession, and a political and ideological reaction against state intervention has thrust right wing populists such as Ronald Reagan and Margaret Thatcher into office.

The growth of the state's economic activities is closely related to the development of monopoly capitalism. The immense expansion in the size of individual firms has created the need for effective coordination of their activities. The nationalisation of unprofitable but essential industries such as coal, rail and steel effectively transferred surplus value from less efficient to more efficient capitals. And the need for a comparatively well educated and healthy workforce has been provided by the expansion of the welfare state (itself largely financed, in Britain at least, out of workers' wages, which have suffered increasingly heavily from taxation since the 1950s).

Some of these changes have also been the outcome of pressure from the organised labour movement: the National Health Service, for example, represented for many workers the triumph of social need over private profit. As in the case of factory legislation analysed by Marx, the long term interests of capital in having a healthy and efficient workforce converged with the demands of the workers' movement.

Equally important, however, has been the role of the state in defending the external interests of capital. The turn of the 19th century saw the effective division of the globe among the Western powers. To enforce their interest in this struggle for economic and political influence, capitalists increasingly turned to the state.

213

The result was an intensification of military competition between states, alongside economic competition between firms, which precipitated two world wars.

During and immediately after the First World War the Russian Marxist Nikolai Bukharin analysed these changes. Bukharin argued that the emergence of the capitalist world system was accompanied by a tendency towards state capitalism within individual countries. State and monopoly capital were becoming increasingly integrated with each other, forming relatively unified national capitals. These changes meant that even if national economies were falling under the monopolistic domination of a few large firms, competition was growing on a world scale between these state capitals. This competition, however, was now military as well as economic, said Bukharin.

This analysis develops Marx's argument in *Capital* where, as we have seen, it is the pressure of competition that forces capitals to behave as capitals. Bukharin's analysis provides an insight into the workings of the world system which explains many of the developments since the First World War. We have seen how the pressure of military competition forced the rulers of Russia to make accumulation for accumulation's sake their dominating motive.

The military struggle between national capitals has also been crucial to the comparative stability and great prosperity which the world economy enjoyed in the 1950s and 1960s. For the diversion of resources to the production of means of destruction paradoxically reduces some of the pressures on the system which force it towards crises.

To understand why this is so we have first to recall that Marx identified two main sectors of the economy, Department I (means of production) and Department II (goods for consumption). The commodities produced in these two Departments are, as he puts it, productively consumed. In other words, they are used to produce more commodities. The means of production—machinery, plant and so on—are obviously necessary if more goods are to be made. But consumer goods too are used to keep labour power alive and working efficiently.

There is, however, a third sector of the economy, which Marx calls Department IIb but which is more usually known as Department III, whose output is not productively consumed. Marx himself was thinking of luxury products, which are consumed by capitalists and make no contribution to further production, since they are paid for by surplus value which might otherwise have been reinvested. Arms are in principle the same as luxury goods: they are not used to make other commodities. At best, they simply lie around in readiness for war until they become obsolete, at worst they are used to destroy people and things. Arms production is waste production.

As we have seen, the effect of competition is to force capitals to reinvest surplus value in improving their methods of production. So the organic composition of capital—that is, the share of the means of production in total investment—rises, and the rate of profit falls. Waste production, however, offsets this process. Surplus value which would otherwise be invested in increasing the productivity of labour and therefore also the organic composition of capital is instead diverted to unproductive uses. 'The impact of war is self evident,' Marx wrote, 'since economically it is exactly the same as if the nation were to drop a part of its capital in the ocean' (G 128). By removing some capital from the production of commodities the pressures which lead towards crises are relieved.

Furthermore, corrected versions of the way that Marx set out the transformation of values into prices of production show that the rate of profit in Department III does not influence the formation of the general rate of profit. This means that even if the organic composition of capital in arms production is higher than in other sectors of the economy this will not bring down the general rate of profit. Department III can provide a market for the products of the other two Departments without undermining the overall profitability of capital.

This stabilising effect of arms production was already evident in the 1930s, when the two countries to rearm first, Germany and Japan, were also the first to recover from the effects of the slump and to achieve full employment. Countries such as Britain and the United States produced the same result only with the onset of the Second World War and the shift to a war economy.

But it was at the end of the Second World War, with the emergence of what has come to be called the 'permanent arms economy' arising from military competition between East and West, that waste production came into its own. Large proportions of

215

the gross national product of both Russia and the US, enormous by the standards of earlier peacetime periods, were devoted to the production and use of arms. The stabilising consequences of this were seen in a fall in the organic composition of capital and stable or rising rates of profit. World capitalism enjoyed a boom unprecedented in its length and scale.

It seemed as if the long boom could go on forever. Magical qualities were attributed to the methods of manipulating state budgets that had been made economically respectable by Keynes, even though the use of these methods under Franklin Roosevelt's 'New Deal' in the US during the 1930s did not prevent an even sharper economic collapse in 1937-8 than that which followed the Wall Street Crash in 1929. One of Keynes's disciples, Michael Stewart, an adviser to the SDP leader David Owen, wrote in his popular introduction *Keynes and After*: 'The basic fact is that with the acceptance of the *General Theory* [Keynes's masterwork], the days of uncontrollable mass unemployment in advanced countries are over. Other economic problems may threaten; this one, at least, has passed into history.'

Today, with 'uncontrollable mass unemployment' standing at over 30 million in the 'advanced industrial countries', we know better. The slump of the 1970s and 1980s reflects the fact that the tendency towards crisis which Marx uncovered in *Capital* has been reawakened.

The burden of the arms economy was spread unevenly. In the Western bloc the US and Britain carried the most. This meant that countries such as Germany and Japan could devote all their resources to large scale productive investments which enabled them to outstrip the others on the world market. Beyond a certain point the erosion of US economic supremacy was unacceptable to the American establishment. The late 1960s and early 1970s saw a major rundown in US arms expenditure in order to divert capital to productive investment. The result was an enormous burst of worldwide competition, a sharp rise in the organic composition of capital, and a fall in the rate of profit. The fourfold rise of the oil price in 1973-4 precipitated the first genuine world recession since the mid-1930s.

The more intelligent sections of the ruling class are well aware of the underlying causes of the slump. The *Financial Times* recently acknowledged that 'the post-war boom began to peter out in the late 1960s, not, as is commonly thought, as a result of the 1973-4 oil shock. The clearest guide to the underlying trend is... profit ratios, in which a serious decline is visible already in the late 1960s for many of the major economies' (7 September 1982). *Financial Times* columnist Samuel Brittan, one of the most celebrated exponents of monetarism, has confessed himself unable to explain this fall in the world rate of profit: 'Why have employers been forced to lower their mark-up in each business cycle?... I am far from convinced that I fully understand this process' (16 September 1982).

Only Marx's *Capital* provides the solution to the problem which so puzzles leading bourgeois pundits. The pressure of competition worldwide has forced capitalist firms and states to invest massively in the latest technology. The cost of investment has risen much more quickly than the size of the workforce. And because workers produce the surplus value on which the system rests, the rate of profit has fallen.

Nor is there any easy way out of the crisis. Capitalist economies in their present weakened state would find it difficult to sustain the enormous rise in arms expenditures which would be necessary to devote the same portion of, say, US gross national product to arms as was achieved in the 1950s. And whichever state took the bulk of this burden would suffer in the competitive struggle for markets.

Moreover, as the system has aged, the size of individual capitals has grown. This means that bankruptcies may be very costly, not just to those directly involved but also to the national capital. The classic example is British Leyland, whose collapse would wipe out the British controlled car industry, along with hundreds of thousands of jobs. So governments of whatever colour intervene to prop up these lame ducks.

The result is that slumps no longer perform their function of destroying capital on a scale sufficient to restore the rate of profit to an adequate level. This is reflected in the phenomenon of permanent inflation. Previously prices rose during booms and fell during slumps. Now they rise continuously. The only variation is the *rate* of inflation, which is slower during recessions than periods of expansion. The problems generated during booms are no longer solved during slumps. So economic upswings are brief, feeble and uncertain, downswings

217

protracted, deep and all embracing.

The power of individual states to ignore the effects of world crisis is greatly undermined by the increasingly international character of capitalism. It is not only that multinationals are able to escape the control of governments by shifting investments and money across national frontiers. The financial system, transformed since 1945 to service these companies, is increasingly internationally integrated, and outside the control of nation states.

Sometimes this may be an advantage, as when the Western banks helped to reduce the damage caused by the 1974-5 recession by lending massively to the Third World. In the early 1980s, however, the chickens are coming home to roost, as the bad debts of countries such as Poland, Argentina, Brazil and Mexico threaten to cause the collapse of major Western banks. Such a development would almost certainly lead to a slump even deeper than the worst of the Great Depression of the 1930s. Marx's argument in *Capital* Volume 3 that the credit system only delays, rather than abolishes, the contradictions of capital accumulation is thus confirmed.

The working class

A third argument used against Marx today is that the working class, at least in the form in which he conceived it, no longer exists. The manual working class is now only a minority of the workforce, it is said, which is dominated by white collar workers enjoying middle class living standards and lifestyles, while, contrary to Marx's expectations, real wages have steadily risen in the past century. These economic changes have led to an erosion of class divisions so that, instead of there being bourgeoisie and proletariat confronting one another as antagonists, industrial (or rather 'post-industrial') societies consist largely of a vast amorphous middle class.

Such an analysis was much touted by the 'revisionist' Labour theorists of the 1950s such as Crosland. It has recently been revived in Britain by the SDP, who claim to be a radical, classless party whose politics fit this new society better than the declining Labour Party. But these claims have also been made by some Marxists—for example, the German socialist Rudolph Bahro who recently bade 'Goodbye to the proletariat'.

As critics of this analysis point out, it focuses on questions of consumption. In other words, it claims that because the lifestyle of the traditional working class has become similar to that of sections of the middle class, capitalism no longer exists. Marx, on the other hand, focuses mainly on the relations of *production*, taking these as the foundation on which he built his theory of class.

There is a connected point. Class for Marx is a theoretical concept, not a descriptive category. In other words, he was concerned to uncover the underlying realities of society, not merely to describe how things appeared to be. Yet most of his critics have concentrated on comparatively superficial developments, such as the fact that many workers have cars and mortgages. They have not confronted the fundamental issue of the distribution of wealth and power in contemporary capitalism.

A person's class, Marx argued, was defined by the position he or she occupies in the relations of production. This involves seeing class as a social relationship. It's not so much a matter of the particular sort of work you do, than of where you fit into the antagonistic relations of exploitation which are at the heart of a class society. So Marx regarded as a member of the working class anyone who was regularly compelled to sell their labour power in order to live, even if they were not engaged in manual labour.

We can see this in a variety of ways. Marx distinguishes between productive and unproductive labour. 'The only worker who is productive is one who produces surplus value for the capitalist,' he writes (C i 644). Many wage earners do not produce surplus value. An important example of these unproductive labourers in Marx's day was domestic servants, then the largest single group of the working population. Rather than producing commodities embodying surplus value, they were paid out of the revenue of the propertied classes in order to provide these classes with personal services. Marx's theory of productive labour contains some difficulties, but it is fairly clear that he regarded all those wage earners involved in producing commodities (including those who transported them to their point of final consumption) as productive workers.

There are two important points to note. First, many productive workers are not manual workers. Marx argues that with the development of the 'collective worker', 'an ever increasing number of types of labour are included in the immediate concept of *productive labour*, and those who perform it are classed as *productive workers*, workers directly exploited by capital and *subordinated* to its process of production and expansion' (**C** i 1039-40). As examples he cites managers, engineers, technologists.

Secondly, 'every productive worker is a wage labourer, but not every wage labourer is a productive worker' (**C** i 1041). The working class therefore includes many who are not productive workers. Marx gives the example of a merchant's clerk, who does not produce commodities, but whose labour enables his employer to grab a share of the total surplus value through his role in the circulation of commodities:

> In the first place, his labour power is bought with the variable capital of the merchant, not with money expended as revenue, and consequently it is not bought for private service, but for the purpose of expanding the capital advanced for it. In the second place, the value of the labour power, and thus his wages, are determined as those of other wage workers, ie by the cost of production and reproduction of his specific labour power, not the product of his labour power (**C** iii 292).

Marx goes on to argue that the lower the merchant's costs, the more surplus value created elsewhere will he be able to obtain with his capital, and therefore he has an interest in squeezing the maximum amount of unpaid labour out of his employees. So the clerk, even if he does not produce surplus value, is in the same position as the productive worker.

The working class is thus for Marx not what it is conventionally thought to be, namely manual factory workers, but all those whose conditions of life force them to sell their labour power, and who find themselves at work subject to constant pressure from an employer who seeks to extract the maximum of unpaid labour from them. What defines the working class is not the sort of work they do, but their place in the relations of production.

This is an important point to grasp, because the structure of the workforce has changed dramatically since Marx's time. The figures for Britain are typical of global trends. In 1911 manual workers made up 75 percent of the workforce; by 1979 they had fallen to 48 percent. This transformation means that a majority of the British workforce today are white collar workers.

Two groups have sharply increased their share of the workforce since the First World War. The first is at the top of the occupational ladder, professionals, managers and administrators, who now form nearly 30 percent of the workforce. A significant number of these are scientists, engineers, laboratory technicians and engineers, all groups that have risen dramatically in size this century. Most of these are, in Marx's terms, productive workers. The majority of 'lower professionals' are teachers and nurses, whose pay and conditions of work mean that they must be regarded as wage earners. The rest form what is called 'the new middle class' or 'service class', whose job is to administer the highly complex economy of advanced capitalism, and whose income and power over fellow employees make them a group separate and alienated from the working class.

The other group that has risen sharply is clerical workers, up from 5 percent of the workforce in 1911 to 16 percent in 1979. The overwhelming majority of these are women—nearly 40 percent of all women employees belong to this category. As a group of wage earners, they are in a similar position to manual workers. Indeed, clerical workers' earnings are lower than those of many manual workers, while the 'industrialisation of office work', with the massive introduction of new technology, means that their work conditions are increasingly similar to those of semi-skilled manual workers.

What has happened, then, is a shift in the structure of the working class, not its abolition. The changes I have described are, indeed, an effect of the tendencies of capitalist development analysed by Marx. For the rising productivity of labour, and the accompanying rise of the organic composition of capital which is its expression in value terms, mean that a smaller number of productive workers than at the beginning of the century can produce a far larger number of goods.

This process explains not simply the shift from manual to white collar work, but accompanying changes in the structure of the economy. Much attention has been paid to the phenomenon of 'de-industrialisation', the decline in the share of the economy taken by manufacturing industry and primary industries such as mining. A majority of the workforce in Britain today work in service industries, which produce services rather than goods which can be consumed. These industries may be privately owned, such as hotels and catering, or part of the state, such as the National Health Service, but they share in common the feature that they are not, on the whole, involved in the physical process of production.

Again, this development is a reflection of the rising productivity of labour, which means that even with much higher living standards than 100 years ago, far fewer people need be involved in material production.

This has been achieved at a price, however. Higher productivity has meant speed-up, 'rationalisation', the elimination of many skills in industry. The proportion of manual workers who are unskilled is higher now than at the beginning of the century, despite considerable improvements in public education and the far greater technological sophistication of the labour process today. Many semi-skilled workers are little more than machine minders who require only a few weeks' training, if that, to be able to perform their jobs.

Moreover, workers in the new service industries are far from being a privileged elite. Hotels, for example, are notorious for low pay and opposition to trade unions. The mass of public sector workers are typists, dustmen, hospital ancillary workers, nurses, cleaners, none of them specially well paid groups. One of the most significant developments of the past 15 years has been the transformation of public sector workers into one of the most militant sections of the trade union movement.

Nor does the fact that real wages have risen considerably in the past century, contradict Marx's analysis. I have shown in earlier chapters that he rejected the 'iron law of wages', according to which workers cannot earn more than their bare physical subsistence. Discussing the most important tendency of capitalist production, that for the organic composition of capital to rise, Marx wrote that 'it does not follow from this that the fund from which the workers draw their revenue is diminished *absolutely*; only that it is diminished *relatively*, in proportion to their total output' (**TSV** ii 566). This is precisely what has happened since Marx's day: the enormous rise in labour productivity has meant that workers' living standards have increased in absolute terms, even though their share of what they have produced has fallen. One study of the post-war American economy, for example, suggests that the rate of surplus value has risen considerably.

Analyses of the distribution of wealth are very imperfect guides to these matters, if only because rich people have a strong interest in concealing their wealth for fear of being taxed more. One estimate suggests that the richest 5 percent of the British population owned 87 percent of all personal wealth in 1911, and 75 percent in 1960. In 1954, at a time when Crosland and Strachey were proclaiming the withering away of capitalism, 1 percent of all shareholders owned 81 percent of stocks and shares. There is no question but that a small minority continues to control the economy.

The capitalist class system is still very much in business. The main changes have been in the structure of the working class, accompanied by a greater concentration of economic power caused by the development of first monopoly capital and now multinational capital. The working class is the overwhelming majority of the population of the advanced capitalist countries. Even excluding the many professionals who are undoubtedly part of the working class, manual and clerical workers made up 64 percent of the British workforce in 1979.

There are some who would accept this analysis, but argue that future trends will erode the working class. They point to the spread of automation, the introduction of robots into many manufacturing processes, and the possibility that, thanks to the new information technology, many workers will now 'telecommute', working at home using their own computer terminals.

The existence of these trends is undoubted, but their significance is greatly overstated. 'Telecommuting', for example, may not affect more than a small minority of higher paid white collar workers. Computer terminals are unlikely suddenly to sprout in every council flat, and it is difficult to see how a miner or hospital porter could do their jobs at home.

The introduction of robots may be of greater significance. Already they are being used in the car industry to do jobs such as welding. But even here it is easy to overstate the trend. Existing robots are inflexible, and often break down. Even if these difficulties are overcome, fully automated factories will require workers to supervise and programme them. These workers will possess enormous economic power.

223

In any case talk of 'de-industrialisation' is in many ways rather parochial. For the rationalisation of Western manufacturing industry is part of a process which is seeing the shift of many types of work to 'newly industrialised countries' in the Third World, where labour is cheap and plentiful. This is already evident in the case of industries such as steel, shipbuilding and textiles. The effect, however, is to introduce all the contradictions of capitalism into these societies. Over the past few years, a number of the more advanced 'backward' countries have seen massive social struggles in which the working class has played a major part— Iran, Poland, Brazil, South Africa, South Korea, India, to name some of them. The expansion and reorganisation of capitalism worldwide inevitably stimulates the organisation and resistance of the working class it brings into existence. In the Third World, as surely as in the First or Second, the bourgeoisie is creating its own gravediggers.

Conclusion

Capitalism has not changed its spots. It is still based on the exploitation of the working class, and liable to constant crises. The conclusion that Marx drew from this analysis, that the working class must overthrow this system and replace it with a classless society, is even more urgent now than in his day. For the military rivalries which are the form increasingly assumed by competition between capitals now threaten the very survival of the planet.

As Marx's centenary approached, the fires of war flickered across the globe—in Lebanon, Iran and Iraq, Kampuchea, Southern Africa, the Horn of Africa, Afghanistan and the South Atlantic. The accumulation of vast armouries of nuclear destruction by the superpowers, missile-rattling in the Kremlin, talk of 'limited' and 'protracted' nuclear war in Washington, these cast a shadow over the whole of humanity.

Socialist revolution is an imperative if we are to change a world in the grip of economic depression and war fever, a world where 30 million rot on Western dole queues and 800 million go hungry in the Third World. To that extent, Marx's ideas are more relevant today than they were 100 years ago. Capitalism has tightened its grip of iron on every portion of the planet since 1883, and is rotten-ripe for destruction, whether at its own hands through nuclear war, or at the hands of the working class. The choice is between workers' power or the 'common ruination of the contending classes'—between socialism or barbarism.

Many people who genuinely wish to do something to remedy the present state of the world believe that this stress on the working class is much too narrow. The existence of nuclear weapons threatens everyone, whether workers or capitalists or whatever. Should not all classes be involved in remedying a problem which affects them all?

What this ignores is that what Edward Thompson has called 'exterminism'—the vast and competing military apparatuses which control the arms race—is an essential part of the working of capitalism today. No sane capitalist desires a nuclear war (although some insane ones who believe that such a war would be the prelude to the Second Coming now hold positions of influence in Washington). But sane or insane, every capitalist is part of an economic system which is bound up with military competition between nation states. Only a class with the interest and power to do away with capitalism can halt the march to Armageddon.

Marx always conceived of the working class as the class whose own self emancipation would also be the liberation of the rest of humanity. The socialist revolution to whose cause he devoted his life can only be, at one and the same time, the emancipation of the working class and the liberation of all the oppressed and exploited sections of society.

Those who accept the truth of Marx's views cannot rest content with a mere intellectual commitment. There are all too many of this sort around, Marxists content to live off the intellectual credit of *Capital*, as Trotsky described them. We cannot simply observe the world but must throw ourselves, as Marx did, into the practical task of building a revolutionary party amid the life and struggles of the working class. 'The philosophers have interpreted the world', wrote Marx, 'the point, however, is to change it.' If Marxism is correct, then we must act on it.

Further reading

The writings of Marx and Engels

One negative consequence of the collapse of Stalinism has been that Progress Publishers in Moscow no longer churns out cheap editions of Marx and Engels in vast quantities. Some of this output is still available, in Britain through Lawrence & Wishart which publishes the two best selections of Marx's and Engels' writings in English in one and three volumes respectively. Lawrence & Wishart is also publishing the monumental 50 volume Marx-Engels *Collected Works*, begun in 1975 and now nearing completion.

Penguin Classics publishes, in association with *New Left Review*, an excellent three volume selection of Marx's *Political Writings* (*The Revolutions of 1848*, *Surveys from Exile*, and *The First International and After*), the *Grundrisse* and a good modern translation of the three volumes of *Capital*. These editions, and those published by Lawrence & Wishart, are to be preferred since, on the whole, they provide complete works rather than selected fragments of Marx's and Engels' writings which can be highly misleading. The Chinese regime still publishes cheap separate editions of many of the most important works in English, though these are not always easy to get hold of.

The best place to start in trying to understand Marx is with

The Communist Manifesto. Engels' *Socialism, Utopian and Scientific* (Bookmarks, 1993) sets Marx's ideas in their historical context and briefly summarises them.

Marx's materialist conception of history is concisely stated in his 1859 Preface to *A Contribution to the Critique of Political Economy*. This text is to some extent a summary of Part 1 of *The German Ideology*, where historical materialism first took shape in something like its mature form. (Part 1 has been published separately by Lawrence & Wishart with some other useful short texts; the rest of *The German Ideology*, Volume 5 of the *Collected Works*, should be avoided like the plague by all except those interested in Marx's obscure quarrels with the Young Hegelians.)

Marx's *Wages, Price and Profit* is the best introduction to the labour theory of value; *Wage Labour and Capital* is also a good starting point (published together by Bookmarks, 1996). Those who wish to sample *Capital*, and it is after all Marx's life-work, should try Volume 1, which is far more historical and concrete than the others. The Penguin edition is the best. Readers intimidated by the opening chapter on commodities might try skipping Part 1 of the book, having first read *Wages, Price and Profit*, and come back to Part 1 after reading the rest of Volume 1.

Marx's skills as a writer and an anatomist of bourgeois society are nowhere better displayed than in his writings on France and especially *The Eighteenth Brumaire of Louis Bonaparte*. His theory of the state is developed much further, however, in *The Civil War in France* (the Beijing edition contains Marx's important drafts of the final Address), and in Engels' *The Origin of the Family, Private Property and the State*.

It is more difficult to suggest what to read on Marx's method since it has to be gleaned chiefly from his longer writings, but the three most important texts are probably *The Poverty of Philosophy*, the Introduction to the *Grundrisse* and the Afterword to the 2nd German edition of *Capital* Volume 1. Engels' *Anti-Dühring* is an important attempt to state and defend Marx's method.

Finally, the publication of Volumes 30-34 of the *Collected Works* means that the second rough draft of *Capital*, usually known as *The Economic Manuscript of 1861-3*, is now available in English. It includes *Theories of Surplus Value*, Marx's critical history of bourgeois economics (also available separately from

Lawrence & Wishart), along with much other interesting material. But it is one of his more difficult works.

General introductions

Chris Harman's *How Marxism Works* (Bookmarks, 4th edition, 1993) is an excellent short basic introduction. The best book length introduction in print is still probably Isaiah Berlin's *Karl Marx* (Oxford, 1978) which, although unsympathetic to its subject, manages to convey the quality of Marx's intellectual, political and cultural context better than any other work I know. The latest edition corrects the worst factual howlers committed in earlier versions.

Of the more demanding general treatments two long out of print works, Sidney Hook's *Towards an Understanding of Karl Marx* (London, 1933) and Karl Korsch's *Karl Marx* (London, 1938) stand out. Jon Elster's *Making Sense of Marx* (Cambridge, 1985) is a detailed, erudite, intelligent but destructive discussion of Marx's writings. His more basic *An Introduction to Marx* (Cambridge, 1986) has all the vices and none of the virtues of the longer book.

Chapter 1: The life of a revolutionary

Franz Mehring's *Karl Marx* (London, 1936), the classic Marxist biography, is now badly dated. David McLellan has written a good modern biography, *Karl Marx* (London, 1973), although he is not a reliable guide to Marx's thought. The 1995 edition has an extensive and up to date bibliography. *Marx Without Myth* by Maximilien Rubel and Margaret Manale (Oxford, 1975) is a detailed chronology of Marx's life and works.

Engels comes vividly alive in Gustav Meyer's *Friedrich Engels* (London, 1936). *The Revolutionary Ideas of Friedrich Engels*, a special issue (2:65) of *International Socialism* to mark the centenary of his death in 1995, contains valuable articles on different aspects of Engels' life and thought by Lindsey German, John Rees, Chris Harman and Paul McGarr.

The philosophical background to Marx's intellectual development is provided by Karl Löwith's *From Hegel to Nietzsche* (London, 1965) and Herbert Marcuse's *Reason and Revolution*

(London, 1968). The two best studies of Marx's development in English are Hal Draper's *Karl Marx's Theory of Revolution* Volume I (London, 1977), and Sidney Hook's *From Hegel to Marx* (Ann Arbor, 1971).

What Marx was like as a person can be gleaned from a variety of sources. Among these are contemporary witnesses, for example *Karl Marx: Interviews and Recollections* (London, 1982) edited by David McLellan, and his letters, either in the *Selected Correspondence* (Moscow, 1965) or in the *Collected Works* from Volume 38 onwards. Perhaps best of all are S S Prawer's *Karl Marx and World Literature* (Oxford, 1978) and the first volume, *Family Life*, of Yvonne Kapp's *Eleanor Marx* (London, 1973).

Chapter 2: Socialism before Marx

Three books by Eric Hobsbawm, *Industry and Empire* (Harmondsworth, 1969), *The Age of Revolution* (London, 1973) and *The Age of Capital* (London, 1977) provide the essential historical background to Marx's epoch. Unfortunately, apart from Engels' *Socialism, Utopian and Scientific*, G D H Cole's *A History of Socialist Thought* Volume 1 (London, 1953) and Frank and Fritzie Manuel's *Utopian Thought in the Western World* (Oxford, 1979), there is not much in English that is any good on the Utopian Socialists. This is a pity since they merit serious, if critical attention.

Chapter 3: Ricardo, Hegel and Feuerbach

Isaak Rubin, a first rate Marxist economist murdered by Stalin, wrote the excellent *A History of Economic Thought* (London, 1979) outlining the development of economics before Marx. (Ignore the highly pretentious Afterword by a French academic socialist.)

Engels' *Ludwig Feuerbach and the End of German Classical Philosophy* is a lucid discussion of both Hegel and Feuerbach. But there is no getting round the fact that Hegel is very difficult. Charles Taylor's *Hegel* (Cambridge, 1975) and the same author's more concise *Hegel and Modern Society* (Cambridge, 1979) represent a serious attempt to make sense of this highly obscure philosopher. If you want to sample Hegel himself, try *The Philosophy of History* (London, 1956) or, if you're feeling braver, *The Logic of Hegel* (Oxford, 1975). His greatest work is *The Phenomenology of Spirit* (Oxford, 1977) whose Preface gives probably the best statement of Hegel's philosophy.

Chapter 4: Marx's method

Marxist philosophy isn't the most accessible of subjects either, in part because of the obscure vocabulary practitioners often use, in part because it is dogged by controversy. I have tried to provide an overview in *Marxism and Philosophy* (Oxford, 1983). Undoubtedly the greatest work of Marxist philosophy is Georg Lukacs' *History and Class Consciousness* (London, 1971), though it is not easy reading. John Rees's forthcoming book *The Algebra of Revolution* (New Jersey, 1997) provides an excellent treatment of the whole subject of the dialectic.

The relationship between Marx's early writings and his later work has been a source of much debate since Louis Althusser argued in *For Marx* (London, 1969) that there was a 'break' between them. The opposite case is defended strongly in Istvan Meszaros's *Marx's Theory of Alienation* (London, 1970) and Bertell Ollman's *Alienation* (Cambridge, 1971). C J Arthur's *Dialectics of Labour* (Oxford, 1986) is a good study of the *1844 Manuscripts*. Norman Geras' *Marx and Human Nature* (London, 1983) and Ali Rattansi's *Marx and the Division of Labour* (London, 1982) are two important discussions of issues covered in this chapter.

Chapter 5: History and the class struggle

Marx's theory of history has also been much debated in Britain over the past 20 years or so. The origins of this debate go back to the attempt by Louis Althusser and Etienne Balibar in *Reading Capital* (London, 1970) systematically to reconstruct historical materialism. Contributions include Edward Thompson's *The Poverty of Theory and Other Essays* (London, 1978), G A Cohen's *Karl Marx's Theory of History—a Defence* (Oxford, 1978), Perry Anderson's *Arguments within English Marxism*

(London, 1980), Chris Harman's 'Base and Superstructure' in *International Socialism* 2:36 (1986) and Alex Callinicos's *Making History* (Cambridge, 1987).

British Marxists have also produced some marvellous historical studies. I am thinking of the writings of, for example, Edward Thompson, Christopher Hill, G E M de Ste Croix, Rodney Hilton, George Rudé, Maurice Dobb, Brian Manning, Eric Hobsbawm, and Perry Anderson. Ste Croix's *The Class Struggle in the Ancient Greek World* (London, 1981) is particularly important as a demonstration of historical materialism's ability to comprehend pre-capitalist societies.

Chapter 6: Capitalism

Paul Sweezy's *The Theory of Capitalist Development* (London, 1968), though wrong in places and largely mistaken politically, is still unequalled as a guide to Marxist political economy. Isaak Rubin's *Essays on Marx's Theory of Value* (Detroit, 1972) and Roman Rosdolsky's *The Making of Marx's 'Capital'* (London, 1977) are the best commentaries on *Capital*.

Two books by authors from Communist Party backgrounds, Ben Fine's and Lawrence Harris's *Rereading Capital* (London, 1979) and John Weeks' *Capital and Exploitation* (London, 1981), provide sophisticated theoretical responses to attacks on Marx by orthodox economists. My account of his theory of crises is heavily indebted to these two books, and to Chris Harman's *Explaining the Crisis* (Bookmarks, 1984). This last book is unfortunately out of print, but Chris Harman has also written a much more recent and popular exposition, *Economics of the Madhouse* (Bookmarks, 1995).

Chapter 7: Workers' power

Marx's and Engels' conception of the revolutionary party is outlined, and critically discussed in Chris Harman's *Party and Class* (Bookmarks, 1983) and John Molyneux's *Marxism and the Party* (Bookmarks, 1986). Lenin's approach is also sketched out in these works. Harman's essay is now reprinted in an excellent collection, *Party and Class,* also including important essays by Tony Cliff, Duncan Hallas and Leon Trotsky (Bookmarks, 1996). For

231

a much more detailed study, see especially the first volume, *Building the Party* (Bookmarks, 1986), of Tony Cliff's *Lenin*.

Lenin's *The State and Revolution* is essentially a study and development of Marx's and Engels' theory of the state. Two of the best academic studies are Hal Draper's *Karl Marx's Theory of Revolution* (4 volumes, New York, 1977, 1978, 1986, 1990) and Alan Gilbert's *Marx's Politics* (Oxford, 1981). Chris Harman's 'The State and Capitalism Today' in *International Socialism* 2:51 (1991), is an important contribution to the Marxist theory of the state.

The question of the relationship between the class struggle and various forms of oppression—sexual, racial etc—is only touched on in this book. Some pointers to this vast and controversial subject can be found in Lindsey German's 'Theories of Patriarchy' in *International Socialism* 2:12 (1981), and *Sex, Class and Socialism* (Bookmarks, 1989), Chris Harman's 'Women's Liberation and Revolutionary Socialism' in *International Socialism* 2:23 (1984), Johanna Brenner's and Maria Ramas' 'Rethinking Women's Oppression' in *New Left Review* 144 (1984), Tony Cliff's *The Class Struggle and Women's Liberation* (Bookmarks, 1984) and Alex Callinicos's *Race and Class* (Bookmarks, 1993).

Chapter 8: Marx today

Tony Cliff's *State Capitalism in Russia* (Bookmarks, new edition, 1996) is basic to an understanding of the self styled 'socialist' countries. Chris Harman extended this analysis in *Class Struggles in Eastern Europe 1945-83* (Bookmarks, 1983) and used it to explain the East European revolutions in 'The Storm Breaks' in *International Socialism* 2:46 (1990). I discuss the significance of 1989 in *The Revenge of History* (Cambridge, 1991) and in the first chapter of *Theories and Narratives* (Cambridge, 1995).

Chris Harman's *Explaining the Crisis* (Bookmarks, 1984), the best single Marxist account of post-war capitalism, is out of print, but he restates and updates his analysis in 'Where Is Capitalism Going?' in *International Socialism* 2:58 and 60 (1993). The articles reprinted in Alex Callinicos, John Rees, Chris Harman and Mike Haynes, *Marxism and the New Imperialism* (Bookmarks, 1994) analyse different aspects of the world situation after the Cold War.

The class structure of contemporary capitalism is explored in Alex Callinicos's and Chris Harman's *The Changing Working Class* (Bookmarks, 1987) and by Lindsey German in *A Question of Class* (Bookmarks, 1996). Harry Braverman's study of the 20th century working class, *Labour and Monopoly Capital* (New York, 1974), is a modern socialist classic.

index